PERFORMANCE MANAGEMENT

D1355466

Michael Armstrong graduated from the London School of Economics. He is a Fellow of the Chartered Institute of Personnel and Development and a Fellow of the Institute of Management Consultants. He has had over 25 years' experience in personnel management, including 12 as a personnel director. He has also practised as a management consultant for over 16 years, and is now chief examiner, employee reward, for the CIPD. He has written a number of successful management books, including *Management Processes and Functions* (1990); (with Phil Long) *The Reality of Strategic HRM* (1994); *Using the HR Consultant* (1994); (with Angela Baron) *The Job Evaluation Handbook* (1995); *Employee Reward* (2nd edition 1999); *Managing Activities* (1999); and *Rewarding Teams* (2000), all published by the CIPD.

Angela Baron has a Masters degree in organisational and occupational psychology, and is a member of the Chartered Institute of Personnel and Development, for whom she is currently the policy adviser on employee resourcing. In that role she has been involved in numerous research projects, including detailed investigations into quality management, the lean organisation and organisational culture. She is also responsible for the CIPD's policy and development work on all aspects of resourcing the organisation, including recruitment and selection, psychometric testing, organisational design and development, career counselling, human resource planning, teamworking, flexible working, employee data, workplace relationships and management style. Her previous collaboration with Michael Armstrong was *The Job Evaluation Handbook* (also published by the CIPD).

Other titles in the series:

The Chartered Institute of Personnel and Development is the leading publisher of books and reports for personnel and training professionals, students, and for all those concerned with the effective management and development of people at work. For details of all our titles, please contact the Publishing Department:

tel. 020-8263 3387

fax 020-8263 3850

e-mail publish@cipd.co.uk

The catalogue of all CIPD titles can be viewed on the CIPD website:

www.cipd.co.uk/Publications

PERFORMANCE MANAGEMENT

The new realities

Michael Armstrong
and
Angela Baron

CHARTERED INSTITUTE OF PERSONNEL AND DEVELOPMENT

First published in 1998

Reprinted 1999, 2000 (twice)

Design by Paperweight
Typeset by
Fakenham Photosetting Ltd, Norfolk
Printed in Great Britain by
The Cromwell Press, Wiltshire

British Library Cataloguing in Publication Data

A catalogue record for this book is available from the
British Library

ISBN 0-85292-727-4

Chartered Institute of Personnel and Development,
CIPD House, Camp Road, London SW19 4UX
Tel: 020–8971 9000 Fax: 020–8263 3333
E-mail: cipd@cipd.co.uk
Website: www.cipd.co.uk
Incorporated by Royal Charted. Registered no. 1079797.

CONTENTS

ACKNOWLEDGEMENTS

Numerous people have assisted in the research for this book; the authors and the Chartered Institute of Personnel and Development are extremely grateful to all those busy practitioners who took the time to complete our survey and talk to us about their practices, and who provided a wealth of literature and documentation for us to draw upon. We are particularly grateful to those organisations who allowed us access to the attitudes and thoughts of their employees through attitude surveys and focus groups. In addition, we would like to mention the following for the immense support that they gave to enable us to complete the project: Gary Annels, Chris Bottomley, Alan Cave, Mike Conway, Sarah Hall, Gillian Henchley, Jose Pottinger, Angela Sheard and Peter Stemp.

FOREWORD

There are a number of stories, legends and myths surrounding the management of performance, but my favourite is that of the individual who, stopping his car next to that of his boss at a set of traffic lights one day, was surprised to see the boss gesticulating at him to wind down the car window. He duly did so, and was even more amazed when the boss said, 'It's appraisal time – I'll put you down for a "3" ... OK?' No wonder performance management got a bad name.

Work carried out for the (then) Institute of Personnel Management in 1991 concluded that performance management was about managing people well. At its best, it can provide an important source of motivation and challenge to achieve better and better results, as well as significant personal development. This book is based on a considerable amount of research mapping current trends in performance management and analysing the attitudes of both appraisers and appraisees. It challenges some of the negative comments about attitudes and gives detailed comment on the practices of a range of organisations.

The authors go on to offer practical guidance on the development of a performance-management process that is likely to be fit for the purpose. No single process can adequately fill the needs of all organisations, and therefore it is important that practitioners have an understanding of the role of performance management and its relationship to other people-management activities. They should also be able to balance the need for a formal framework with adequate flexibility to allow individual managers to tailor processes to their individual requirements.

Performance management is ultimately about communication: communicating what is expected from people and how best this can be achieved, allowing individuals to

develop themselves and their contribution to the organisation, rather than squeezing them into boxes and labelling
them a '3' or a 'B'. In stressing this throughout the book, the
authors offer practitioners both thought-provoking analysis
and practical guidance to ensure that no one is 'put down for
a "3"' without an adequate and two-way exchange of information with their manager.

Ron Collard
(Former) IPD vice-president, organisation and human
resource planning

INTRODUCTION

What this book is about

This book is about what organisations, teams, managers, team leaders and individuals do (and could do better) to manage their performance in order to achieve success. It draws extensively on research that was carried out in 1997 and 1998 for the (then) Institute of Personnel and Development (IPD) by the authors with the help of Professor David Guest and Zella King of Birkbeck College*. The aim of the research was to identify and explore the new realities of performance management in best-practice organisations in the UK.

The research project was initiated because there have been considerable developments in how organisations are introducing and operating processes for performance management since the last comprehensive research on this subject was conducted by the (then) Institute of Personnel Management in 1991. The 1997–98 research included the analysis of 562 questionnaires completed by respondents following a postal survey, visits to 35 organisations, 12 focus groups in six organisations, six attitude surveys and two telephone surveys of organisations (one on 360-degree feedback and the other on how people are trained in performance-management processes and skills). In addition, we interviewed a number of consultants and trade-union officials. The outcomes of the research are described fully in Part II of this book.

Aim of the book

Our aim is to provide useful information about the latest thinking and developments in the practice of performance management. We set out to explore 'the new realities' of how organisations are approaching the vital tasks of managing for performance and developing the capabilities of their people, and to offer some stimulating insights and guidance for practitioners.

* The IPD became the Chartered Institute of Personnel and Development (CIPD) in July 2000.

Plan of the book

Part 1 – The Foundations of performance management

In Part I, performance management is defined (Chapter 1) and then the management of performance is examined from the overall point of view of how organisations can improve their effectiveness (Chapter 2). Chapter 3 is devoted to a short history of performance management, whereas Chapter 4 examines its essential elements, including an overall model and a description of each of the key processes.

Performance management and performance appraisal have often had a bad press, and in Chapter 5 we summarise some of the more important criticisms.

Part 2 – Performance management in action

This part incorporates summaries of the findings of our research, covering:

☐ an analysis of the questionnaires completed by respondents (Chapter 6)

☐ summaries of the information on performance-management practices derived from our visits to organisations (Chapter 7)

☐ case-studies describing some of the most interesting 'best-practice' approaches (Chapter 8)

☐ an analysis of what people feel about performance management derived from the focus groups, interviews and discussions with trade unions (Chapter 9)

☐ an analysis of the outcomes of the attitude surveys (Chapter 10)

☐ an assessment of the impact of performance management derived from an analysis of completed questionnaires, and information derived from visits and literature research (Chapter 11).

Part 3 – The Application of performance management

Here we discuss three important aspects of the application of performance management: development (Chapter 12), pay (Chapter 13) and team performance (Chapter 14).

Part 4 – Performance-management processes

This part describes the various processes and skills used in performance management.

Part 5 – Developing and maintaining performance management

This part covers methods of introducing performance management, training people in the skills required and evaluating its effectiveness.

Part 6 – Conclusions

We summarise our conclusions on performance-management best practice.

PART 1

THE FOUNDATIONS OF PERFORMANCE MANAGEMENT

1 PERFORMANCE MANAGEMENT – DEFINITION, CONCERNS AND SCOPE

Performance management is a fairly imprecise term, and performance-management processes (or systems, as some people persist in calling them) manifest themselves in many different forms. There is no one right way of managing performance: the approach must depend on the context of the organisation – its culture, structure, technology – the views of stakeholders and the type of people involved. But it is still possible, and desirable, to define in very broad terms what performance management is about and to discuss generally the concerns and scope of fully realised processes of managing performance. These are set out in this chapter as points of reference when later in this book we examine the new realities of performance management in its many different guises.

Performance management defined

Performance management is a strategic and integrated approach to delivering sustained success to organisations by improving the performance of the people who work in them and by developing the capabilities of teams and individual contributors. Performance management is:

□ *strategic* in the sense that it is concerned with the broader issues facing the business if it is to function effectively in its environment, and with the general direction in which it intends to go to achieve longer-term goals

□ *integrated* in four senses:

■ (1) *vertical integration* – linking or aligning business, team and individual objectives

■ (2) *functional integration* – linking functional strategies in different parts of the business

■ (3) *human resource (HR) integration* – linking different aspects of human resource management (HRM), especially organisational development and human resource development and reward, to achieve a coherent approach to the management and development of people

■ (4) *the integration of individual needs* with those of the organisation, as far as this is possible

❑ concerned with *performance improvement* in order to achieve organisational, team and individual effectiveness. Organisations, as stated by Lawson (1995), have 'to get the right things done successfully'. Performance is not only about *what* is achieved but also about *how* it is achieved. Management is involved in direction, measurement and control. But these are not the exclusive concerns of managers: teams and individuals jointly participate as stakeholders.

❑ concerned with *development*, which is perhaps the most important function of performance management. Performance improvement is not achievable unless there are effective processes of continuous development. This addresses the core competences of the organisation and the capabilities of individuals and teams. 'Performance management' should really be called 'performance and development management'.

An alternative but complementary definition is provided by Fletcher (1993a):

> The real concept of performance management is associated with an approach to creating a shared vision of the purpose and aims of the organisation, helping each employee understand and recognise their part in contributing to them, and in so doing, manage and enhance the performance of both individuals and the organisation.

Concerns of performance management

Concern with outputs, outcomes, process and inputs

Performance management is concerned with outputs – the

achievement of results – and with outcomes – the impact made on performance. But it is also concerned with the processes required to achieve these results (competencies) and the inputs in terms of capabilities (knowledge, skill and competence) expected from the teams and individuals involved.

One of the trends we noted in our research was the focus on inputs in the form of competencies: 31 per cent of the organisations we contacted who had performance-management processes included some form of competence assessment. On the basis of the 1991 IPM survey, Fletcher and Williams (1992) suggested that 'The interest in competencies perhaps signifies a much more explicit concern with means and not just ends.' But they also remarked that if competencies are not defined on the basis of empirical research to determine which of them are associated with effective performance, then 'there is a danger that the competencies in themselves will lack validity and the assessments made by managers may lack reliability and validity'. (Methods of defining valid competencies are described in Chapter 17.)

Concern with planning

Performance management is concerned with planning ahead to achieve future success. This means defining expectations expressed as objectives and in business plans.

Concern with measurement and review

'If you can't measure it, you can't manage it.' Performance management is concerned with the measurement of results and with reviewing progress towards achieving objectives as a basis for action.

Concern with continuous development and improvement

Performance management is concerned with creating a culture in which organisational and individual learning and development are a continuous process. It provides means for the integration of learning and work so that everyone learns from the successes and challenges inherent in their day-to-day activities.

Concern for communication

Performance management is concerned with communication. This is done by creating a climate in which a continuing dialogue between managers and the members of their teams takes place to define expectations and share information on the organisation's mission, values and objectives. This establishes mutual understanding of what *is to be* achieved and a framework for managing and developing people to ensure that it *will be* achieved (Armstrong and Murlis 1994).

Concern for stakeholders

At its best, performance management is concerned with satisfying the needs and expectations of all the organisation's stakeholders – owners, management, employees, customers, suppliers and the general public. Ideally, employees are treated as partners in the enterprise whose interests are respected, whose opinions are sought and listened to, and who are encouraged to contribute to the formulation of objectives and plans for their team and for themselves. Performance management should respect the needs of individuals and teams as well as those of the organisation, recognising that they will not necessarily coincide.

Ethical concerns

Performance management processes should operate in accordance with agreed ethical principles. These have been defined by Winstanley and Stuart-Smith (1996) as follows:

- *respect for the individual* – people should be treated as 'ends in themselves' and not merely as 'means to other ends'
- *mutual respect* – the parties involved in performance-management processes should respect each other's needs and preoccupations
- *procedural fairness* – the procedures incorporated in performance management should be operated fairly to limit the adverse impact on individuals
- *transparency* – people affected by decisions emerging from performance-management processes should have the

opportunity to scrutinise the basis on which decisions were made.

The scope of performance management

Performance management is about managing the organisation. It is a natural process of management, not a system or technique (Fowler 1990). It is also about managing within the context of the business (its internal and external environment). This will affect how it is developed, what it sets out to do and how it operates. The context is very important: Jones (1995) goes as far as to say 'manage context not performance'.

Performance management concerns everyone in the business – not just managers. It rejects the cultural assumption that only managers are accountable for the performance of their teams and replaces it with the belief that responsibility is *shared* between managers and team members. In a sense, managers should regard the people who report to them as customers for the managerial contribution and services they can provide. Managers and their teams are jointly accountable for results and are jointly involved in agreeing what they need to do and how they need to do it, both in monitoring performance and in taking action. In their recent report, David Guile and Nickie Fonda argue that underlying the current debates about organisational competitiveness is an assumption that the drive to enhance performance is making ever-greater demands on the knowledge and skills of the workforce, and that people will carry a much greater responsibility for their own performance (Guile and Fonda 1998).

In short, best-practice performance-management processes are part of a holistic (ie all-embracing) approach to managing for performance, which is the concern of everyone in the organisation (this theme is developed in the next chapter). However, as our research demonstrated, this is not necessarily universal practice and, consequently, performance management is carried out with varying degrees of success and commitment from employees.

2 THE MANAGEMENT OF PERFORMANCE

An organisation exists to achieve a purpose, which is to meet the needs and expectations of its stakeholders: the people working there or associated with it, customers or clients, owners, trustees or governing bodies, suppliers and the public at large. This chapter examines the general considerations affecting the management and improvement of performance, dealing in turn with:

☐ the features of an effective organisation
☐ the concept of performance
☐ the processes involved in the management of performance.

Features of an effective organisation

Every organisation is effective in its own particular way within its own particular context. Perhaps the only feature that is generally recognised is the importance of defining objectives and of planning to achieve them.

This interest in objectives was, of course, started by Peter Drucker (1955). He identified five key characteristics of objectives:

☐ They enable the organisation to explain the whole range of business statements in a small number of general statements.
☐ They allow the testing of these statements in actual experience.
☐ They enable behaviour to be predicted.
☐ They facilitate the examination of the soundness of decisions while they are still being made rather than after they fail.
☐ They provide for performance in the future to be improved as a result of the analysis of past experience.

Richard Beckhard (1969) followed this up when he stated that in a 'healthy organisation':

> The total organisation, the significant sub-parts, and individuals manage their work against goals and plan for the achievement of these goals.

These views provided the basis for the management-by-objectives movement and much of the earlier approaches to performance management. But other commentators looked at effectiveness from the point of view of the context, structure, process, and the people within organisations. In *Thriving on Chaos*, Tom Peters (1988) proposed the following approaches:

☐ Break organisations into the smallest possible independent units.

☐ Give every employee a business person's strong sense of revenue, cost and profit.

☐ Achieve ever-closer involvement with the customer.

☐ Minimise organisational layers.

☐ Achieve flexibility by empowering people.

☐ Learn to love change through a new view of leadership at all levels.

☐ Pursue fast-paced innovation.

In *When Giants Learn to Dance*, Rosabeth Moss Kanter (Kanter 1989) described the 'post-entrepreneurial' organisation as representing a triumph of process over structure. She suggests that relationships and communication, and the flexibility temporarily to combine resources, are more important than the formal channels and reporting relationships represented in an organisation chart: 'What is important is not how responsibilities are divided but how people can pull together to pursue new opportunities.'

In *The Frontiers of Excellence* Robert Waterman (1994) provides definitions of what makes top companies different:

☐ They are better organised to meet the needs of their *people*, so that they attract better people than their competitors do, and their people are more greatly motivated to do a superior job, whatever it is they do.

□ They are better organised to meet the needs of *customers*, so that they are more innovative in anticipating customer needs, more reliable in meeting customer expectations, better able to deliver their product or service more cheaply, or some combination of the above.

Another important feature of an effective organisation is the pursuit of high performance by developing competence. As Richard Boyatzis (1982) said in *The Competent Manager*:

> You may view competency as the key that unlocks the door to individuals in realising their maximum potential, developing ethical organisational systems, and providing maximum growth opportunities for personnel.

The means by which businesses achieve high performance was modelled by Sears, the American retailing company (Rucci, Kirn and Quinn 1998), and is depicted in Figure 1.

Implications for the management of performance

Four implications for the management of performance can be

Figure 1
THE SEARS MODEL: EMPLOYEE – CUSTOMER – PROFIT CHAIN

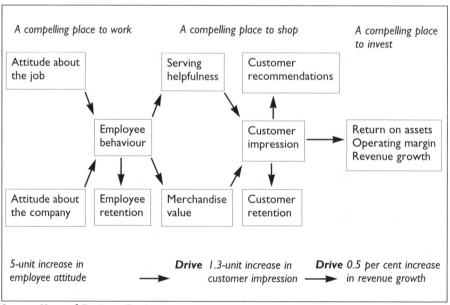

Source: *Harvard Business Review*

derived from these views on organisational performance and from the Sears model:

1   The importance of *goals*, and the measuring and monitoring of performance in relation to goals.

2   The importance of *context* (structure, process and people) – it can be argued that managing the context will make more impact on organisational success than any narrowly focused 'systems' of performance management.

3   The importance of *competence* – achieving high performance by developing core, team and individual levels of competence.

4   The importance of the *value chain* – achieving revenue growth and shareholder value through the two key contributors to organisational effectiveness, namely employees and customers.

Before looking at how these four approaches can contribute to improving organisational effectiveness, it is necessary to consider what is meant by 'performance' and 'management'.

Performance

If you can't define performance, you can't measure or manage it. It has been pointed out by Bates and Holton (1995) that 'Performance is a multi-dimensional construct, the measurement of which varies, depending on a variety of factors.' They also state that it is important to determine whether the measurement objective is to assess performance outcomes or behaviour.

There are of course different views on what performance is. It can be regarded as simply the record of outcomes achieved. On an individual basis, it is a record of a person's accomplishments. Kane (1996) argues that performance 'is something that the person leaves behind and that exists apart from the purpose'. Bernadin, Kane, Ross, Spina and Johnson (1995) are concerned that:

> Performance should be defined as the outcomes of work because they provide the strongest linkage to the strategic

goals of the organisation, customer satisfaction, and economic contributions.

The *Oxford English Dictionary* defines performance as the 'accomplishment, execution, carrying out, working out of anything ordered or undertaken'. This refers to outputs/outcomes (accomplishment), but also states that performance is about doing the work, as well as being about the results achieved. Performance could therefore be regarded as behaviour – the way in which organisations, teams and individuals get work done. Campbell (1990) believes that 'Performance is behaviour and should be distinguished from the outcomes because they can be contaminated by systems factors.'

A more comprehensive view of performance is achieved if it is defined as embracing both behaviour and outcomes. This is well put by Brumbrach (1988):

> Performance means both behaviours and results. Behaviours emanate from the performer and transform performance from abstraction to action. Not just the instruments for results, behaviours are also outcomes in their own right – the product of mental and physical effort applied to tasks – and can be judged apart from results.

This definition of performance leads to the conclusion that, when one is managing the performance of teams and individuals, both inputs (behaviour) and outputs (results) should be considered. Performance is about *how* things are done as well as *what* is done. This is the so-called 'mixed model' (Hartle 1995) of performance management, which covers competency levels and achievements as well as objective-setting and review. And it is this model that our research showed as the one now interesting many organisations.

Factors affecting performance

Performance is affected by a number of factors, all of which should be taken into account. These comprise:

- □ *personal factors* – the individual's skill, competence, motivation and commitment

☐ *leadership factors* – the quality of encouragement, guidance and support provided by managers and team leaders

☐ *team factors* – the quality of support provided by colleagues

☐ *systems factors* – the system of work and facilities provided by the organisation

☐ *contextual (situational) factors* – internal and external environmental pressures and changes

Cardy and Dobbins (1994) point out that traditional approaches to performance appraisal attribute variations in performance to personal factors, when they could be caused in part or entirely by situational or systems factors. Deming (1986) made the same point even more forcibly. Performance reviews must therefore consider not only what individuals have done but also the circumstances in which they have had to perform. And, importantly, this analysis should extend to the performance of the manager as a leader.

Processes for managing performance

It has been well said by Mohrman and Mohrman (1995) that managing performance is 'running the business'. It is not a set of techniques, and it is certainly not all about 'performance-management systems' (although performance-management *processes* can play an important part). Kermally (1997) believes that 'performance management should support corporate strategy formulation and monitor value drivers, ie those elements that really make the business profitable'.

If an all-embracing or holistic approach to the management of performance is adopted, the following aspects of what makes organisations, teams and individuals perform well must be considered:

☐ the context of the organisation

☐ culture

☐ functionality

☐ job design (for individuals)

☐ teamwork

- [ ] organisational development
- [ ] purpose and value statements
- [ ] strategic management
- [ ] human resource management.

Organisational context

Organisations can be regarded as open systems that are continually dependent upon and influenced by their environment. As Katz and Kahn (1964) wrote, 'Systems theory is basically concerned with problems of relationship, of structure and of interdependence.' The emphasis is on transactions across boundaries – between the system and the environment, and between the different parts of the system. The socio-technical model of organisation is based on the principle that, in any system of organisation, the technical or task aspects are interrelated with the human aspects. Managing performance is about managing within this context. So far as possible it is concerned with *managing* the context, or at least influencing it.

The external global and national environment – business, economics, politics and society – is constantly changing, and indeed may be turbulent, even chaotic. It imposes changes on the performance requirements of the organisation, including the need for continuous improvement to maintain competitive edge. The social and technical systems in the internal environment are therefore also in a constant state of change, so performance-management processes must help to shape this change, as well as respond to it.

Contingency theory suggests that the internal structure of an organisation and its systems are a direct function of its environment. The action theory contingency model as developed by Silverman (1970) (and as illustrated in Figure 2) traces the factors linking organisational performance to critical environmental pressures. Contingency theory states that whatever is done within an organisation must fit its circumstances. That is why no performance-management 'system' can safely be transferred from one organisation to another. Best fit is therefore more crucial than best practice.

Our research established the 'best-practice' organisations

Figure 2
ACTION THEORY CONTINGENCY MODEL

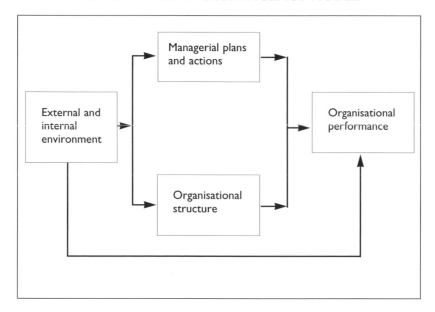

were those that emphasised the contextual issues. BP Exploration (BPX), for example, identified these as:

□ the business BPX does
□ the way BPX does business
□ the shape BPX is in.

These issues are changing rapidly; the processes for managing performance are expected to facilitate such changes and assist adaptation to them.

Culture

Culture can be described as the glue that holds organisations together and performance management, both in philosophy and design, is inevitably influenced by the prevailing organisational culture. This may be embedded in deeply held beliefs, reflecting what has worked in the past and composed of responses that have been accepted because they have met with success. Culture will dominate the internal environment of the organisation, which will also be influenced by structure, size, working practices, the employee-relations climate and the type of people employed. Culture dictates both the behaviour and the attitudes of individuals.

The components of organisational culture are values, norms, and management style:

☐ *Values* are expressed as beliefs in what is good for the organisation and what sort of behaviour is desirable. Values are reflected in how people interact, customer care, innovation, social responsibility and how employees are developed. They influence both the focus of performance management (for example on customer care, quality or innovation) and how performance management is carried out (for example, the things that are measured).

☐ *Norms* are unwritten rules that define expectations of behaviour, such as how managers treat individuals and how individuals relate to their managers. Norms govern how performance management operates.

☐ *Management style* describes the way in which managers behave and how they exercise power and authority. A command-and-control style of management is likely to produce a task-oriented style of performance management, whereas a non-directive participative style of management is more likely to support a partnership approach to performance management, with an emphasis on involvement, empowerment and ownership.

It is possible to change this culture, and therefore the consequences for performance management, and organisational development philosophy provides useful lessons. Bandura (1986) states that people make conscious choices about their behaviour. These choices are influenced by information from the environment, and are based upon the things that are important to them, the views they have about their own abilities to behave in certain ways and the consequences they think will result from whatever behaviour they decide to engage in. Boyett and Conn (1995) believe that 'people don't resist change, they resist *being* changed'. The implication is that performance-management processes can be a powerful tool in helping to achieve change by providing for the joint identification by the manager and the individual of the targeted behaviour required and the skills required to reach that target.

Functionality

How organisations function is a contextual factor that directly affects the design and operation of performance-management processes. There are three issues that affect performance management:

1   The organisation may operate globally or, for example, across Europe. It may be controlled rigidly from headquarters not only as regards the results it has to achieve, but also *how* those results are achieved. This centralisation can extend to HR processes, including performance management. At the other extreme, the centre will be concerned only with business plans and achievements, and will leave the local plant to develop its own HR and other practices. Between these two extremes, the centre may provide guidelines on practices such as performance management, for example insisting that it is carried out in accordance with certain general principles, but will leave local management to decide how to apply the principles in their own environment.

2   Organisations within one country may devolve authority to a greater or lesser degree to business units, subsidiaries or divisions. Again there may be total central control, total freedom, or freedom to act within certain parameters.

3   Organisational structures impinge on performance because, in a sense, they are the framework for getting things done. The traditional view of an organisation as being highly structured with extended hierarchies and clearly defined lines of command and control is no longer valid in the new situations that organisations are finding themselves in. Such structures can inhibit rather than enhance performance if, as is usually the case today, the emphasis is on flexibility, teamwork and rapid response.

Pascale (1990) believes that the new organisational paradigm functions by moving:

□   *from* the image of organisations as machines, with the

emphasis on concrete strategy, structure and systems *to* the idea of organisations as organisms, with the emphasis on the 'soft' dimensions – style, staff and shared values

□ *from* a hierarchical model, with step-by-step problem-solving, *to* a network model, with parallel nodes of intelligence that surround problems until they are eliminated

□ *from* the status-driven view that managers think and workers do as they are told *to* a view of managers as 'facilitators', with workers empowered to initiate improvements and change

□ *from* an emphasis on 'vertical tasks' within functional units *to* an emphasis on 'horizontal tasks' and collaboration across units

□ *from* a focus on 'content' and the prescribed use of specific tools and techniques *to* a focus on 'process' and a holistic synthesis of techniques

□ *from a* military model *to* a commitment model.

This list not only describes the basis upon which new organisations are being structured to meet contextual challenges but is also a useful guide to the organisational factors that should be taken into account when developing performance-management processes.

Job design

Job design for individual contributors can be defined as the specification of the contents, methods and relationships of jobs in order to satisfy technological and organisational requirements as well as the social and personal requirements of the jobholder.

Job design's aims, all directly affecting performance, are:

1 to specify job context, role expectations and relationships

2 to satisfy the requirements of the organisation for productivity, operational efficiency and quality of product or service

3 to satisfy the needs of the individual for interest, challenge and accomplishment.

These aims are interrelated, and effective job design can go some way towards integrating organisational and individual needs. It is certainly a means of providing intrinsic motivation and, given the right levels of competence and an appropriate context, a basis for improving performance.

A job will maximise interest and challenge, and will therefore motivate, if it has the following characteristics:

☐ It is a complete piece of work, in the sense that the worker can identify a series of tasks or activities that culminate in a recognisable end-product.

☐ It affords the individual as much variety, decision-making responsibility and control as possible in carrying out the work.

☐ It provides direct feedback through the work itself on how well employees are doing their jobs.

These characteristics were advocated by the job enrichment movement of the 1960s (Herzberg 1968). In more recent years, the concept of empowerment has been developed as a vehicle for enhancing performance. Empowerment is the process of giving people more scope or 'power' to exercise control over, and take responsibility for, their work. In 1990s jargon, its aim is to give people more 'space'. Empowerment has been termed the 'elixir of the 1990s' (Burdett 1991) and, ideally, the philosophy of performance management embraces this concept.

Teamwork

Flatter and process-based organisations emerged as the most favoured structure in the 1990s through processes of de-layering and business process re-engineering. One of the most important developments emerging from these initiatives was the perceived need for better teamwork arising from the use of multifunctional, multidiscipline teams and the needs of production for single-cell manufacture and other forms of organisation. This move was accelerated by the introduction of new technology such as CIM (computer-integrated manufacturing) and the emphasis on providing customer focus through teams in financial and service industries, often self-managed.

It seems logical, therefore, that more attention should be

given to performance management for teams as well as individuals. But one of the more remarkable findings from our research was the almost total neglect of this aspect of managing for performance. It will be addressed as a specific subject in Chapter 14.

Organisational development

Organisational development is concerned with the planning and implementation of programmes (interventions) designed to improve the effectiveness with which an organisation functions and manages change.

Organisational development approaches have a strong humanistic foundation. The basic philosophy was defined by Bennis (1960) as follows:

☐ a new concept of people, based on increased knowledge of their complex and shifting needs, which replaces an over-simplified, push-button notion of people

☐ a new concept of power, based on collaboration and reason, which replaces a model of power based on coercion and threats

☐ a new concept of organisational values, based on humanistic-democratic ideas, which replaces the mechanistic value system of bureaucracy.

This philosophy of organisational development (OD) has been dismissed by many hard-headed commentators as idealistic. But some of the messages it contains have been absorbed into the philosophy of performance management and should not be ignored. At least the OD practitioners of the 1970s saw the organisation as an entity, and based their approaches on a coherent view of how the various processes should be developed and managed. This provides impetus to the concept of performance management as a holistic and integrating process.

Purpose and value statements

High-level performance that meets the needs of all stakeholders is more likely to be achieved if it is purposeful and in accordance with an agreed set of core values. A statement of purpose defines overall what the organisation is setting out to do. It is therefore more outcome-oriented than a typical mission statement, and can provide a lead in formulating statements of functional, team and individual role purposes. Purpose statements define what is to be achieved, whereas value statements define the behaviour expected in attaining the purpose. They both cover such aspects as teamwork, quality, customer care and respect for the individual. Bass Brewers is a good example of a company that has predicated its performance-management processes on the statements of purpose and values prepared by its parent company, Bass plc.

Strategic management

Strategic management has been defined by Pearce and Robinson (1988) as:

> the set of decisions and actions resulting in the formulation and implementation of strategies designed to achieve the objectives of an organisation.

The purpose of strategic management has been expressed by Rosabeth Moss Kanter (1984), who states that strategic plans 'elicit the present actions for the future' and become 'action vehicles – integrating and institutionalising mechanisms for change'.

A frequently expressed aim of performance management is to integrate individual or team objectives with those of the organisation – often described as a 'cascading' process, which implies that it is entirely top-down. This concept is challenged by the philosophy of empowerment, which suggests that employees should contribute to the formulation of the objectives that directly affect them.

Michael Porter (1997) suggests that strategy is about choice – that is, not just about winning the race, but about choosing the right race to win. He states that companies are collections of discrete activities in which competitive advantage resides. The aim of strategy is to achieve, maintain and extend best practice by:

☐ employing the most up-to-date equipment, inputs, information technology and management techniques

□ eliminating waste, defects and delays

□ stimulating continuous organisational improvement

□ operating closer to the productivity frontier.

Strategic management sets the scene for the management of performance, and Porter believes that the general manager as strategist:

□ defines and communicates the company's unique position

□ decides which industry changes and customer needs to respond to

□ guides people in making choices that arise in their individual activities and in day-to-day decisions.

He has also expressed the view (Porter 1985) that:

> Performance management can only be effective where the organisation has a clear corporate strategy and has identified the elements of its overall performance which it believes are necessary to achieve competitive advantage.

Another way of putting this is that organisations have to establish what their critical success factors are. These constitute the areas of corporate performance – the 'drivers' – vital for the achievement of the organisation's goals. Thus they provide the agenda for deciding what aspects of performance should be focused on by the organisation, its managers, its teams and its individual contributors.

Another perspective on strategy is provided by Prahalad and Hamel (1990). They suggest that the performance of top executives should be judged on their ability to identify, cultivate and exploit the core competences of their organisations – the things that they do well that make growth possible. Core competences are bundles of skills and technology that enable a company to provide benefit to customers and constitute the collective learning in an organisation. The core-competence company organises itself around skills and capabilities and is concerned with acquiring, possessing and making operational the capabilities of its people. Core competences are 'the wellspring of new business development. They should constitute the focus for strategy at the corporate level ... Only if the company is conceived of as a hierarchy of core competences, core products, and market-focused business units will it be fit to fight.'

The significance of the core-competence concept for managing performance is that, if the core competences can be defined in terms of 'this is what the organisation is good at doing but needs to do even better', then they can provide the basis for the management of performance. This can be undertaken within the framework provided by the core competencies that indicate the areas of competency that have to be developed at unit, team and individual level.

Human resource management

All human resource management (HRM) activities are, or should be, business-driven and focused on improving performance by acquiring and developing a competent, well-motivated and committed workforce. Formal perform- ance-management processes are simply part of what should be an integrated and coherent approach to the management of performance. As David Guest (1996) points out:

> While performance management is potentially useful in directing attention to performance ... It risks becoming too bureaucratic, it risks being misused. Too many appraisal schemes are narrow and individualistic in focus.

Guest suggests that the following are high-performance HRM practices:

- harmonised terms and conditions for all staff
- use of psychological tests in selecting all staff
- formal system of communicating values to staff
- deliberate development of a learning organisation
- design of jobs to make full use of skills and abilities
- staff being responsible for their own quality
- regular use of attitude surveys
- formal appraisal of all staff at least annually
- staff being informed about company performance and prospects

□   internal promotion if at all possible

□   a policy of job security

□   a merit element in the pay of staff.

Guest suggests that the HRM route to high performance should be built on the requirements for commitment, quality and flexibility. Fit is important – that is, with the business strategy and across the various aspects of HRM strategy.

Implications for performance management

Managing for performance is about managing the business effectively within its context. As Mohrman and Mohrman (1995) emphasise, it is necessary to tie all aspects of managing performance to business objectives and to regard the organisation as a nest of performing units. The focus should be on running the business. Performance management should be treated as part of the normal process of management and its processes should fit the way work is done.

The importance of regarding performance management as no more, or no less, than one aspect among others of an integrated approach to managing for performance cannot be overestimated. The context within which the organisation functions, its purpose, values and business strategy, its core competences, its culture and its management style all provide the basis upon which processes for managing the performance of individuals and teams are developed and implemented. The rest of this book will mainly concentrate on performance management for individuals and teams, but the message we want to convey is that *performance management is a holistic process that pervades every aspect of running the business.*

The problem is that the history of performance appraisal and performance management as summarised in Chapter 3 shows that, until quite recently, it has concentrated on rating individual merit. It has been a top-down system run by the personnel department and isolated from what the business does and what people do in it. That is why performance appraisal got a bad name.

3 A SHORT HISTORY OF PERFORMANCE MANAGEMENT

Antecedents

No one knows precisely when formal methods of reviewing performance were first introduced. According to Koontz (1971), the emperors of the Wei dynasty (AD 221–265) in China had an 'Imperial Rater' whose task was to evaluate the performance of the official family. Centuries later, Ignatius Loyola (1491–1556) established a system for formal rating of the members of the Society of Jesus (the Jesuits).

The first formal monitoring systems, however, evolved out of the work of Frederick Taylor and his followers before World War I. Rating for officers in the US armed services was introduced in the 1920s, and this spread to the UK, as did some of the factory-based US systems. Merit-rating came to the fore in the USA and the UK in the 1950s and 1960s, when it was sometimes rechristened performance appraisal. Management by objectives then came and went in the 1960s and 1970s and, simultaneously, experiments were made with the critical incident technique and behaviourally anchored rating scales. A revised form of results-oriented performance appraisal emerged in the 1970s, which still exists today. The term 'performance management' was first used in the 1970s, but it did not become a recognised process until the latter half of the 1980s.

Merit-rating and performance appraisal (earlier versions)

W D Scott was the American pioneer who introduced rating of the abilities of workers in industry prior to World War I. He was very much influenced by Taylor and invented the 'man to man comparison' scale, which was Taylorism in action (it is possible to argue that many of the developments in this area that followed, even to this day, have been influenced by Taylor). The W D Scott scale was modified and used to rate the efficiency of US Army officers. It is said to have supplanted the seniority system of promotion in the army and initiated an era of promotion on the basis of merit. The perceived success of this system led to its adoption by the British Army.

The pioneering efforts of Scott were developed in the 1920s and 1930s into what was termed the graphic rating scale, used for reports on workers and for rating managers and supervisors. A typical manager's or supervisor's scale included assessments of various qualities, for example:

Consider his success in winning confidence and respect through his personality:

| inspiring | favourable | indifferent | unfavourable | repellent |

Times have changed. The justification made for the use of this sort of rating scale was that they were 'educational'. They ensured, it was said, that those making the reports analysed subordinates in terms of the traits essential for success in their work. The educational impact on employees was described as imparting knowledge that they were being judged periodically on essential traits considered vital and important. The original scale was said to have been based on thorough research by W D Scott and colleagues into what were the key criteria for rating people at work. But the principle of the scale and the factors used were seized on with enthusiasm by organisations on both sides of the Atlantic as merit-rating or, in the 1950s, performance appraisal, flourished. This was without any research into or analysis of the extent to which the factors were relevant (or even whether dubbing someone 'repellent' was a good idea). Our survey revealed that some organisations are today using lists of competencies that include items suspiciously like some of the traits identified 70 years or more ago. They seemed to have been lifted down from some shelf (or extracted from a 'dictionary of competencies') without any research into the extent to which they were appropriate in the context of the organisation. Merit-rating still exists in some quarters, even if it is now called performance management.

Merit-rating often involved (and still involves under the guise of performance appraisal) the quantification of judgements against each factor, presumably in the belief that the quantification of subjective judgements makes them more objective. Some companies use the total merit score as the basis for ranking employees, and this is translated into a forced distribution for performance-pay purposes; for example, the top 10 per cent in the ranking get a 5 per cent increase, the next 20 per cent a 4 per cent increase, and so on. We heard of one manufacturing company that, to iron out rating inconsistencies, used a diabolical device they called 'factorising'. An average score was calculated for the whole company and the allocation of points in each department was equated to the company average. Inevitably, line managers objected strongly to the implied assumption that there were no differences between departmental performances.

Attacks on merit-rating and performance appraisal

Although merit-rating in different guises persists, a strong attack on the practice was mounted by McGregor in his highly influential *Harvard Business Review* article, 'An uneasy look at performance appraisal' (1957). He suggested that the emphasis should be shifted from appraisal to analysis:

> This implies a more positive approach. No longer is the subordinate being examined by his superior so that his (*sic*) weaknesses may be determined; rather he is examining himself, in order to define not only his weaknesses but also his strengths and potentials ... He becomes an active agent, not a passive 'object'. He is no longer a pawn in a chess game called management development.

McGregor went on to propose that the focus should be on the future rather than the past in order to establish realistic targets and to seek the most effective ways of reaching them. The accent of the review is therefore on performance, on actions relative to goals:

> There is less of a tendency for the personality of the subordinate to become an issue. The superior, instead of finding

himself in the position of a psychologist or a therapist, can become a coach helping a subordinate to reach his own decisions on the specific steps that will enable him to reach his targets.

In short, the main factor in the management of performance should be the analysis of the behaviour required to achieve agreed results, not the assessment of personality. This is partly management by objectives, which is concerned with planning and measuring results in relation to agreed targets and standards, but retains the concept that performance is about behaviour as well as results (a notion that management by objectives ignored).

A mainly forgotten, but still relevant, research project conducted by Rowe (1964) in the UK came to broadly the same conclusion as McGregor – that managers do not like 'playing at being God' in rating the personalities of their subordinates:

> Managers admitted they were hesitant [to appraise] because what they wrote might be misunderstood, because they might unduly affect a subordinate's future career, because they could only write what they were prepared to say and so on.

One comment made to Rowe was that, 'You feel rather like a schoolmaster writing an end-of-term report'. Rowe concluded:

☐ Appraisers were reluctant to appraise.
☐ The follow-up was inadequate.
☐ No attempt should be made to clarify or categorise performance in terms of grades. The difficulty of achieving common standards and the reluctance of appraisers to use the whole scale made them of little use.

These comments, especially the last one, are as relevant today as they were more than 30 years ago – and commentators are still producing these precepts as original truths. It is remarkable how much re-inventing of the wheel goes on in the field of performance management. Another example is the replacement of the discredited management by objectives by performance management, at least in its earlier versions.

The attack on merit-rating, or on the earlier versions of performance appraisal (as it came to be known in the 1950s), was often made on the grounds that it was mainly concerned with the assessment of traits. These could refer to the extent to which individuals were conscientious, imaginative, self-suffi-cient, co-operative, or possessed qualities of judgement, initiative, vigour or original thinking. Traits represent 'pre-dispositions to behave in certain ways in a variety of different situations' (Chell 1992). Trait theorists typically advance the following definition of personality: 'More or less stable internal factors that make one person's behaviour consistent from one time to another and different from the behaviour other people would manifest in comparable situations' (Hampson 1982). But the belief that trait behaviour is inde-pendent of situations and the people with whom an individ-ual is interacting is questionable. Trait measures cannot predict how a person will respond in a particular situation (Epstein and O'Brien 1985). And there is the problem of how anyone can be certain that someone has such-and-such a trait. Assessments of traits are only too likely to be prompted by subjective judgements and prejudices.

Management by objectives

The management-by-objectives movement claimed that it overcame the problems of trait rating.

Background

The term was first coined by Peter Drucker (1955), when he wrote:

> What the business enterprise needs is a principle of manage-ment that will give full scope to individual strength and responsibility and at the same time give common direction of vision and effort, establish teamwork and harmonise the goals of the individual with the common weal. The only principle that can do this is management by objectives and self-control.

Drucker emphasised that 'an effective management must direct the vision and efforts of all managers towards a common goal'. This would ensure that individual and corpor-ate objectives were integrated and would also make it possible for managers to control their own performance: 'Self-control means stronger motivation: a desire to do the best rather than just enough to get by. It means higher performance goals and broader vision'.

McGregor's (1960) contribution arose from his *Theory Y* concept. He wrote that:

> The central principle which derives from Theory Y is that of integration: the creation of conditions such that the members of the organisation can achieve their own goals *best* by directing their efforts towards the success of the organisation.

This is McGregor's principle of 'management by integration and self-control', which, he emphasised, should be regarded as a strategy – a way of managing people. McGregor developed the concept in a way more in line with current thinking on performance management than the bureaucratic focus of management by objectives prevailing in the late 1960s. He wrote that:

> The tactics are worked out in the light of the circumstances. Forms and procedures are of little value ... 'selling' management a programme of target setting and providing standardised forms and procedures is the surest way to *prevent* the development of management by integration and control.

This principle may not have entered the vocabulary of performance management, but is fully absorbed into current thinking about it. Many writers and management consultants recycle McGregor's philosophy without ever acknowledging its source.

The management-by-objectives system

Management by objectives was defined by John Humble (1972), a leading British enthusiast, as:

> a dynamic system which seeks to integrate the company's need to clarify and achieve its profit and growth goals with the manager's need to contribute and develop himself (*sic*). It is a demanding and rewarding style of managing a business.

He described management by objectives as a continuous process of:

☐ reviewing critically and restating the company's strategic and tactical plans

- clarifying with each manager the key results and performance standards he must achieve, and gaining his contribution and commitment to these, individually and as a team member
- agreeing with each manager a job improvement plan which makes a measurable and realistic contribution to the unit and company plans for better performance
- providing conditions (an organisation structure and management information) in which it is possible to achieve the key results and improvement plan
- using systematic performance review to measure and discuss progress towards results
- developing management training plans to build on strengths, to help managers to overcome their weaknesses and to get them to accept responsibility for self-development
- strengthening the motivation of managers by effective selection, salary and succession plans.

Humble emphasised that these techniques are interdependent and illustrated the dynamic nature of the system as shown in Figure 3.

Figure 3
THE MANAGEMENT-BY-OBJECTIVES CYCLE

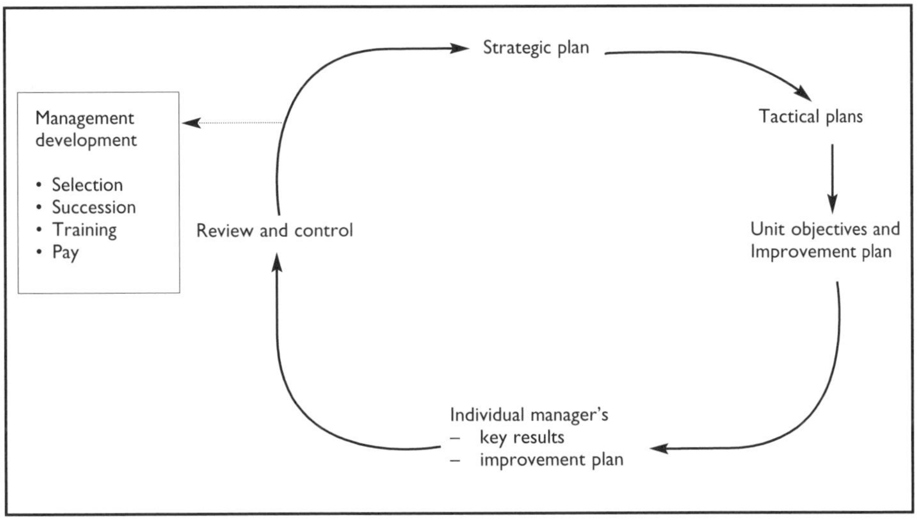

Except for the insistence that this system is exclusively for managers, much of what Humble wrote would be acceptable today as good, if not necessarily best, performance-management practice.

But management by objectives had become thoroughly discredited by the end of the 1970s – why?

Criticisms of management by objectives

One of the first, and most formidable, attacks on management by objectives was made in the *Harvard Business Review* by Levinson (1970). His criticisms were as follows:

☐ Every organisation is a social system, a network of interpersonal relationships. A person doing an excellent job by objective standards of measurement may fail miserably as a partner, superior, subordinate or colleague.

☐ The greater the emphasis on measurement and quantification, the more likely the subtle, non-measurable elements of the task will be sacrificed. Quality of performance frequently loses out to quantification.

☐ It (management by objectives) leaves out the individual's personal needs and objectives, bearing in mind that the most powerful driving force for individuals comprises their needs, wishes and personal objectives.

Another critic writing in the *Harvard Business Review* (a favourite medium for attacks on performance appraisal) was Schaffer (1991), who wrote:

> Ironically, management by objectives programmes often create heavy paper snowstorms in which managers can escape from demand making. In many MBO programmes, as lists of goods get longer and thicker, the focus is diffused, bulk is confused with quality, and energy is spent on the mechanics rather than the results. A manager challenged on the performance of her (*sic*) group can safely point to the packet of papers and assert: 'My managers have spent many hours developing their goals for the year.'

The cause of the demise of management by objectives was no doubt the fact that the process became oversystematised (often under the influence of package-oriented management consultants) and that too much emphasis was placed on the quantification of objectives. The originators of the concept may not have advocated lots of forms, and they recognised, as John Humble had, that qualitative performance standards could be included in the system, by which was meant 'a statement of conditions which exist when the result is being satisfactorily achieved'. But these principles were often ignored in practice. In addition, management by objectives often became a top-down affair with little dialogue, and it tended to focus narrowly on the objectives of individual managers without relating them to corporate goals (although that is what was supposed to happen, and it was certainly a major part of Drucker's original concept). The system also tended to concentrate on managers, leaving the rest of the staff to be dealt with by an old-fashioned merit-rating scheme, presumably because it was thought that they did not deserve anything better.

A later comparison of management by objectives and performance management by Fowler (1990) criticised the former because:

□ it was not right for all organisations – it required a highly structured, orderly and logical approach which did not fit the opportunistic world of the entrepreneur

□ only limited recognition was given to the importance of defining the organisation's corporate goals and values – the emphasis was on the role of the individual manager

□ line managers perceived it as a centrally imposed administrative task

□ it became a formal once-a-year exercise bearing little relationship to managers' day-to-day activities

□ there was overemphasis on quantifiable objectives to the detriment of important qualitative factors

□ the system was administratively top-heavy – form-filling became an end in itself.

Critical-incident technique

The critical-incident technique was developed by Flanagan (1954). On the basis of his research, he came to the conclusion that, to avoid trait assessment (merit-rating) and overconcentration on output (management by objectives), appraisers should focus on critical-behaviour incidents which were real, unambiguous and illustrated quite clearly how well individuals were performing their tasks. Flanagan advocated that managers should keep a record of these incidents and use them as evidence of actual behaviour during review meetings, thus increasing objectivity. He defended this proposal against the suggestion that he was asking managers to keep 'black books' on the grounds that it was positive as well as negative examples that should be recorded, and that it would be better to make a note at the time rather than rely on memory, which is selective and may recall only recent events.

The critical-incident technique did not gain much acceptance, perhaps because the 'black book' accusations stuck, but also because it seemed to be time-consuming. In addition, the problem was raised of converting the incident reports into an overall rating.

But the concept of critical incidents has had considerable influence on methods of developing competence frameworks, where it is used to elicit data about effective or less effective behaviour. The technique is used to assess what constitutes good or poor performance by analysing events observed to have a noticeably successful or unsuccessful outcome, thus providing more factual, 'real' information than by simply listing tasks and guessing performance requirements. Used in this way the critical-incident technique produces schedules of 'differentiating competencies' which can form the basis for assessing and, if desired, rating competency levels. (Differentiating competencies define the behavioural characteristics that high-performers display, as distinct from those characterising less effective people – ie the performance dimensions of roles.)

Even if the Flanagan concept of critical incidents has not survived as a specific assessment technique, it does survive as the basis for review processes that rely on factual evidence rather than opinion. The critical-incident method can also be used to develop behaviourally anchored rating scales, as described below.

Behaviourally anchored rating scales

Behaviourally anchored rating scales are designed to reduce the rating errors that it was assumed are typical of conventional scales. They include a number of performance dimensions such as teamwork, and managers rate each dimension on a scale, as in the following example:

A   Continually contributes new ideas and suggestions. Takes a leading role in group meetings but is tolerant and supportive of colleagues and respects other people's points of view. Keeps everyone informed about own activities and is well aware of what other team members are doing in support of team objectives.

B   Takes a full part in group meetings and contributes useful ideas frequently. Listens to colleagues and keeps them reasonably well informed about own activities, while keeping abreast of what they are doing.

C   Delivers opinions and suggestions at group meetings from time to time, but is not a major contributor to new thinking or planning activities. Generally receptive to other people's ideas and willing to change own plans to fit in. Does not always keep others properly informed or take sufficient pains to know what they are doing.

D   Tendency to comply passively with other people's suggestions. May be withdrawn at group meetings but sometimes shows personal antagonism to others. Not very interested in what others are doing or in keeping them informed.

E   Tendency to go own way without taking much account of the need to make a contribution to team activities. Sometimes uncooperative and unwilling to share information.

F   Generally uncooperative. Goes own way, completely ignoring the wishes of other team members and taking no interest in the achievement of team objectives.

It is believed that the behavioural descriptions in such scales discourage the tendency to rate on the basis of generalised assumptions about personality traits (which were probably highly subjective) by focusing attention on specific work behaviours. But there is still room for making subjective judgements based on different interpretations of the definitions of levels of behaviour.

Behaviourally anchored rating scales take time and trouble to develop and are not in common use, except in a modified form as the dimensions in a differentiating competency framework. It is this application that has spread into some performance-management processes.

Performance appraisal (1970s version)

In the 1970s a revised approach to performance appraisal was developed under the influence of the management-by-objectives movement. It was sometimes called 'results-oriented appraisal' because it incorporated the agreement of objectives and an assessment of the results obtained against these objectives. Ratings were usually retained of overall performance and in relation to individual objectives. Trait ratings were also used but, more recently, these have been replaced in some schemes with competence ratings. This form of performance appraisal received a boost during the late 1980s because of the use of performance-related pay based on performance ratings.

Appraisals, as defined by ACAS (1988),

> regularly record an assessment of an employee's performance, potential and development needs. The appraisal is an opportunity to take an overall view of work content, loads and volume, to look back at what has been achieved during the reporting period and agree objectives for the next.

Appraisal schemes often included ratings of performance factors such as volume of work, quality of work, knowledge of job, dependability, innovation, staff development and communication and an overall rating. Some schemes simply reviewed the achievement of objectives but still included the overall rating. Scope might be allowed for self-assessment, and the forms frequently included spaces for work improvement plans, training requirements and the assessment of potential. There was usually an arrangement for 'counter-signing' managers to make comments, generally the appraiser's manager – the appraisee's 'grandparent'.

In principle, many organisations and personnel specialists believed that formal appraisals were desirable. The ACAS (1988) booklet stated that:

> Appraisals can help to improve employees' job performance by identifying strengths and weaknesses and determining how their strengths may be best utilised within the organisation and weaknesses overcome.

But many criticisms were made of the ways in which appraisal schemes operated in practice. Levinson (1976) wrote that 'It is widely recognised that there are many things wrong with most of the performance appraisal systems in use.' He thought that the most obvious drawbacks were that:

☐ judgements on performance are usually subjective, impressionistic and arbitrary

☐ ratings by different managers are not comparable

☐ delays in feedback occur, which create frustration when good performance is not quickly recognised and anger when judgement is rendered for inadequacies long past

☐ managers generally have a sense of inadequacy about appraising subordinates, and paralysis and procrastination result from their feelings of guilt about playing God.

Levinson stated that 'Performance appraisal needs to be viewed not as a technique but as a process involving both people and data, and as such the whole process is inadequate.' He also pointed out that appraisal was not usually recognised as a normal process of management and that individual objectives were seldom related to the objectives of the business.

A slightly more balanced comment was made by Long (1986) on the basis of the (then) Institute of Personnel Management's research into performance appraisal:

> There is no such thing as the perfect performance review system. None are infallible, although some are more fallible than others. Some systems, despite flaws, will be managed fairly conscientiously, others, despite elegant design, will receive perfunctory attention and ultimately fail. The relative success or failure of performance review, as with any other organisational system, depends very much on the attitudinal response it arouses.

The requirements for success were indeed demanding. These were stated by Lazer and Wikstrom (1977) as follows:

> A 'good' performance appraisal scheme must be job related, reliable, valid for the purposes for which it is being used, standardised in its procedures, practical in its administration and suited to the organisation's culture.

The problem was that performance appraisal was too often perceived as the property of the personnel department. This was where the forms were kept and where decisions were made about performance-related pay. Line managers frequently criticised the system as being irrelevant. They felt they had better things to do; at worst, they ignored it and, at best, paid lip-service to completing the forms, knowing that they had to make ratings to generate performance pay. Indeed, managers have been known to rate first in accordance with what pay increase individuals should have and then write their comments to justify their marks. In other words, human beings behaved as human beings. Individuals were said to be wary of appraisals and to be as likely to be de-motivated by an appraisal meeting as the opposite.

Perhaps the worst feature of performance appraisal schemes in the 1970s and 1980s (and some still surviving through the 1990s) was that appraisal was not regarded as a normal and necessary process of management. If ratings were based on a review of the extent to which individual objectives were attained, those objectives were not linked to the objectives of the business or department. Appraisal was isolated and therefore irrelevant.

The concept of 'Appraisal: an idea whose time has gone?' was advanced by Fletcher (1993a). He stated that:

> What we are seeing is the demise of the traditional, monolithic appraisal system ... In its place are evolving a number of separate but linked processes applied in different ways according to the needs of local circumstances and staff levels. The various elements in this may go by different names, and perhaps the term appraisal has in some ways outlived its usefulness.

Enter performance management

Early days

The first recorded use of the term 'performance management' is in Beer and Ruh (1976). Their thesis was that 'performance is best developed through practical challenges and experiences on the job with guidance and feedback from superiors'. They described the performance-management system at Corning Glass Works, the aim of which was to help managers give feedback in a helpful and constructive way, and to aid in the creation of a developmental plan. The features of this system, which the authors said distinguished it from other appraisal schemes, were as follows:

☐ emphasis on both development and evaluation

☐ use of a profile defining the individual's strengths and development needs

☐ integration of the results achieved with the means by which they have been achieved

☐ separation of development review from salary review.

Although this was not necessarily a model performance-management process, it did contain a number of characteristics still regarded as good practice.

The concept of performance management then lay fallow for some years, but began to emerge in the USA in the mid-1980s as a new approach to managing performance. However, one of the first books exclusively devoted to performance management was not published until 1987 (Plachy 1987). He described what had become the accepted approach to performance management as follows:

> Performance management is communication: a manager and an employee arrive together at an understanding of what work is to be accomplished, how it will be accomplished, how work is progressing toward desired results, and finally, after effort is expended to accomplish the work, whether the performance has achieved the agreed-upon plan. The process recycles when the manager and employee begin planning what work is to be accomplished for the next performance period. Performance management is an umbrella term that includes performance

planning, performance *review*, and performance *appraisal*. Major work plans and appraisals are generally made annually. Performance review occurs whenever a manager and an employee confirm, adjust, or correct their understanding of work performance during routine work contacts.

In the UK the first published reference to performance management was made at a meeting of the Institute of Personnel Management (IPM) Compensation Forum in 1987 by Don Beattie, then personnel director, ICL, who described how it was used as 'an essential contribution to a massive and urgent change programme in the organisation' and had become a part of the fabric of the business.

By 1990 performance management had entered the vocabulary of HRM in the UK as well as in the USA. Fowler (1990) defines what has become the accepted concept of performance management:

> Management has always been about getting things done, and good managers are concerned to get the right things done well. That, in essence, is performance management – the organisation of work to achieve the best possible results. From this simple viewpoint, performance management is not a system or technique, *it is the totality of the day-to-day activities of all managers.* (Emphasis added.)

Performance management established

Full recognition of the existence of performance management was provided by the research project conducted by the (then) Institute of Personnel Management (1992). The following definition of performance management was produced as a result:

> A strategy which relates to every activity of the organisation set in the context of its human resources policies, culture, style and communications systems. The nature of the strategy depends on the organisational context and can vary from organisation to organisation.

It was suggested that what was described as a 'performance management system' (PMS) complied with the textbook definition when the following characteristics were met by the organisation:

- It communicates a vision of its objectives to all its employees.
- It sets departmental and individual performance targets that are related to wider objectives.
- It conducts a formal review of progress towards these targets.
- It uses the review process to identify training, development and reward outcomes.
- It evaluates the whole process in order to improve effectiveness.

In addition, 'performance management organisations':

- express performance targets in terms of measurable outputs, accountabilities and training/learning targets
- use formal appraisal procedures as ways of communicating performance requirements that are set on a regular basis
- link performance requirements to pay, especially for senior managers.

In the organisations with performance management systems, 85 per cent had performance pay and 76 per cent rated performance. The emphasis was on objective-setting and review, which, as the authors of the report noted, 'leaves something of a void when it comes to identifying development needs on a longer-term basis ... there is a danger with results-orientated schemes in focusing excessively on *what* is to be achieved and ignoring the *how*.' It was noted that some organisations were moving in the direction of competency analysis, but not very systematically.

Two of the IPM researchers (Bevan and Thompson 1991) commented on the emergence of performance-management systems as integrating processes that mesh various HRM activities with the business objectives of the organisation. They identified two broad thrusts towards integration:

- *reward-driven integration*, which emphasises the role of performance pay in changing organisational behaviour and tends to undervalue the part played by other human resource development (HRD) activities. This appeared to be the dominant mode of integration.

☐ *development-driven integration*, which stresses the importance of HRD. Although performance pay may operate in these organisations, it is perceived to be complementary to HRD activities rather than dominating them.

Some of the interesting conclusions emerging from this research were that:

☐ 'No evidence was found that improved performance in the private sector is associated with the presence of formal performance management programmes.'

☐ 'An overwhelming body of psychological research exists which makes clear that, as a way of enhancing individual performance, the setting of performance targets is inevitably a successful strategy.'

☐ 'The process of forming judgements and evaluations of individual performance is an almost continuous one. Most often it is a subconscious process, relying on subjective judgements, based on incomplete evidence and spiced with an element of bias.'

☐ 'There was little consistency of viewpoint on the motivating power of money. The majority (of organisations) felt that the real motivators at management levels were professional and personal pride in the standards achieved, or loyalty to the organisation and its aims, or peer pressure.' One line manager commented that he was self-motivated: 'The money comes as a result of that, not as the cause of it.' While the principle of pay for performance was generally accepted, the reservations were about putting it into practice: 'It was often viewed as a good idea – especially for other people – but not something that, when implemented, seemed to breed either satisfaction or motivation.'

☐ 'The focus has been on the splendid-sounding notion of the performance-orientated culture and of improving the bottom line, and/or the delivery of services. Whilst this is well and good, the achievement of such ends has to be in concert with the aims and the development needs of individuals.'

Why performance management?

Performance management arrived in the late 1980s partly as a reaction to the negative aspects of merit-rating and management by objectives referred to earlier. Of course, it at first incorporated many of the elements of earlier approaches; for example, rating, objective-setting and review, performance pay and a tendency towards trait assessment. Some of these features have changed, and the 'new realities' of performance management will be spelt out in Chapter 5. Conceptually, however, performance management is significantly different from previous approaches, although in practice the term has often simply replaced 'performance appraisal', just as 'human resource management' has frequently been substituted for 'personnel management' without any discernible change in approach – lots of distinctions, not many differences.

Performance management may often be no more than new wine in old bottles or, to mix metaphors, a 'flavour of the month'. But it exists, and our research demonstrates that interest is growing – why?

The market economy and entrepreneurial culture of the 1980s focused attention on gaining competitive advantage and getting added value from the better use of resources. Performance orientation became important, especially in the face of global competition and recession. The rise of HRM also contributed to the emergence of performance management. The aims of HRM are to:

☐ adopt a strategic approach – one in which HR strategies are integrated with business strategies

☐ treat people as assets to be invested in to further the interests of the organisation

☐ obtain higher levels of contribution from people by HRD and reward management

☐ gain the commitment of employees to the objectives and values of the organisation

☐ develop a strong corporate culture expressed in mission and value statements and reinforced by communication.

Advocates of performance management believe that it is a practical approach to the achievement of each of these aims.

The use of performance management in the best-practice companies is not because it is a better technique than performance appraisal, but because it can form one of a number of integrated approaches to the management of performance. The appeal of performance management in its fully realised form is that it is holistic: it pervades every aspect of running the business and helps to give purpose and meaning to those involved in achieving organisational success.

We conclude this chapter by providing a summary of the most recent developments in the history of performance management (Table 1, adapted from Fowler 1990).

Table I

MANAGEMENT BY OBJECTIVES, PERFORMANCE APPRAISAL AND PERFORMANCE MANAGEMENT COMPARED

Management by objectives	Performance appraisal	Performance management
Packaged system	Usually tailor made	Tailor made
Applied to managers	Applied to all staff	Applied to all staff
Emphasis on individual objectives	Individual objectives may be included	Emphasis on integrating corporate, team and individual objectives
Emphasis on quantified performance measures	Some qualitative performance indicators may also be included	Competence requirements often included as well as quantified measures
Annual appraisal	Annual appraisal	Continuous review with one or more formal reviews
Top-down system, with ratings	Top-down system, with ratings	Joint process, ratings less common
May not be a direct link to pay	Often linked to pay	May not be a direct link to pay
Monolithic system	Monolithic system	Flexible process
Complex paper work	Complex paper work	Documentation often minimised
Owned by line managers and personnel department	Owned by personnel department	Owned by line management

4 THE ESSENCE OF PERFORMANCE MANAGEMENT

In this chapter we describe the essence of performance management in terms of what it is, what it sets out to do, why it is necessary and how it works. We also examine the somewhat vexed subjects of performance rating and, briefly, performance-related pay, and consider documentation and some of the issues concerning performance management, namely, fairness, transparency, equity and discipline. We continue with summaries of the principles of performance management and the benefits it can provide, and conclude with a list of criteria for success.

What is performance management?

A definition of performance management was given at the beginning of Chapter 1. But as Mohrman and Mohrman (1995) say: 'Performance management practices must derive from and be tailored to fit each organisation's changing requirements. This will lead to a wide diversity of practices.'

It is, however, helpful to have a general notion of what performance management is about, and so here are some definitions:

> An effective performance management system aligns individual performance with the organisation's mission, vision and objectives.
>
> American Compensation Association (1996)

> Performance management is a process for establishing shared understanding about what is to be achieved, and an approach to managing and developing people in a way which increases the probability that it will be achieved in the short and longer term.
>
> Armstrong (1994)

Performance management is a means of getting better results from the organisation, teams and individuals within an agreed framework of planned goals, objectives and standards.

Armstrong and Murlis (1994)

The performance management process is the process by which the company manages its performance in line with its corporate and functional strategies and objectives. The objective of this process is to provide a pro-active closed loop system, where the corporate and functional strategies are deployed to all business processes, activities, tasks and personnel, and feedback is obtained through the performance measurement system to enable appropriate management decisions.

Bitici, Carrie and McDevitt (1997)

The essence of performance management is the development of individuals with competence and commitment, working towards the achievement of shared meaningful objectives within an organisation which supports and encourages their achievement.

Lockett (1992)

A systematic approach to improving individual and team performance in order to achieve organisational goals.

Hendry, Bradley and Perkins (1997)

A clear focus on how each employee can contribute to the overall success of the organisation lies at the heart of performance management systems.

IDS (1997)

Performance management is a way of translating corporate goals into achievable objectives that cascade down throughout the organisation to produce optimum results.

IRS Management Review (1996)

Performance management aims to improve strategic focus and organisational effectiveness through continuously securing improvements in the performance of individuals and teams.

Philpott and Sheppard (1992)

Performance management is about 'directing and supporting employees to work as effectively and efficiently as possible in line with the needs of the organisation'.

Walters (1995)

These definitions frequently refer to performance management as a process of aligning or integrating organisational and individual objectives to achieve organisational effectiveness. It is interesting to note that only one definition mentions development and only two refer to teams. Yet, in our view, development is the prime purpose of performance management – a view which is shared by Chris Bones (1996), who says that 'performance does not need managing. It needs encouraging, developing, supporting and sustaining.'

What does performance management set out to do?

The basic aims

Two simple propositions provide the foundation upon which performance management is built:

1 When people (individuals *and* teams) know and understand what is expected of them, and have taken part in forming these expectations, they will use their best endeavours to meet them.

2 The capacity to meet expectations depends on the levels of capability that can be achieved by individuals and teams, the level of support they are given by management, and the processes, systems and resources made available to them by the organisation.

These propositions imply that the basic aims of performance management are to share understanding about what is to be achieved, to develop the capacity of people and the organisation to achieve it, and to provide the support and guidance individuals and teams need to improve their performance.

Another way of putting the overall aim of performance management is that it exists to establish a culture in which individuals and groups take responsibility for the continuous improvement of business processes and of their own skills and contributions. It is about *sharing* expectations. Managers can clarify their expectations of what they want individual team members and their teams as a whole to do, and individuals and groups can communicate their expectations of what they should be able to do, of how they should be managed, the support and resources they need and how their talent should be used. The aim is to achieve consensus because, as Fletcher (1993) put it, 'Our perceptions of what is real and valid in the world depend on a consensus of shared beliefs.' One of the aims of performance management could be expressed as being to clarify the psychological contract.

Performance management is very much concerned with interrelationships – between managers and individuals, between managers and teams, between members of teams, and between individuals and groups and other stakeholders. These relationships are reciprocal, and performance management aims to improve their quality. It was interesting to note the number of comments made by members of the focus groups we convened as part of our research to the effect that formal or semi-formal meetings between managers and individuals provided 'quality time'. They were occasions for reaching better understanding of each other's concerns that are impossible (or at least difficult) to create in the hurly-burly of everyday working life.

Detailed aims

In more detail, the aims of performance management are to:

☐ help to achieve sustainable improvements in organisational performance

☐ act as a lever for change in developing a more performance-oriented culture

☐ increase the motivation and commitment of employees

☐ enable individuals to develop their abilities, increase their job satisfaction and achieve their full potential to their own benefit and that of the organisation as a whole

☐ enhance the development of team cohesion and performance

☐ develop constructive and open relationships between individuals and their managers in a process of continuing dialogue which is linked to the work actually being done throughout the year

☐ provide opportunities for individuals to express their aspirations and expectations about their work.

Performance management aims – suggested by other commentators

The American Compensation Association (1996) states that organisations rely on performance management to:

☐ document job responsibilities

☐ help define performance expectations

☐ provide a framework for supervisors and employees to communicate with each other

☐ provide ongoing opportunities for supervisors to coach and encourage personal development

☐ align individual performance expectations with organisational goals.

Egan (1995) suggests that:

> Most employees want direction, freedom to get their work done, and encouragement, not control. The performance management system should be a control system only by exception. The solution is to make it a collaborative development system in two ways. First, the entire performance management process – coaching, counselling, feedback, tracking, recognition, and so forth – should encourage development. Ideally, team members grow and develop through these interactions. Second, when managers and team members ask what they need [in order] to be able to do bigger and better things, they move to strategic development. The message from the company should be: 'We are not only going to help you develop in order to do a great job in meeting today's needs. We are going to tie your development to the company's development.'

Lockett (1992) believes that performance management should focus on two objectives:

1   ensuring that people are motivated to perform effectively to the boundaries of their ability.

2   stretching these boundaries through an effective programme of personal development.

The performance improvement aspect inevitably looms large in definitions of what people expect performance management to achieve. Daniels (1987) takes a somewhat instrumental view: 'Performance management is a way of getting people to do what you want them to and like doing it.' (Some people might regard this as recipe for manipulation!)

IDS (1997) commented, on the basis of their study of performance-management practices, that one of the central aims of the companies they contacted was to link individual performance more closely to organisational goals. In general, however, IDS suggested that performance management can help organisations to:

☐ set objectives for employees over the coming year

☐ review employees' performance against objectives and agree plans for improvement the following year

☐ pay employees for good performance

☐ develop employees for future roles to aid succession-planning and individual career aspirations

☐ collect information on gaps in skills and training needs.

These items include developmental aims as well as performance-improvement objectives. Pay is also mentioned, by implication, as a motivator.

Why organisations introduce performance management

The IRS 1998 survey elicited the following reasons from 24 organisations for introducing performance management:

Organisation	Reasons given
☐ American Express Services Europe	Cultural change
☐ Arts Council of England	Link pay to performance
☐ British Medical Association	Customer service
☐ Building Research Establishment	Link pay to performance
☐ Bury Healthcare NHS Trust	Market demand
☐ Edinburgh International Conference Centre	Quality – providing the customer with what the customer wants
☐ Emhart Fastening Teknologies (Europe)	Cultural change
☐ Halifax Building Society	Cultural change
☐ Jamont UK	Improve performance and identify training needs

☐ London Borough of Bromley	Feedback from staff
☐ Mansfield Shoe Group	Quality, reduce costs and improve customer service
☐ Natural History Museum	Link pay to performance
☐ NBC Health Trust	Market demands, competitiveness, identify training needs and feedback from staff
☐ NHS Executive Trust	Link pay to performance, quality and skills development
☐ Northern Ireland Audit Office	Improve customer service
☐ Nottingham City Hospital NHS Trust	Devolve control to line managers
☐ Pearl Assurance	Improve customer service
☐ Pfizer	Cultural change
☐ PHH Relocation	Link pay to performance and skill development, and improve efficiency of organisation
☐ Public Record Office	Improve efficiency and devolve control to line managers
☐ Scottish Power	Link pay to performance for managers, identify training needs and link pay to skill development for other staff
☐ Sericol	Improve competence
☐ South Derbyshire Health Authority	Improve efficiency, reduce costs and embrace government initiative
☐ Westminster City Council	Initially link pay to performance, now achieve better performance, and increase effectiveness in meeting council objectives.

Why is performance management necessary?

The reasons given by the organisations listed above appear to be powerful ones for introducing performance management, and the aims listed earlier in this chapter seem to be equally worthy. But it can be argued, especially by line managers, that if it *is* a normal process of management, why bother to introduce formal and possibly bureaucratic procedures for doing it?

Indeed, in any organisation there will be some good managers for whom adopting the performance-management process is just 'doing what comes naturally'. They can be invaluable as champions, developers and coaches. But there may be many more who need the encouragement, support and guidance that can be provided by a well-defined framework for managing performance, especially if they have taken part in its development. Performance management provides structures built round the natural planning, monitoring and reviewing processes of management. Generally people like to have some structure within which they can operate, as long as the structure is appropriate and does not constrain them unduly. And they need to appreciate how they can use the processes to their advantage as well as to that of the organisation by performing better themselves or by helping others to perform better. Performance management also provides the impetus for planned and systematic learning activities and events that might otherwise be lacking. Finally, the skills developed and nurtured by performance management are ones everybody can use to their own benefit as well as to that of others.

The one proviso is that performance management should not be imposed as a rigid, monolithic system that everyone has to operate exactly as and when they are told. A reasonable degree of scope should be allowed for individuals to operate it flexibly according to their needs.

How does performance management work?

We must emphasise again that there is no one right way of 'doing' performance management. It must be tailored to the circumstances and needs of the organisation, and it must be operated flexibly in accordance with the needs of the individuals affected by it. Having said that, it is possible to set out a typical sequence of processes that in one form or another are found in most performance-management arrangements, certainly in all the organisations we visited during the course of our research. This can be regarded in a sense as a model of performance management that illustrates its various components. But it should not be regarded as an ideal upon which all approaches to performance management should be modelled in every respect.

The performance-management cycle

Performance management is a process, not an event. It operates as a continuous cycle, as shown in Figure 4.

Figure 4
THE PERFORMANCE-MANAGEMENT CYCLE

plan
act
monitor
review

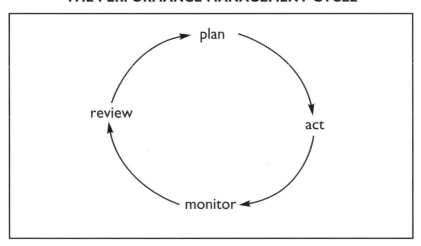

This is broadly in line with Deming's model for continuous quality management. A variation on this model has been produced by Torrington and Hall (1995), as shown in Figure 5.

Figure 5
PERFORMANCE-MANAGEMENT CYCLE
(Torrington and Hall)

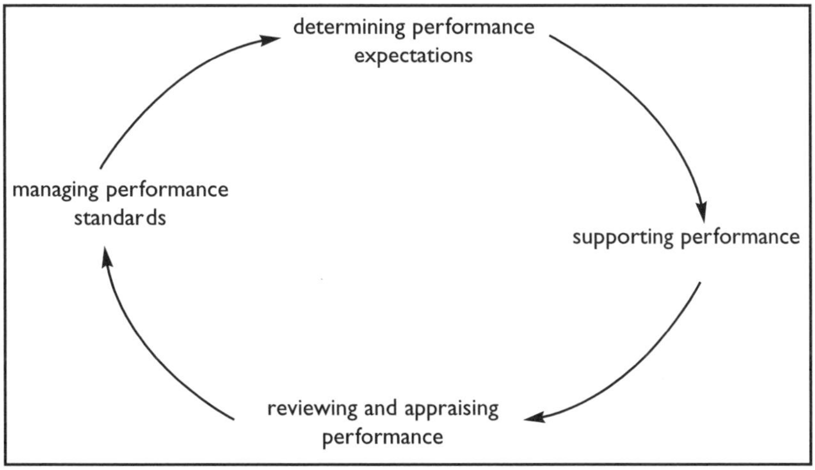

determining performance expectations
supporting performance
reviewing and appraising performance
managing performance standards

The performance-management sequence

The sequence of processes carried out in this cycle and the likely outcomes are illustrated in Figure 6. The activities carried out at each stage are described below.

Figure 6
THE PERFORMANCE-MANAGEMENT SEQUENCE*

*(Adapted from Cave and Thomas 1998)

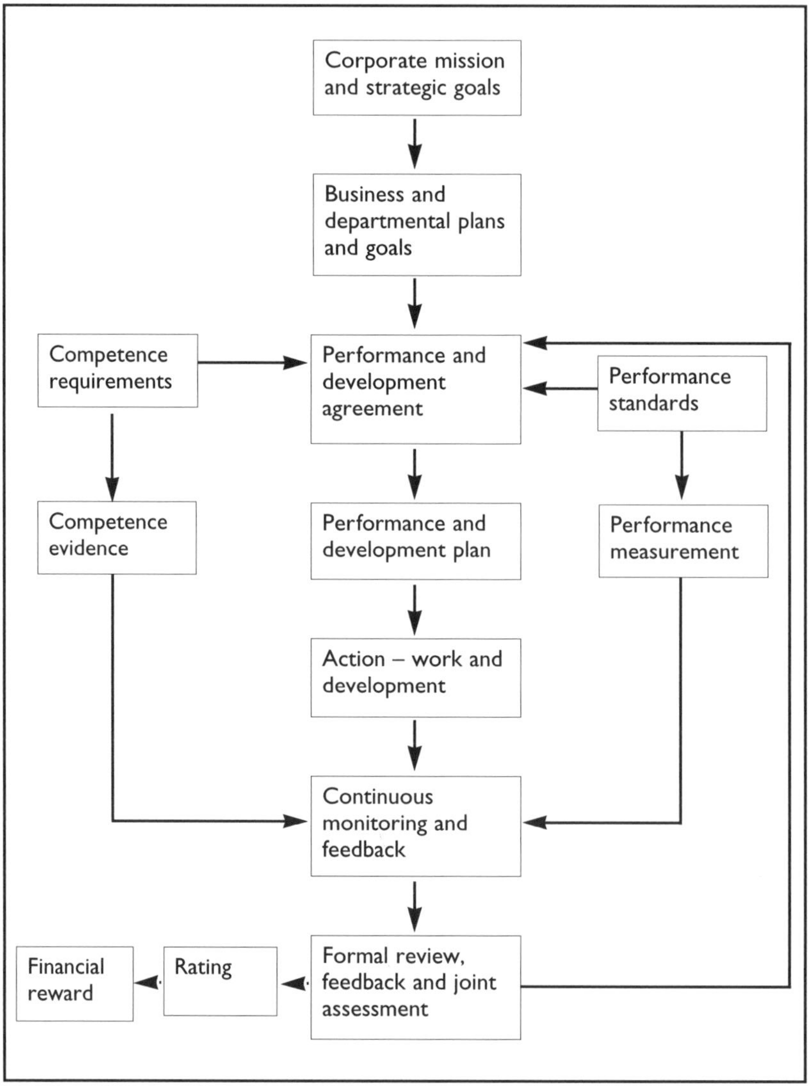

Corporate mission and strategic goals

These provide the starting-point of the performance-management process. The aim is to ensure that each of the activities in the sequence is aligned to those goals and contributes to their achievement.

Business and departmental plans and goals

These flow directly from the corporate goals but some iteration may take place so that departmental views about what can be achieved are taken into account before the business goals are finalised.

Performance and development agreement

The performance and development agreement, sometimes called the performance contract, is the agreement on objectives and accountabilities reached by individuals with their managers. The agreement is usually reached at a formal review meeting and recorded during or after the meeting on a performance review form. The processes of discussion and agreement are easier if both parties (the manager and the individual) prepare for the meeting by reviewing progress against agreed work or learning objectives, considering what plans need to be made to improve performance or develop competences and skills, thinking about future objectives, and examining any areas where the manager could provide more support through help, guidance, coaching or the provision of additional resources or facilities. Many organisations ask both managers and individuals to complete a pre-review meeting questionnaire (examples are given later in this chapter) which will provide an agenda for the review. A performance agreement defines the work to be done, the results to be attained, the performance standards to be achieved and the competence levels required.

For individuals, the work to be done is agreed in terms of key result areas or principal accountabilities or, sometimes, in the case of relatively routine jobs, by reference to main tasks or duties. In more dynamic roles, existing accountabilities may have to be re-assessed and new ones agreed as part of a revised agreement. In some cases, it may simply be necessary to confirm existing arrangements. The individual agreement should be based on an open, two-way and unambiguous discussion. This covers the areas listed below:

□ what the person is doing now

□ what the person might have to do in the future because of changing requirements

□ how the work should be done (competence or process requirements)

□ what the expected output and outcomes of the work (performance requirements and standards) are

□ what knowledge, skills and ability are required to do the work (input requirements)

□ any core values the individual would be expected to uphold – these may refer to such areas as quality, teamwork, customer service, responsibility to the community and care for environmental issues. The purpose of the discussion would be to define expectations on how the person's behaviour should support these values. The core values may be expressed in a list of competencies

□ what support the person requires – from the manager, from co-workers, from resources or information.

As Antonioni (1994) emphasises, it is essential that agreement is concluded on process goals (how the work is done) as well as output goals (what has to be achieved). And looking at it from a total quality management (TQM) view, he also stressed that the most important need 'centres on information regarding key external and internal customers' needs and expectations. Each internal customer has performance requirements that must be made explicit.'

The discussion on individual or team goals in the light of how they fit in with these internal customer expectations may lead to a reconsideration of departmental goals, and even of corporate goals – especially if people are being asked to do more than they can reasonably be expected to accomplish.

Basically the same process can be followed for teams ie agreeing what work should be done, how it should be done, what should be achieved, and what team skills are required.

Further consideration is given to the objective and competence agreement and definition aspects of the performance and development agreement in Chapters 16 and 17.

The performance and development plan

The performance and development-planning part of the performance-management sequence is primarily a joint exploration of what individuals need to do and know to improve their performance and develop their skills and competencies, and how their managers can provide the support and guidance they need.

The performance aspect of the plan obtains agreement on what has to be done to achieve objectives, raise standards and improve performance. It also establishes priorities – the key aspects of the job to which attention has to be given. Agreement is also reached at this stage on the basis upon which performance will be measured and the evidence that will be used to establish levels of competence. It is important that these measures and evidence requirements should be identified and fully agreed now, because they will be used jointly by managers and individuals and collectively by teams to monitor progress and demonstrate achievements.

Methods of measuring performance and analysing evidence of levels of competence are considered in Chapters 15 and 17.

For individuals, this stage includes the preparation and agreement of a *personal development plan* (PDP). This provides an action plan for individuals with the support of their managers and the organisation. It may include formal training but, more importantly, it will incorporate a wider set of development activities such as self-managed learning, coaching, project work, job enlargement and enrichment, an element of self-assessment by the individual. If multi-source assessment (360-degree feedback) is practised in the organisation, this will be used to discuss development needs.

Personal development planning is a key part of the performance and development management process, and is considered fully in Chapter 12.

Action – work, development and support

Performance management helps people to get into action so that they achieve planned and agreed results. It is a work- and people-related activity, and focuses on what has to be done, how it is done and what is achieved. But it is equally concerned with developing people – helping them to learn – and providing them with the support they need to do well, now and in the future.

The emphasis should be on managing performance throughout the year. This will involve continuous monitoring and feedback and formal reviews, as described below.

It is also necessary to enhance what Alan Mumford (1989) calls 'deliberate learning from experience', which means learning from the problems, challenges and successes inherent in people's day-to-day activity. The premise is that every task individuals undertake presents them with a learning opportunity. This will be the case as long as they are encouraged to reflect on what they have done and how they have done it, and draw conclusions on what they need to do when they are next presented with a similar task or have to undertake a different task requiring the use of the newly acquired skills.

Support should also be provided on a continuing basis through coaching and counselling, and by providing the facilities and resources necessary to meet expectations. As Marchington and Wilkinson (1996) state, 'performance management requires ongoing and unsolicited support in order to be effective; that is, the telephone call or the "chance" conversation just to check that all is going well, which many busy managers tend to overlook in their efforts to satisfy formal organisational requirements.'

Continuous monitoring and feedback

Perhaps one of the most important concepts of performance management, and it bears frequent repetition, is that it is a continuous process of managing and developing performance standards which reflects normal good practices of direction-setting, monitoring and measuring performance, providing feedback and taking action accordingly. Performance management should not be imposed on managers as something 'special' that they have to do. Neither should it be imposed on individuals and teams as something 'special' that is done to them. Performance management does no more than provide a framework within which managers, individuals and teams work together to gain a better understanding of what is to be done, how it is to be done, what has been achieved, and what has to be done to do even better in the future.

These sentiments could be dismissed as no more than managerialist rhetoric. And indeed they are managerialist, in the sense that they promote the notion of continuous improvement to support the achievement of the purposes of the organisation, and therefore of its management. But organisations are there to achieve a purpose, and it can be argued that if performance management helps them to do so, then to describe it pejoratively as managerialist is to miss the point. Of course, this argument is only valid if management appreciates that performance management should respect the needs of all stakeholders. Individual needs for job satisfaction, growth, security, recognition and reward have to be understood and reconciled with the needs of the organisation. And the continuous process of managing performance throughout the year can be carried out in a way that respects different needs as well as recognising mutual interests.

As stated by the American Compensation Association (1996), it is important to develop performance management on the basis of 'open, honest, positive, two-way communication between supervisors and employees throughout the period'. From the viewpoint of performance, this means instant feedback to individuals and teams on the things they have done well or not so well. If people can be provided with the information they need to monitor their own performance, so much the better. If it is not available readily, they can be encouraged to seek it. The aim is to provide intrinsic motivation by giving people autonomy and the means to control their work.

Interim informal reviews can be held as required – monthly, quarterly etc. They can be used to provide more structured feedback and, importantly, to revise objectives and plans in response to changing circumstances.

Progress in implementing the personal development plan can also be monitored during the year.

Formal review and feedback

Formal review meetings between managers and individuals, or team leaders and their teams, may be held annually, but may also take place more frequently – twice a year or even quarterly – in fast-moving environments. They provide an occasion for structured feedback and reflection. The feedback will summarise and draw conclusions from what has been happening since the last review, but it will be based on events and observations rather than opinion. These should have been raised at the time – there should not be any surprises during the formal discussion. But the conversation – and that is what it should be – will concentrate on analysis and review of the significant points emerging from the period under consideration. It will recognise successes and identify things that have not gone according to plan in order to learn lessons for the future. It should be a joint affair – both parties are involved. Therefore there may well be an element of self-assessment by the individual.

The review meeting itself can be used to give individuals the opportunity to comment on the leadership, support and guidance they get from their managers. This is a form of upward feedback and it may be structured into the discussion through pre-meeting questionnaires or check-lists.

If the purpose of the review is primarily developmental, as it should be, the managers will not be exercising judgement. This is not an *appraisal* session, in the sense of a top-down expression of the opinion of managers about the performance and behaviour of their subordinates. It is for this reason that we dislike the word *appraisal*, with its connotation of unilateral judgement from above.

The review may also consider developmental career moves. The latter may often be lateral to new roles at a broadly similar level that will extend the individual's knowledge, skills and competencies and provide the basis for further career development.

The review should be rooted in the reality of what the individual has been doing. It is concrete, not abstract, and it allows managers and individuals together to take a positive look at how performance can become even better in the future, and how any problems in achieving objectives or meeting standards can be resolved by the individual alone or jointly by the individual and the manager – for example by coaching or arranging training. The points that may be covered in a review include:

☐ the achievement of objectives, including an analysis of why they have or have not been achieved

☐ the level of competency achieved under each competency heading

☐ the contribution made by the person to upholding core values

☐ achievements in implementing the personal development plan

☐ areas for future consideration – development of strengths, aspects of performance that need to be improved, training needs

☐ feelings about the work – nature, scope, demands, opportunity to use abilities and develop skills etc

☐ aspirations – different types of work, career

☐ comments from the individual about the support given by his or her manager.

In a sense, the review is partly a stock-taking exercise answering the questions 'Where have we got to?' and 'How did we get here?' But there is much more to it than that. It is not just an historical exercise, dwelling on the past and conducting post mortems. The true purpose of the review is to look forward to what needs to be done by people to achieve the overall purpose of their jobs, to meet new challenges, to make even better use of their skills, knowledge and abilities, and to develop their skills and competencies to further their career and increase their employability, within and outside the organisation.

The role of managers during the meeting is to provide constructive feedback but also to *listen* to what individuals have to say about their performance and development needs. Managers are not there to sit in judgement. They are there to coach, not to criticise. As Chris Bones (1996) says, they have 'to move from critical parent to development coach'.

The review should identify areas for improvement in the

future and assess development needs. It therefore provides the foundation for a new performance agreement and performance and personal development plans. Typically, the meeting is divided into two parts: the first consists of the performance review and the second of a discussion leading to agreement on new or revised objectives and the formulation of the performance and development plans. The review meeting may also discuss the feedback from multisource assessments, as described in Chapter 19.

It cannot be emphasised too strongly that the prime purpose of the review is developmental. It should not be regarded as a top-down appraisal exercise. It is these judgmental, top-down connotations of the word 'appraisal' that have led a number of organisations we visited to replace it with 'review'. And that seems to us to be a highly desirable change.

The main output of the review in the performance-management sequence is the revised performance agreement, and this, together with the conclusions reached at the review, is usually documented on a performance review form. The contents of such a form are described later in this chapter.

The review may also generate performance ratings (and if so, it takes on the character of an appraisal session) and these are discussed below, together with the other output from some, but not all, performance management schemes – namely performance-related pay decisions based on the ratings.

Overall performance rating

Performance appraisal schemes have almost always included an overall rating of the individual's performance. Early performance management systems normally incorporated rating, especially when they were associated with performance-related pay, as was frequently the case. It is interesting to note, however, that the 1997 IPD research found that 43 per cent of all the organisations with performance management did not require an overall rating.

Arguments for and against rating

The arguments *for* rating are these:

☐ It is not possible to have performance-related pay without an overall rating (assuming performance-related pay is wanted or needed).

☐ It provides a convenient means of summing up judgements so that high or low performances can easily be identified (as long as the judgements are consistent and fair).

☐ It can provide a basis for predicting potential on the somewhat dubious assumption that people who perform well in their existing jobs will perform well in the future in different jobs. This is dubious because past performance is only a predictor of future performance when there is a connecting link ie there are elements of the present job that are also important in a higher-level job.

☐ They let people know where they stand, at least in the mind of their manager. (But this is only desirable if the manager's opinion is honest, justified and fair, and the numbers or letters convey what is really felt and have real meaning in themselves.)

The arguments *against* ratings are these:

☐ To sum up the total performance of a person with a single rating is a gross oversimplification of what may be a complex set of factors influencing performance, some of which, such as systems factors, may be beyond the person's control.

☐ Consistency between raters is difficult, if not impossible, to achieve.

☐ Ratings are likely to be based on largely subjective judgements (explicit standards against which these judgements are made are absent). They could therefore well be unfair and discriminatory.

☐ Managers might find it difficult to answer the question 'What do I have to do to get a higher rating?' if there are no explicit definitions in the rating scale of the standards of performance expected of anyone in that particular role, which is most unlikely.

☐ Rating encourages managers to be dishonest. Either they rate everyone in the middle of a five-point range or the second point down in a four-point range (this is the so-called central tendency) – or they decide first on what they want a performance-related pay (PRP) increase to be and rate accordingly.

☐ Rating turns what may – should – have been an open, positive and constructive discussion into a top-down judgemental exercise.

☐ The positive developmental aspects of the review may be overshadowed by the knowledge that the end-product will be a rating that will inform a pay decision. In practice, the review and the preparation for it may be dominated by its pay implications, destroying its main purpose.

☐ To label people with a letter or a number is both demeaning and demotivating.

☐ Ratings convey opinions about past performance. They say nothing about the future.

☐ Ratings may encourage 'impression management': people try hard to make a good impression rather than getting on with their work.

These are powerful arguments, supported by much of the evidence we collected during our research. One group personnel director, for example, said that 'It denigrates the whole performance management process.' A team-leader member of a focus group exclaimed, 'The rating system is crap, really – excuse me!' And a senior manager in a large financial services organisation told us that 'In the old system, one number was your life. Every other HR process was locked in behind the appraisal.' The following comment on ratings was made by the American Compensation Association (1996):

> To reduce the subjectivity of performance management systems and increase the focus on continuous improvement, organisations have tended to move away from rating categories or labels toward summary statements that are behaviour orientated and more focused on future improvements.

And Fletcher (1993a) made the point that in the UK:

> The use of ratings to compare individuals (even overall performance ratings), for so long a central element of appraisal forms and processes, is now declining.

Some people we talked to about rating recognised the problem, but said, 'We've got to do it because we have PRP.' In fact, some organisations manage PRP quite effectively without ratings at the time of the performance review, as we shall describe in Chapter 12.

If, in spite of these objections, it is felt that the system must have ratings, then there are three considerations:

□ how many levels
□ how to describe the levels
□ how to achieve an acceptable degree of consistency, equity and fairness in ratings.

How many levels?

The American Compensation Association (1996) accepts that the number of levels in a rating scale is probably one of the most controversial issues in performance-management design. The possibility is posed that the degree to which discriminatory judgements can be made will increase if there are more than, say, five levels. But the ACA then asks the question, 'How does one objectively differentiate performance at each of the five levels?' It comments that it is difficult to communicate the rationale for ratings in a way that ensures that employees understand performance expectations at different rating levels.

The first choice is between having an odd number of levels eg three or five and an even number eg four or six. The argument in favour of an odd number is that this represents the normal distribution of ability, with most people in the middle. The argument used to support an even number is that this will frustrate the tendency of managers to centralise ratings. The typical number of levels is four or five, but some organisations favour three on the grounds that this is the limit to which accurate discrimination is possible.

There has been much debate on what constitutes the 'best' number of rating levels. Milkowich and Wigdor (1991), in their report on a research project, came to this conclusion:

The weight of evidence suggests the reliability of ratings drops if there are fewer than three or more rating categories. Recent work indicates that there is little to be gained from having more than five response categories. Within this range (three to five) there is no evidence that there is one best number of scale points in terms of scale quality.

Describing the levels

Levels can be defined numerically (1, 2 etc) or, more commonly, alphabetically (A, B etc). Some organisations just rely on verbal descriptions in order to minimise the 'putting people into boxes' problem. It is preferable to avoid the use of above average – 'above average, average, below average' – what is average? And should one really label anyone for the next 12 months as 'below average'?

The tendency is to avoid negative descriptions in the levels and to leave out an 'unsatisfactory' or 'unacceptable' level on the grounds that anyone in this category should have been dealt with at the time the performance problem emerged under the normal disciplinary procedure – action should not be delayed until the performance review.

An increasingly popular approach is to have a rating scale that provides positive reinforcement at each level. This is in line with a policy of continuous improvement. The example given below emphasises the positive and improvable nature of individual performance:

Highly effective Frequently exceeds agreed targets and standards and consistently performs in a thoroughly proficient manner beyond normal expectations.

Effective Achieves agreed targets and standards and meets the normal expectations of the role.

Developing A contribution that is stronger in some aspects of the role than others, where most objectives and standards are met but, in some areas, further development is required to become fully effective in meeting performance expectations.

Improvable A contribution that generally meets or almost meets the standards expected but there is clearly room for improvement in a number of definable areas.

Note that these definitions ask raters to focus on definitions that compare performance to performance expectations and avoid ratings that compare employees, such as 'average' or 'below average'.

Achieving consistency

There are five methods of attempting to achieve an acceptable degree of consistency in ratings:

1   *Forced distribution.* This requires managers to conform to a pattern that quite often corresponds to the normal curve of distribution, on the rather dubious assumption that performance levels will be distributed normally in each part of the organisation. A typical distribution would be A = 5 per cent, B = 15 per cent, C = 60 per cent, D = 15 per cent, E = 5 per cent. But managers and employees rightly resent being forced into pre-determined categories, and this approach produces win–lose situations.

2   *Ranking.* Staff are ranked in order of merit, and then performance ratings are distributed through the rank order, for example the top 5 per cent get an A rating, the next 15 per cent a B rating and so on. This is another form of forced distribution that still depends on the objectivity and fairness of the rankings.

3   *Training.* 'Consistency' workshops are run for managers to discuss how ratings can be objectively justified and to test rating decisions on case-study performance review data. This can build a level of common understanding about rating levels.

4   *Peer reviews.* Groups of managers meet to review the pattern of each other's ratings and challenge unusual decisions or distributions. This process of moderation is time-consuming, but is possibly the best way to achieve a reasonable degree of consistency, especially when the moderating group members share some knowledge of the performances of each other's staff as internal customers.

5   *Monitoring.* The distribution of ratings is monitored by a central department, usually HR, which challenges any unusual patterns and identifies and questions what

appear to be unwarrantable differences between departments' ratings.

Performance-related pay

It was once assumed that performance management was
inevitably associated with PRP, and some organisations still
introduce it mainly to support PRP decisions (see the IRS
survey results referred to earlier in this chapter) and not for
developmental purposes. The arguments against mixing
developmental and reward factors in performance reviews
have already been mentioned in this chapter.

It is interesting to note that 85 per cent of the organisations
with performance management covered by the 1992 IPM
survey had performance-related pay, whereas only 43 per cent
of the organisations with performance management responding to the 1997 IPD survey had PRP. Too much should not be
read into these figures, however. These were not matched
samples. But there is evidence that organisations are concentrating more on the developmental than the reward aspects of
performance management.

The link between performance management and pay for
performance is discussed fully in Chapter 13.

Documentation

We have often said in this book, but it bears repetition, that
it is the *process* of performance management as practised in
the organisation as a whole and by line managers, teams and
individuals that matters, not the content of the 'system'. And
the content often consists largely of forms of varying degrees
of complexity.

The biggest danger faced by any organisation designing or
redesigning performance-management processes is to
'overengineer' the system – to produce lengthy and overelab-
orate forms, the only effect of which will be to convince line
managers that this is a bureaucratic burden imposed upon
them by top management or the HR department, or both.

Performance management is *not* a form-filling exercise,
and indeed a case can be made for not having any forms at all.

Managers, teams and individuals could be encouraged simply to record the conclusions of their reviews and their performance and development agreements on blank sheets of paper, which would then be used as working documents during the process of managing for performance and seeking continuous improvements that goes on throughout the year.

But there is something to be said for having a format that helps to structure the agreement, planning and review process. And the mere existence of a form demonstrates that performance management is something that everyone is expected to take seriously. The emphasis, however, should always be on the use of the form as a working document by both the manager and the individual or team. Increasingly, organisations are arranging for forms to remain in the possession of those who completed them. The forms are not sent to the HR department to gather dust in a dossier, and the only information required centrally is about training and development needs and, sometimes, data on people with potential for career and management succession-planning. The identification of people with potential can be recorded on the form, although some organisations conduct separate surveys for this purpose.

The two main categories of documents are those for completion before the meeting and those for completion during or after the meeting.

Pre-meeting documentation

The pre-meeting documentation can consist of forms to be completed by both the manager and the individual. For managers, these could include a review of the job content, the individual's achievements, development needs and potential, and possible objectives for the next period. Individuals could also review the content of their jobs, their achievements and aspirations, and what objectives they would like to set for themselves. In addition, they could be given the opportunity to express their thoughts on where they feel they need support from their managers and how that might be provided. The following are the questions, which largely mirror each other, for managers and individuals that could be included in a pre-meeting form.

Managers

1   What are the key results areas for this job?

2   How well has the job-holder done since the last formal review? (Consider achievements in comparison with agreed objectives and standards of performance.)

3   What are the key competency requirements in this role?

4   What level of competency has the job-holder displayed in each of these areas?

5   What feedback should I give to the job-holder on his/her performance? (Think about the evidence you have got to support this feedback.)

6   Is the best use being made of the job-holder's skills and abilities? If not, what should be done about it?

7   Are there any areas in which the job-holder could benefit from additional training, coaching or experience? (Specify the areas and how the needs can be met.)

8   What potential has the job-holder for promotion or taking on higher levels of responsibility?

9   What steps should be taken to develop the job-holder to advance his/her career?

10 Have I given the job-holder the support he/she needs? If not, what should I do about it?

Individuals

1   What are the key results areas of my job?

2   How well have I done since the last formal review? (Consider achievements in comparison with agreed objectives and standards of performance.)

3   What are the key competency requirements for my role?

4   What level of competency have I achieved in each of these areas?

5   What feedback should I give my manager on my performance (with particular reference to successes and any problems I have met in achieving objectives)? (Think about the evidence you have got to support this feedback.)

6   Is the best use being made of my skills and abilities? If not, what should be done about it?

7   Are there any areas in which I could benefit from additional training, coaching or experience? (Specify the areas and how the needs can be met.)

8   What are my aspirations for the future?

9   How would I like my career to develop?

10 Has my manager given me the support I need? If not, what would I like him/her to do about it?

Review meeting documentation

There is no standard format. But an examination of the forms used by the organisations covered in our survey revealed the following typical features:

□ *A section (or separate form) for the performance and development agreement.* This includes subsections for entering agreed objectives and standards of performance and competence targets, and for the personal development plan. The performance measures may be specified, and the personal development plan may set out the development need and how it is proposed to meet it, with details of the learning method proposed, who provides it (if it is not self-managed) and timings. The agreement may refer to any specific competencies that the individual has agreed should be developed.

□ *A section (or separate form) for recording the results of the formal performance and development review.* This incorporates agreed comments on the achievement of objectives, the level of competency attained and progress in implementing the personal development plan.

□ *Space for additional comments.* These, coming from the manager and the individual, would draw attention to any special points made during the meeting by either party. A separate space may be included to record the reviewer's and reviewee's views on potential, progression and development.

□ A space for *ratings* may be included and, especially if a rating has been made, a section for the reviewee's manager to comment on the review.

Some companies incorporate preparation forms in the document pack for reviewers and reviewees that act as a check-list on the points they want to make at the review meeting. An evaluation form in which the reviewee comments on how the reviewer conducted the meeting may also be included.

The two principles to bear in mind when designing the documentation are, first, keep it simple and, second, ensure that the different sections of the form are aligned to the sequence of areas for discussion at the meeting. The basic format of a performance and development review document is illustrated in Table 2.

Performance management issues

The most important issue, of course, is that performance management achieves what it sets out to achieve in the manner in which it is expected to achieve it. Too often, the reality does not match the vision, and the rhetoric remains rhetoric – unfulfilled pledges and promises, no more. Sadly, the cynicism of many academics about performance management rhetoric is justified. It can be said of some managements who introduce performance management with a flourish of trumpets what was said of Lloyd George: 'Count not his broken promises a crime: he meant them, how he meant them at the time.'

Performance management is difficult. Performance management is demanding. It is not an easy option. Grand designs can too readily produce edifices that soon crumble to dust. Engelmann and Roesch (1996) list the following negative consequences of poorly designed or poorly administered performance-management schemes, or schemes that lack management commitment (and, it could have been added, the ownership and support of other stakeholders):

☐ poor motivation and self-esteem because employees receive inadequate feedback on their work performance

☐ little or no focused communication about performance between supervisors and employees

Table 2 (Part 1)
PERFORMANCE AND DEVELOPMENT REVIEW FORM

PERFORMANCE AND DEVELOPMENT AGREEMENT AND REVIEW	
Name:	Forename(s):
Job title:	Department:
Reviewer's name:	Job title:

PERFORMANCE AND DEVELOPMENT AGREEMENT	
Objectives	Performance measures
Competencies	Agreed actions

PERSONAL DEVELOPMENT PLAN			
Development need	How it is to be met	Action by whom	Target completion date

Table 2 (Part 2)
PERFORMANCE MANAGEMENT AND DEVELOPMENT FORM

PERFORMANCE AND DEVELOPMENT REVIEW	
Objectives	Achievements
Competencies	Actions taken
Development needs	Actions taken
Comments by reviewer:	
Signed: Date:	
Comments by reviewee:	
Signed: Date:	

□ inefficient use of supervisors' time

□ litigation over alleged discriminatory actions.

The criteria for the successful design and operation of performance management to avoid these and other problems of lack of enthusiasm, positive dislike, or misunderstanding are exacting. They are set out as a fitting conclusion to this chapter because, in the light of our research, they do compose the new realities of performance management. But there are other issues, and these are discussed below.

Fairness

Performance management can be perceived as unfair if it involves the top-down imposition of objectives and the top-down appraisal and rating of performance. It will then function as a means of obtaining compliance rather than genuine commitment and understanding. Performance management is more likely to be perceived as fair if there is genuine sharing of the processes for defining objectives and reviewing performance, agreement on performance measures, and agreement on the evidence that has been produced against which performance is measured.

To increase the likelihood of fairness in ratings or assessments it is desirable to get a second opinion – usually from the appraiser's manager. An appeal system against ratings perceived to be unfair may be necessary.

Transparency

The performance process must be open. Everyone must understand how it works, the part they play and how any decisions arising from performance management that affect them are reached.

Equity

Performance management could be applied inequitably. This is especially the case if it involves ratings that can be affected by prejudice on the grounds of gender, race or disability. Townley (1990) recommended that the following actions to avoid discrimination should be adopted:

□ Criteria should be job-related, preferably be developed

from job analysis, identify behaviour rather than personal traits, and have precise rather than vague standards.

☐ There should be a check on appraisers through a review by the next level of management, and appraisers should not be drawn predominantly from one sex or ethnic group.

☐ There should be evidence of the system's being valid and reliable.

☐ There should be provision for open discussion of the evaluation with the employee, the latter having the opportunity to question or challenge any written comments.

☐ There ought to be an opportunity for appeal, preferably to a committee with minority membership.

☐ Employees should have written guidelines on how to complete appraisals, with formal training provided for appraisals, including equal opportunities awareness.

☐ There should be adequate provision of follow-up opportunities, access to training courses, developmental assignments etc.

Discipline

If performance management is to meet its developmental objectives, it is best to divorce it entirely from any disciplinary proceedings. The outcome of a review discussion should never be used as the basis for disciplinary action and, preferably, it should not be used as evidence in a disciplinary hearing.

Disciplinary actions in accordance with a disciplinary procedure should be taken on the basis of incapability at the time the alleged inadequate performance or behaviour took place. It should not wait until a performance review is conducted several months later.

Principles of performance management

The principles of performance management have been well summarised by IRS (1996) as follows:

☐ It translates corporate goals into individual, team, departmental and divisional goals.

- ☐ It helps to clarify corporate goals.
- ☐ It is a continuous and evolutionary process, in which performance improves over time.
- ☐ It relies on consensus and co-operation rather than control or coercion.
- ☐ It creates a shared understanding of what is required to improve performance and how this will be achieved.
- ☐ It encourages self-management of individual performance.
- ☐ It requires a management style that is open and honest and encourages two-way communication between superiors and subordinates.
- ☐ It requires continuous feedback.
- ☐ Feedback loops enable the experiences and knowledge gained on the job by individuals to modify corporate objectives.
- ☐ It measures and assesses all performance against jointly agreed goals.
- ☐ It should apply to all staff.
- ☐ It is not primarily concerned with linking performance to financial reward.

To this list should be added that performance is about providing support as well as direction.

Benefits of performance management

The benefits to the organisation, managers and individuals of well-conceived and well-run performance management processes are summarised below.

For the organisation

Such processes:

- ☐ align corporate, individual and team objectives
- ☐ improve performance
- ☐ motivate employees
- ☐ increase commitment
- ☐ underpin core values
- ☐ improve training and development processes

- help to develop a learning organisation
- enlarge the skill base
- provide for continuous improvement and development
- provide the basis for career-planning
- help to retain skilled employees
- support total quality and customer service initiatives
- support culture-change programmes.

For managers

Such processes:

- provide the basis for clarifying performance and behaviour expectations
- afford a framework for reviewing performance and competence levels
- improve team and individual performance
- support leadership, motivating and teambuilding processes
- provide the basis for helping underperformers
- may be used to develop or coach individuals
- offer the opportunity to spend structured 'quality' time with teams and team members
- provide the basis for providing non-financial rewards to staff (eg recognition, opportunity for growth and development).

For individuals

Such processes offer:

- greater clarity of roles and objectives
- encouragement and support to perform well
- the provision of guidance and help in developing abilities and performance
- opportunities to spend 'quality time' with their managers
- opportunities to contribute to the formulation of objectives and plans and to improvements in the way work is managed and carried out
- an objective and fair basis for assessing performance.

Criteria for success

1   Performance management processes fit the culture of the organisation, the context in which it operates and the characteristics of its people and work practices.

2   There is commitment and support from top management.

3   There is shared ownership with line managers and employees generally.

4   Processes are aligned to the real work of the organisation and how, in general, performance is managed.

5   It can be demonstrated that performance management adds value in terms of both short-term results and longer-term development.

6   Performance-management processes are integrated with strategic and business-planning processes.

7   Performance-management processes are integrated with other HR processes.

8   Performance-management processes can operate flexibly to meet local or special circumstances.

9   Performance-management processes are readily accepted by all concerned as natural components of good management and work practices.

10 All stakeholders within the organisation are involved in the design, development and introduction of performance management. These comprise top management, line managers, team leaders, team, individual employees and trade-union or employee representatives.

11 Performance-management processes are transparent and operate fairly and equitably.

12 Managers and team leaders take action to ensure that there is a shared understanding generally of the vision, strategy, goals and values of the organisation.

13 Performance-management processes recognise that there is a community of interests in the organisation and respect individual needs.

14 Performance-management processes are used by managers and team leaders to help people feel that they are valued by the organisation.

15 Performance-management processes help to align organisational and individual goals (but this is not a matter of a top-down 'cascade' of objectives). Individuals and teams are given the opportunity to put forward their views on what they can achieve, and their views are listened to.

16 The focus of performance management is on the development of people and the provision of the support they need. Financial rewards are a secondary consideration if, indeed, they are associated with performance management.

17 There are competence frameworks in place developed specially for the organisation with the full involvement of all concerned.

18 The aims and operation of performance management and how it can benefit all concerned are communicated thoroughly and effectively.

19 Training in performance-management skills is given to managers, team leaders and employees generally.

20 The effectiveness of performance management is continually monitored and evaluated.

21 The opinions of all stakeholders are sought about how well the scheme is working, and action is taken as required to improve the various processes.

5   CRITIQUES OF PERFORMANCE MANAGEMENT AND APPRAISAL

The critical arena

The aim of this chapter is to provide insight into some of the more problematic aspects of performance management. Most of the adverse critisisms have been directed at performance appraisal, in particular performance appraisal carried out in isolation from other tools for managing performance. These criticisms fall broadly into two categories:

- □ 'It's a good idea but it doesn't work' (*mainly practitioners and some academics*).
- □ 'It's a bad idea and it doesn't work' (*mainly academics*).

'It's a good idea but it doesn't work'

Those who believe that it does not work assert that managers often do not like doing appraisal because they see it as an imposed bureaucratic chore that has nothing to do with their real work. It is claimed that individuals either dread the appraisal meeting because it is potentially threatening (even though managers are notoriously unwilling to criticise openly), or because they perceive it as an irrelevant bore, their managers merely 'going through the motions'. There is said to be general dissatisfaction among both managers and individuals with rating systems, which they see as being applied inconsistently and unfairly.

As Furnham (1996) comments, 'The question is why this fundamental process (performance appraisal) is so rare and, when done at all, is frequently done badly?' He suggests the following reasons for this situation:

- □ Pusillanimity – managers are too scared to give negative or corrective feedback.
- □ Managers have not been trained in the skills of appraisal.
- □ Managers argue that, rather than having a couple of specific hour-long meetings over the year, they give subordinates consistent feedback on a day-to-day basis. (But what they fail to realise is that discussions about software, the sales figures and the strategic plan do *not* constitute appraisal.)
- □ The organisation, despite much rhetoric, does not take the whole process seriously.

It is true that traditional performance appraisal can too easily become, as Armstrong and Murlis (1994) describe it, 'a dishonest annual ritual'. And there is no doubt that in quite a few organisations performance appraisal, old style, fails to work in the ways described above. Our research confirmed that many people – both managers and their staff – dislike or distrust rating, and believe that performance-related pay can function unfairly. However, our research, as described in Part II, revealed that most people approved of the performance review (and personal-development aspects of performance management), and carried it out conscientiously.

'It's a bad idea and it doesn't work'

The heaviest, and in some ways, the most salutary criticisms have come from the academics, based on their research, together with the notorious attack by William Deming, the leading total quality management (TQM) guru. The rest of this chapter contains summaries of their ideas and research.

Deficiencies and the Perpetuation of Power: Latent functions in performance appraisal
G Barlow (1989)

Argument

'Institutionally elaborated systems of management appraisal and development are significant rhetorics in the apparatus of bureaucratic control.' They reward what is perceived to be successful performance and penalise deviance.

Appraisal systems impose artificial rationality. 'Ambiguity

and complexity will not be eliminated from the pluralistic processes and alliances of organisational life as it actually is.'

Evidence from field study in the petrochemicals industry

The study established from managers that the appraisal system 'served neither to motivate nor control'. Managers saw the appraisal system as a bureaucratic ritual. The system:

> institutionalised an ideology which sought to enlist partici- pants' positive effort and continued compliance, despite the inegalitarian nature of business organisations.

Conclusion

The conclusion was that:

> The dynamic of power relationships is bound up with their intangibility ... Such relationships evolve from the myriad intangible observations and devices by means of which one person learns how to relate to and work with another. Formalised appraisal systems discount the influences of such dynamics because they cannot be enumerated satisfactorily. In doing so they ride roughshod over what frequently is precari- ous and tenuous.

What's Wrong with Performance Appraisal? A critique and a suggestion K Grint (1993)

Dislike of appraisal systems

There seems to be considerable, although not universal, dis- like of and dissatisfaction with all performance-appraisal sys- tems to some degree. Crudely speaking, HR managers seem favourably inclined, line managers much less so.

Problems with appraisals

The problems with appraisals are:

☐ the complexity of the variables being assessed

☐ the subjective elements that confuse the assessment

☐ the fact that rewards and progress are in the hands of a single 'superordinate' (ie appraiser/manager)

☐ the fact that individuals have to work with their appraisers after the appraisal

□ the fundamental issue relating to the appraisal by individuals of individuals who act only in social situations – the comment is made that a major aim of appraisal schemes is to limit the collective aspects of work and individualise the employment relationship. 'F W Taylor would indeed have been impressed.'

The unreal nature of assessments

The extent to which assessments bear a close or, indeed, any relationship to reality is questioned because:

□ the assessor sees the assessed only from one specific position

□ of the impossibility of 'being able to reduce the complex nature of any individual to a series of scales in a tick list'

□ the multifaceted identity of people may lead to views about individuals varying widely – different people read each other very differently

□ as people ascend the hierarchy, they are likely to be less and less aware of what their subordinates think about them and their performance

□ the possibility of ever achieving objective appraisals of a subordinate by a superior is remote.

Conclusions

'Rarely in the history of business can such a system have promised so much and delivered so little.' But in spite of the relatively long and generally unhappy life of appraisal schemes, they should not be abandoned. Instead they should be considered more sceptically: people might have to accept their 'subjective fate'.

Image and Substance: The management of performance as rhetoric or reality?
M Bowles and G Coates (1993)

Arguments

□ Appraisal is shifting from concern with performance to concern with people in terms of their identification with the job and the organisation. 'Believing in the organisation is the criterion rather than performing for it.'

☐ Managers are mostly appraised by results, but results alone cannot reflect performance, because it is still affected by many other factors. Deming (1986) is right: job performance cannot be disentangled from systems effects.

☐ The emphasis given to collective effort and teamwork conflicts with the individualistic ethic of performance-appraisal practice.

☐ The nature of performance appraisal, which involves one individual making judgements on another, 'tends to reinforce authority relations and defines dependency'.

Research

A UK survey of 48 organisations in the Midlands established that the major benefit of what some people considered successful systems was their getting people to achieve work goals. The problems faced by organisations experiencing some difficulties were measuring performance and the extra demands made on managers.

Conclusions

☐ 'Performance appraisal requires subtle psychological and social skills which may not be acquired by many managers.'

☐ Performance appraisal seems often to be 'an opportunistic means to address performance issues' rather than 'a well thought out, coherent and systematic attempt to impart a new philosophy and practice of organisational relations'.

☐ 'The absence of clear indices of measurement will often cause images of performance to be exploited.' Performance may have less to do with physical outputs and more about exhibiting the correct 'mind set'.

☐ An ethic is required that 'conveys trust, integrity and faith in the ability of employees to contribute to a creative management practice'.

☐ Management should provide the 'enabling' conditions through which work is performed.

☐ 'The active involvement of employees in the management of performance potentially allows a constructive dialogue with management, to determine what factors foster performance.'

Appraisal into UK Universities
B Townley (1990/1991)

An analysis of 30 university appraisal schemes generated the following general comments on appraisal:

☐ Appraisal is regarded as a technical function that is considered in isolation.

☐ Appraisal should be viewed as 'an assemblage of signs whose meaning is constructed dependent on the context of its introduction and operation'.

☐ A failure to contextualise appraisal will ignore the 'different, sometimes conflicting interests' that influence the form of appraisal adopted.

☐ Seeing appraisal in the context in which it operates 'points to the diversity of functions into which a single system may be invested'.

☐ Appraisal can become a 'mechanism around which interests are negotiated, counter-claims articulated and political processes expressed. Designers of appraisal schemes would do well to remember this.'

☐ One university is quoted as stating that 'the term appraisal usually implies a judgement by a superior of a subordinate, that is, a process which is unilateral and top down'.

Performance Appraisal and the Emergence of Management
Barbara Townley (1993)

Quoting another writer, Townley argues that management is 'institutionally empowered to determine and/or regulate certain aspects of the actions of others' (Willmott 1984). The 'radical critique' of the concept of control is central to an understanding of management.

> Power is exercised through its intersection with knowledge, for example, methods of observation, techniques of registra-

tion – mechanisms for the supervision and administration of individuals and groups.

Appraisal is defined as a managerial activity: 'the provision of data designed to ensure that resources are used efficiently in accomplishing organisational objectives'. The role of appraisers is structured through setting the agenda. Management is inextricably linked to control over the labour process.

One of the inherent paradoxes of appraisal is that 'the information required to ensure effective work organisation will not be forthcoming if it is thought that this will jeopardise the individual'.

Appraisal operates as a form of 'panepticon' (a concept for prison design originated by Jeremy Bentham in the nineteenth century which incorporates a central observation tower from which the activities of all the inmates can be seen). The process of appraisal takes this form because it combines hierarchy, unilateral observation and 'a normalising judgement'. Anonymous and continuous surveillance are methods of articulating a monitoring role.

Appraisal is the 'exercise of control at a distance both spatially and temporally'. It 'illustrates how knowledge of the individual and the work performed articulates the managerial role as a directional activity'.

Performance Appraisal in Practice
I Carlton and M Sloman (1992)

A review of the appraisal system in a merchant bank revealed the following problems:

☐ Managers were hostile to what they perceived as bureaucracy and disliked form-filling.

☐ Ratings linked to pay were disliked. As one line manager said, 'Performance appraisal is a load of rubbish. You decide on the rating you want to put in the box and then make up a few words of narrative in other sections to justify it.'

☐ Ratings drift occurred. Managers tended to over-rate people because of the link between appraisal and pay. As one manager commented when challenged, 'I knew that his performance did not justify the rating but I thought it would demotivate him if I marked him down.'

□ The separation of appraisal and pay decisions was considered to be impossible because 'managers only fill in one form and if they do not perceive a clear link with salary, they will not do it'.

Playing God? The performance of appraisal
T Newton and P Findlay (1996)

Arguments

□ Most writers on appraisal are overinfluenced by the 'neo-human relations' writers of the 1950s and 1960s (eg Douglas McGregor), who provide 'unitarist prescriptions that are generally insensitive to both context and outcome' and assume that appraisal will serve the supposed common interest of employer and employee.

□ Appraisees are not going to view appraisal as a 'helping/counselling exercise' if there is the possibility that the data will be used in assessing promotion or demotion.

□ Participative approaches to appraisal are suspect because they constitute 'a desire through which management control may be enhanced by appearing to disperse it.'

□ Appraisal can be regarded as a management strategy 'aimed at eliciting a measure of voluntary compliance from employees' and encouraging workers to regulate and police their own behaviour.

□ The 'neo-human relations' assumption that appraisal can equally serve the appraiser and the appraisee is rejected.

Conclusion

'A greater understanding of the organisational context in which appraisal takes place and, consequently, of appraisal itself, requires an acknowledgement of the differences of interests between appraisers and appraisees.'

Policing Performance
D Winstanley and K Stuart-Smith (1996)

Argument

Traditional approaches to performance management fail

because they are flawed in implementation, demotivate staff and 'are often perceived as forms of control which are inappropriately used to "police" performance'.

Criticisms of performance management

☐ Conclusive evidence that it leads to improved performance is lacking.

☐ It can produce undesirable side-effects: demotivation on the one hand and overbureaucratisation on the other.

☐ It is difficult to set performance objectives that cover intangibles, are flexible in response to change and cover the whole job.

☐ Not enough time is given to the process.

☐ It is a form of 'Taylorism': in the perception of appraisees, it can 'become akin to a police state', in which evidence is collected, dossiers built up and 'supervision becomes a matter of spying through keyholes'.

☐ It is managerialist in that it takes a unitary view of the organisation. This is referred to as the 'radical critique' of performance management, namely that 'it operates within a unitarist paradigm and is not able to treat organisations as pluralities of interests'.

☐ The question is asked, 'Are individuals in the process treated as "ends in themselves" or merely "means to other ends"?' (It is suggested that the latter approach is typical.)

☐ It reinforces modes of 'intrusive control'.

Ethical principles

Four ethical principles should be built into the performance management process:

☐ respect for the individual
☐ mutual respect
☐ procedural fairness
☐ transparency of decision-making.

Performance-management model

The model used consists of three main processes:

   ☐ setting the objectives

   ☐ managing performance to objectives

   ☐ measuring performance against objectives.

Proposals

It is suggested that a stakeholder perspective should be adopted in the design of performance-management systems, one that offers a wider role to individuals as 'creators' rather than 'victims' of performance management. Because pluralism is endemic in organisations, it should not be only the power-holder's voice that is heard: 'Where consensus exists it can be built in, but where it does not, dissenters are not silenced.'

The approach should be one of 'stakeholder synthesis', which goes beyond the analysis of the interests of stakeholders to gaining their views about business strategy and incorporating these views in the system design.

The case-study

The case-study describes how 'multi-fiduciary stakeholder analysis' was used to develop performance-management processes at the British School of Osteopathy. This included interviews with key stakeholders to agree strategic objectives for the organisation, the use of the 'Delphi technique' to obtain individual views that would not be dominated by those of other people, focus group meetings with tutors and customers (students), and questionnaires and depth interviews with customers (patients).

Conclusion

The focus must move away from measurement and judgement towards 'developing understanding and building up trust to allow a genuine dialogue to take place'.

Performance Management and the Psychological Contract
Stiles, Gratton, Truss, Hope-Hailey and McGovern (1997)

A survey of three companies revealed that there was a considerable degree of managerial apathy and even scepticism towards carrying out appraisal. The reasons were:

- the perceived bureaucracy of the appraisal system, which diverted managers from their 'real job'
- the lack of positive outcomes in terms of both development and pay
- variations between individual managers in judging performance
- defensive use of appraisal – lumping everyone together in average or even high/low categories.

The research also found:

- strong rhetoric in each firm about development and the notion of employability but, because of business pressures, the rhetoric was not converted into reality (development opportunities, if any, were confined to knowledge workers)
- unwillingness among employees to accept that lateral moves were as important as vertical ones
- PRP decisions generated by performance appraisal rating or ranking
- (in a survey of organisational commitment) low levels of commitment in all three companies and low levels of trust in two of the companies.

Use of performance management to change the psychological contract

- There was a focus on performance management in all companies in order to effect change.
- But changes were driven in a top-down, systematic manner and the absence of consultation produced cynicism and a lack of trust among employees.
- Values and objectives espoused by the firm were undermined by short-term pressures and the continuation of the old belief systems, giving conflicting messages to employees.

Other messages

- Concern was expressed by employees over the fairness and accuracy of the performance-management system: little or no negotiation in objective-setting, question marks over the achievability of the targets, variability and inconsistency in appraisal, lack of opportunities for development, and a large degree of mystification about the workings of the appraisal were indicative of this concern.

☐ There was evidence that employees believed changes to the performance-management system had increased the transactional nature of the contract (eg emphasis on the link to pay, little concern about development).

☐ All organisational changes can be viewed as producing incidents of contract violation, new policies and processes making statements at odds with the *status quo*.

☐ The manner of introducing the contract did little to restore the good faith of employees: there was a lack of procedural justice (giving employees involvement in determining decisions about change, giving input during objective-setting and performance evaluations).

Out of the Crisis
W Deming (1986)

In the twelfth of his 14 points, Deming made the following pronouncement:

> Remove the barriers that rob hourly workers and people in management of their right to pride in workmanship. This implies, *inter alia*, abolition of the annual merit rating (appraisal of performance).

He also defined 'evaluation of performance, merit rating or annual review' as the third deadly disease of management.
The further points he made were that:

☐ rating the performance of individuals is unsound because differences in performance are largely due to systems variations

☐ targets and objectives for individuals damage customer-focused teamwork

☐ targets too often make no reference to the customer and results are limited if 'stretching' can be achieved only by suboptimisation, while, on the other hand, soft targets may be negotiated

□ formal appraisal schemes reinforce managers' reluctance to engage in coaching and open, direct regular dialogue with people

□ reliance on pay as a motivator destroys pride in work and individual creativity.

Commentary

Two issues dominate the academic critiques. The first is that the process is problematic because of the complexity and difficulties involved in one person's attempting to sum up the performance of another: 'Performance appraisal requires subtle psychological and social skills which may not be acquired by many managers' (Bowles and Coates 1993).

The second issue is that of appraisal as a means of oppressive or coercive control:

□ Appraisal is a system of bureaucratic or management control (Barlow 1989, Newton and Findlay 1996, Townley 1990/1991).

□ Appraisal enlists compliance (Barlow 1989).

□ Appraisal reinforces authority relations and defines dependency (Barlow and Coates 1993).

□ Appraisal implies that rewards and progress are in the hands of a single 'superordinate' (Grint 1993).

□ Appraisal aims at voluntary compliance (Newton and Findlay 1996).

□ Appraisal is a form of control used to 'police' performance (Winstanley and Stuart-Smith 1996).

Other issues raised include the following:

□ The tendency of managements to adopt a unitary frame of reference ('we're all in it together, our interests coincide') when, in reality, organisations are more likely to be pluralistic in the sense that there are divergent interests that should be acknowledged (Newton and Findlay 1996, Townley 1990/1991, Winstanley and Stuart-Smith 1996).

□ Appraisal ignores system factors (Bowles and Coates 1993, Deming 1986).

☐ Appraisal ignores the collective aspect of work and there is a conflict between the individualistic approach to appraisal adopted by managements and their emphasis on teamwork (Engelmann and Roesch 1996).

☐ Appraisal is an inconsistent and fundamentally subjective process (Grint 1993).

☐ Appraisal is a bureaucratic process to which managers are hostile (Carlton and Sloman 1992, Stiles *et al* 1997).

☐ Managements indulge in rhetoric about development but often do not put their espoused views into practice (Stiles *et al* 1997).

The views expressed by the academic commentators and by Deming provide a different perspective from that offered in prescriptive books and articles – and it is an interesting perspective. It penetrates beyond the rhetoric (a favourite term of abuse employed by the academics) to the forces actually at work when appraisal systems are operated. It has to be recognised that in many organisations (but not, on the whole, those we contacted) performance management, or rather appraisal, *can* be no more than a means of enlisting compliance, as these writers assert. It is also probable that much appraisal is carried out badly, although this was not confirmed by the focus groups conducted as part of our research (see Chapter 9). And when appraisal schemes involve top-down judgement, they *can* be instruments through which unilateral power is exercised. It is also unrealistic to predicate managements' performance-improvement programmes on the assumption that everyone else will support them.

Systems factors must also be taken into account. If judgements about performance are made, they must consider not only what the individual has or has not achieved, but also the context in which this performance has taken place and the influence of the system of work and other extraneous factors on that performance. This will include the quality of leadership displayed by managers and their interest in the development of their staff.

There *is* a danger that performance management may become bureaucratic and, if it includes performance ratings, the latter *may* be inconsistent and be based on subjective opinions. Finally, as we have emphasised and shall continue to emphasise, performance management is about teams as well as individuals.

All these aspects of how performance management functions in organisations should be borne in mind when considering its introduction or amendment. When management says it wants to create 'shared understanding', does it really believe what is being said? And will something be done about the processes (including for example, communication, training, guidance, counselling and evaluation) required to ensure that it happens? If not, the accusation of many academics that much of what is said about performance management is meaningless will be justified. And if management says it believes in a stakeholder approach, will something be done about it that does recognise that the organisation is a community of interests, all of which may not necessarily coincide? The doubts expressed on the likelihood of this happening by the writers quoted in this chapter may well be justified in many organisations.

So there is much to be learned from these critiques. However, there are two reservations that can be expressed about them. First, the almost obsessive focus on the use and misuse of power gives the impression that some commentators believe organisations are not entitled to have a sense of purpose or a sense of direction, are not entitled to believe that to perform well is better than to perform badly and are not entitled to define what they mean about performing well. Yet that is what organisations have to do, and it does not seem unreasonable that they should develop processes that help them to do it. For commentators to emphasise that there are ways to meet these requirements without dressing up the use of naked power in the rhetoric of performance is right. A stakeholder approach that recognises the diversity of interests is appropriate in association with the ethical principles suggested by Winstanley and Stuart-Smith. Managements should listen and act on the views of other stakeholders, but to deny the right of managers as stakeholders to define *their* expectations, as by implication some of the writers do, is going too far. And reading these contributions certainly produces the impression that many of the writers express the beliefs as universal truths that 'if managements say they believe in something, they never mean it, and won't do anything about it' (managerialist rhetoric) or 'if management does appear to be doing something about it, they still don't really mean it' (going through the motions). Is this really so?

The second reservation concerns the basis upon which these critiques have been made. They have mainly concentrated on performance appraisal as practised in the 1980s, when the failings they have identified were indeed rife. But they have set up a straw man that was too easily demolished. They do not appear to have noticed that some organisations – such as the ones covered by our research – have moved on. For example, only 45 per cent of those with performance management responding to the IPD questionnaire used ratings. Performance appraisal in the crude judgemental sense was not therefore practised in the majority of organisations. This is a distinct step forward. And evidence from interviews and focus groups is that performance-management processes are increasingly conforming to Winstanley and Stuart-Smith's ethical principles. There are probably, of course, many organisations not covered by our survey of which this is not true. The precepts of the academics are relevant in these cases and therefore constitute a valuable contribution to this study of the new realities of performance management.

PART II

PERFORMANCE MANAGEMENT IN ACTION

6   THE IPD* PERFORMANCE MANAGEMENT SURVEY

The survey was carried out in the spring and early summer of 1997. The aim was to establish current practice in performance management in the UK and, as a consequence, the survey questionnaire was structured to ascertain, first, what respondents understood to be the meaning of the term 'performance management' and, secondly, what activities were carried out in their organisations under that umbrella heading. The survey questionnaire also attempted to gather data to enable the use of various tools of performance management to be tested against a number of measures of organisational effectiveness such as quality, innovation, efficiency and return on investment.

Further aims of the survey were to identify the extent to which performance management was integrated with other people-management processes, such as those concerned with career management, development and reward. We were also anxious to acquire data relating to the reasons for making formal efforts to manage performance, the outcomes of performance management and how these outcomes are used.

Methodology

The survey was mailed to a total of 2,750 personnel practitioners in UK establishments. The sample reflected a mix of public sector, private-sector manufacturing and private-sector service, and organisational size ranging from 25 to over 5,000 employees. A total of 562 forms were returned in a usable condition, giving a response rate of 20.4 per cent.

Use of performance management

Of all the responding organisations, 388 (69 per cent) said that they operate formal processes to manage performance. Of the

* The IPD became the Chartered Institute of Personnel and Development (CIPD) in July 2000.

31 per cent who do not operate formal processes, 48 per cent have definite plans to do so within the next two years, whereas a further 25 per cent are undecided. Only 11 per cent have no plans to implement formal performance-management processes. The remaining statistics in this summary refer to the 388 organisations with performance management.

Performance management is applied as follows:

- senior managers – 96 per cent
- managers or team leaders – 90 per cent
- technical and clerical staff – 85 per cent
- professional staff – 81 per cent
- manual workers – 53 per cent (a significantly lower proportion).

Sixty-four per cent of respondents say they use only one set of formal performance-management processes, and 35 per cent say their formal processes differ between groups of employees.

Features of performance management

The main features of the performance-management processes used by respondents are shown in Table 3.

Table 3
FEATURES OF PERFORMANCE MANAGEMENT

Feature	Percentage
Objective setting and review	85
Annual appraisal	83
Personal development plans (PDPs)	68
Self-appraisal	45
Performance-related pay (PRP)	43
Coaching/mentoring	39
Career management	32
Competence assessment	31
Twice-yearly appraisal	24
Subordinate (180-degree) feedback	20
Continuous assessment	17
Rolling appraisal	12
360-degree feedback	11
Peer appraisal	9
Balanced scorecard	5

As might be expected, the most common features are objective-setting and review and annual appraisal. The high proportion of organisations using PDPs is significant: this is a feature of performance management not mentioned in the 1991 survey. Further than half the organisations have PRP. This is lower than might have been expected, and contrasts with the 74 per cent of organisations operating it in 1991. Competence assessment is also used by quite a high proportion of the respondents. Again, this was not a prominent feature in 1991.

Effectiveness of key features

Respondents were asked to assess the effectiveness of each of the features. Their replies are set out in Table 4.

Table 4

EFFECTIVENESS OF KEY FEATURES OF PERFORMANCE MANAGEMENT

Features	Very effective (percentage)	Mostly effective (percentage)	Partly effective (percentage)	Not effective (percentage)	No comment (percentage)
Objective-setting and review	27	48	18	2	5
Annual appraisal	7	59	28	2	2
Self–appraisal	22	43	30	2	3
PRP	6	36	37	14	7
PDPs	19	40	31	3	7

Objective-setting and review, annual appraisal, PDPs and self-appraisal are all strongly endorsed. PRP did not receive such support; fewer than half of the respondents thought it was very or mostly effective, and there were a substantial number of people (14 per cent) who thought PRP was not effective.

Views on different aspects of performance management

Respondents were asked to indicate the extent to which they agreed with the following statements as a description of performance-management processes in their organisations. Their replies are set out in Table 5.

Table 5

STATEMENTS ABOUT PERFORMANCE MANAGEMENT (PM): EXTENT OF AGREEMENT

Feature	Fully agree (percentage)	Partly agree (percentage)	Partly disagree (percentage)	Fully disagree (percentage)
PRP is an essential part of PM	13	24	22	37
Line managers own and operate the PM process	38	40	14	3
PM is an integrated part of the employee–manager relationship	43	42	9	1
PM is integrated into other people-management processes	25	47	19	3
The focus of PM is developmental	32	41	21	4
PM integrates individual and organisational goals	47	36	10	3
PM motivates individuals	16	59	20	2
PM is used to manage organisational culture	17	41	28	9
The effectiveness of PM is measured in qualitative rather than quantitative terms	14	48	28	5
PM sets stretching and challenging goals	27	52	16	2
PM is bureaucratic and time-consuming	3	53	35	25
The aims of PM are well communicated and fully understood	21	45	25	5

The majority of respondents either fully agreed or partly agreed with the following statements about performance management:

☐ It is an integrated part of the employee–line-manager relationship (85 per cent).

☐ It integrates individual and organisational goals (83 per cent).

☐ It sets stretching goals (79 per cent).

☐ It is owned by line managers (78 per cent).

- It motivates individuals (75 per cent).
- It is developmental (73 per cent).
- It is integrated into other people-management processes (72 per cent).
- Its aims are well understood (66 per cent).
- It is measured in qualitative terms (62 per cent).

The majority of respondents either partly or fully disagreed with the following statements:

- PRP is an essential part of performance management (59 per cent).
- Performance management is bureaucratic and time-consuming (60 per cent).

Respondents were particularly positive about the integrating, motivating and developmental aspects of performance management, but the majority disliked PRP. Although most respondents did not feel that performance management is bureaucratic and time-consuming, a substantial minority (36 per cent) thought it was.

Rating

The proportion of respondents who said an overall rating was given for performance was 54 per cent. This compares with the 64 per cent of organisations that had had rating in 1991. It is interesting to note that 24 per cent of organisations with PRP did not require an overall rating.

The majority of those with rating (67 per cent) used numerical or alphabetical categories. The following approaches were adopted to achieve consistency in rating:

- grandparenting (30 per cent)
- management-group review (21 per cent)
- forced distributions (5 per cent).

Management-group or peer reviews are becoming increasingly popular. Clearly, forced distribution is not much favoured.

Who keeps the documentation?

The performance-review documents are retained as follows:

- □ by personnel departments – 69 per cent
- □ by line managers – 71 per cent
- □ by individuals – 61 per cent.

There is an increasing tendency for line managers and individuals literally to be given ownership of performance-management documentation; some organisations ask only that PDPs and training proposals be sent to the HR department.

Evaluation of performance management

Nearly half of respondents (44 per cent) stated that they had a formal system for evaluating performance management. The formal methods used comprised opinion surveys (49 per cent of those carrying out evaluations), written feedback (35 per cent) and focus groups (20 per cent). Inconsistently, 59 per cent of those claiming to carry out formal evaluations used informal, verbal, methods, which calls into question the validity of the feedback.

Criteria for measuring performance

In the order in which they were ranked as very important, these are the criteria used for measuring performance:

- □ achievement of objectives
- □ quality
- □ customer care
- □ competence
- □ contribution to team
- □ working relationships
- □ aligning personal objectives with organisational goals
- □ flexibility
- □ productivity
- □ skill/learning target achievement
- □ business awareness
- □ financial awareness.

Views about performance management

The views of various categories of staff about performance as assessed by respondents are given in Table 6.

Table 6

VIEWS ON PERFORMANCE MANAGEMENT

Respondent	Very effective (percentage)	Moderately effective (percentage)	Partly effective (percentage)	Not effective (percentage)
Senior managers	17	64	11	1
Other managers/ team leaders	12	59	16	4
Other staff	4	41	34	9
Personnel	12	49	22	6

'Other staff' seem to be notably less enamoured of performance management than their managers. Interestingly enough, personnel people seem to be less enthusiastic than senior managers and, to a smaller degree, other managers and team leaders.

Changes to performance management

Quite a large proportion of respondents (56 per cent) were proposing to make changes to their performance arrangements over the following 12 months.

Impact on performance management

Nearly half of respondents (48 per cent) thought that their performance-management processes were very or moderately effective in improving overall performance. Leaving out the 'don't knows' or 'no comments', this leaves 37 per cent who think that performance management is ineffective or only slightly effective.

Development of performance management

A new performance-management scheme had been developed by 44 per cent of respondents within the previous two years.

It took less than one year in 43 per cent of the organisations, between one year and two years in 30 per cent of them, whereas 21 per cent took more than two years. Implementation took less than one year in the case of 56 per cent of respondents, between one and two years in 24 per cent, whereas 14 per cent of the respondents took over two years.

A substantial proportion of organisations takes quite a considerable amount of time and, presumably, trouble to develop and implement performance management.

7 PERFORMANCE MANAGEMENT IN PRACTICE

In this chapter we summarise the information about the performance-management practices in the 35 organisations we visited during the course of the research project. Eight detailed case-studies are given in Chapter 8. The information from these visits demonstrates the rich variety of performance-management practices in different organisations. Some basic features such as objective-setting and performance review or appraisal meetings are similar, but the way in which these activities are carried out, the emphasis on development, pay or both, the use of ratings, personnel-development planning, and the application of competence models vary widely.

When analysing the data collected from the case-study organisations, we identified a number of broad trends:

☐ Performance management is regarded as a number of inter-linked processes rather than a single system.

☐ Performance management is seen as a continuous process, not a once-a-year event.

☐ There is increasing emphasis on inputs (competence) as well as outputs (achievements of objectives).

☐ The focus is on development rather than pay.

☐ There is a shift towards line managers' accepting and owning performance management as a natural process.

☐ There is a rejection of bureaucracy.

These themes are discussed below and illustrated with examples from the organisations we visited in the course of our research.

Performance management as an interlinked process

As stated by Hartle (1995), performance management 'should be integrated into the way the performance of the business is managed and it should link with other key processes such as business strategy, employee development, and total quality management'. This appeared to be the case for many of the organisations we visited, although for significantly different reasons.

Many of our case-study organisations reported more than one reason that prompted them either to introduce a new process for managing performance or to revise an old one. A major bank cited the need to improve customer service, competition from building societies and foreign banks, and the need to assess performance against criteria relevant for a rapidly changing organisation. Inevitably, these factors were also prompting change in other areas, such as development needs, career management and organisational structure. At **Seeboard** the decision to introduce performance management was taken in response to a number of very different factors: as part of a broader process of cultural change in the group; reflecting a recognition of the need to focus on performance and development; recognition of the need to improve communications with staff, particularly as regards the business response to customer needs; to encourage two-way communication between managers and individuals; and a business reorganisation centred around the installation of a new customer information computer system. Inevitably, in cases such as these the numerous and diverse pressures to manage performance tend to have an impact on other people-management processes, and therefore drive a process of integrating various practices within an overall people-management strategy.

In some instances the impetus behind the development of performance management was the need to make changes in other areas. For example, **NatWest UK** initiated a culture-change programme in 1993, during which change to HR processes and systems was seen as fundamental in engendering changed behaviour. Changing the appraisal process was key, because the old appraisal process, effectively a 'rating system for reward', was 'driving the wrong behaviour'. The stated objectives of the performance-management scheme are to:

□ make rewards more performance-related (this perception of a need to introduce a performance-oriented culture was a response to a more competitive financial services market)

□ give managers more discretion in reward decisions

□ distribute rewards more fairly across grades (analysis of the old system showed that people at lower grades were less likely to be given high or exceptional performance rankings than people at higher grades

□ make the reward system more flexible and simpler (it was felt that the *total value* of reward – salary, bonus, profit-sharing – was not understood by staff)

□ make managers more locally accountable for their unit's performance and the level of rewards to individuals.

In almost all of the cases we studied, there was more than one factor driving the development of performance management, and the complexity of the problems meant that one tool alone – a performance-management process – would not necessarily result in improvement; on the contrary, a number of linked people-management activities were needed. It was therefore common to find performance management carefully aligned with communications strategies, competency development, job design and evaluation, payment systems and motivation practices.

Perhaps the commonest links were between performance management and career progression or development of skills and capabilities. Such links were to be found in all the organisations we visited to a greater or lesser extent. For example, at **3M Healthcare**, supervisors assess each individual's capabilities and potential for future career progression, and assign one of three development codes: *well-placed* (development plans achievable in current role for the next year), *career-broadening* (ready for a lateral move for broadening experience) and *increased responsibility* (ready for a different job involving increased responsibility). These are reviewed by management teams, which are also expected to provide multiple perspectives on the individual and ensure consistency.

The vast majority of the organisations visited said that the most important outcome of performance appraisal for the personnel department was a summary of training needs, and in many cases this was the only data that they required. In most cases where objectives were set, there were at least some development objectives relating to new skills or competencies that the individual would need to acquire, and PDPs are a key issue in many instances. For example, at **Kent County Council**, their scheme is based on a process of performance management (ie not performance appraisal) made up of the following elements:

☐ individual action-planning and performance review
☐ personal development planning.

At **Eastbourne College of Art and Technology**, the focus of the appraisal process is on development more than performance. Appraisers have a check-list for lesson observations, and judgements of staff performance are derived from professional knowledge and training about what constitutes a 'good' teacher. At **Control Risks Group**, the arrangements are based on performance review. Recent changes include refocusing the system on development and career progression rather than pay. They have also looked at core competencies using language that describes what they mean in terms of organisational development. Specific individual objectives are set that are linked to team and organisational objectives, alongside which developmental objectives are identified. The training and development information generated from objective-setting comes back to the personnel department, who assess the core competencies for development plans and feed into succession-planning.

Links between performance management and other aspects of people management give rise to the need for a new agenda of development activity. At **Assidoman Packaging**, the process involves the systematic identification of training needs. Expectations have had to be managed, because it is not always possible to address all the identified needs. At **Contship Container Lines**, the fact that development is now seen as stemming directly from key tasks and accountabilities means that training can become more focused on the demands of individuals' jobs. At a major **food manufacturer**, the human resources planning (HRP) process runs in parallel with the appraisal and objective-setting process. Each business prepares a plan, which includes an assessment of the HR implications (management and front-line) or organisational objectives, a review of the personal competencies of each senior individual within the unit and their 'promotability call' on a one-year and three-year basis, a succession-planning profile showing expected vacancies, likely people to fill them and their development needs, and an implementation plan, showing how the development needs will be met. The outcome of the central-planning process is often that individuals' development objectives are revised to conform with their planned development under the HRP.

Performance management as a continuous process

Most of the organisations were breaking away from the 'once-a-year' approach to performance management and encouraging managers to meet more regularly with their staff and attempt to embed a performance philosophy into the manager–subordinate relationship. However, many still carried out an annual cycle of identifying key areas for improvement, reviewing needs and monitoring progress. For example, at **Seeboard**, they operate a system called performance and development review (PDR), which is based on 'hard' targets or key performance indicators (KPIs) set at individual and team level, and a 'soft' competency review that enables training needs to be identified. The system involves an initial review with each staff member, in which key tasks are identified, a competency profile is drawn up and personal-development needs identified. This process is now repeated in each subsequent annual and interim review, and at any other time when responsibilities or targets change. This is intended to be an ongoing, rather than an annual, process.

At **Contship Container Lines**, Paul Stone, HR director, defined performance management as 'not just a term – it's a whole way of life'. Throughout the year, the individual is expected to keep a portfolio of successes and development (called the record of achievement and development) which charts progress towards key tasks, achievement of goals and objectives, and development activities; it also includes the manager's acknowledgement of the events, with comments. At the end of the year, the manager looks at the evidence collected by the individual and makes a simple rating of performance. This avoids the need for a formal review or appraisal process at the end of the year.

Increasing emphasis on inputs

The use of competencies in performance-management processes is one of the major growth areas since the IPM survey of 1991. The proportion of respondents to the 1997 questionnaire who said they were using a competence approach was 31 per cent, and this is probably increasing. Certainly, a majority of the organisations visited were using competencies in some respect within their performance-management process. This reflects a growing concern with what individuals 'bring to the party' and with the way in which this relates to their performance and orientation to their jobs, rather than simply measuring output in the form of achievement against objectives. However, the development, operation and use of competency frameworks differed considerably between respondents.

At the **NSPCC** (National Society for the Prevention of Cruelty to Children), there is considerable emphasis on competency in the performance-management process. The Society's approach to the development of competency frameworks is to use whatever is available and customise it for in-house use. This involves working with the Management Charter Initiative (MCI) and National Vocational Qualifications (NVQs) in relevant areas, as well as producing some in-house core competencies for fundraisers and child care officers. At **NatWest**, a competency framework, including activity role profiles, is used for developmental purposes:

> I'd say using the competencies was the first step to local ownership. You are asking an individual member of staff 'What is it that you need to do your job?' and for the first time you're asking them to take personal responsibility.
>
> *Julia Muhs, personnel assistant to the director of human resources, NatWest UK*

The competencies and the need to develop them translates into a personal development plan, and the whole links in to what it is you're trying to achieve within the organisation. You've got a set of values and you're actually getting across all those values. I think it's all connected. But it's not a hard model in terms of saying 'OK, you've got that set of competencies and I'll give you a 5'.

Chris Bottomley, director of human resources, NatWest UK

Performance management at **Volkswagen UK Ltd** is also competence-based. It was developed in-house and started from the proposition that jobs could be grouped into a series of job families in which people can do the same job at different levels. Hence they developed 10 critical competencies for each job family. These can be performed at three or four levels, giving 30 or 40 competency definitions altogether. The system includes company-wide competencies also. Because they have all been written by groups of employees, they use simple, easily understood language. Individuals first assess themselves against the competencies for their job and then agree those assessments in discussion with their managers. The number of competencies 'ticked' or agreed as attained by the individual are added up, and from this a rating is achieved that is then directly related to the incremental move the individual makes on the pay scale. The competencies can be reviewed by the individual as often as he or she likes. However, pay is only reviewed twice a year, and if new competencies are deemed to have been attained, the relevant pay rise will be paid only at the next pay review. The ability of individuals to attain high levels of competency may be curtailed by the nature of their job, so job changes are encouraged to minimise the risk of this. However, in many cases it is a matter of development. People are therefore expected to develop quickly and move swiftly through the pay scale when they are new to a job, but more slowly as they progress up the competency ladder. Performance against objectives is not formally measured, the important read-across being from objective to competence. All assessment is done on competence, the reason being that, if competence is not attained, individuals will not achieve objectives.

Severn Trent Water has developed an interesting definition of competency as 'groupings of knowledge, skills and behaviours which may well be required in whole or in part within a variety of managerial situations'. There are four elements in their performance-management process against which managers are assessed. These are:

☐ strategic contribution – what managers need to do in terms of the achievement of targets

☐ role performance – what managers need to do in terms of maintaining and continually improving their core role

☐ common responsibilities and behaviours – a measure of behaviour in accordance with company values

☐ competency assessment – what managers need to do in terms of developing their underlying skills and knowledge.

This process has been specifically designed to provide an integrated approach to managing performance by giving direction, targets and feedback, and ensuring appropriate individual and team development; so it is a good example of integration between objective-setting and competence assessment.

Objectives

This shift in focus has not lessened the importance of objective-setting for many of the organisations we visited. The cycle of setting and reviewing objectives has survived as a common feature in many cases. The emphasis in the organisations we approached seemed to be on a cascading, top-down approach. There was some evidence of dialogue, iteration and agreement or top-down/bottom-up approaches, but generally these were rarer. A good point was made by one HR director: 'It is important to make people think about the long-term. If you don't build this in, they will just focus on the short-term, on this year's pay rise and bonus.' A problem inherent in cascading objectives was, furthermore, referred to by an HR manager in a manufacturing company:

> The problem is that there is some objection to the toughness of objectives, because they have been literally transposed downwards. We have taken pains to explain to people that if we don't produce the volume, then we don't get our Return on Asset target for our parent company; and to set more lenient

targets for the machines that we actually want to produce for the whole site is ludicrous. And it's not just they who are being leaned on, but everyone.

Eastbourne College of Art and Technology operated one of the best top-down/bottom-up objective-setting processes we found. This is linked with the whole college-operating plan, which is derived from a strategic plan that is submitted to the Further Education Funding Council (FEFC), and is reviewed and updated each year:

> Some [objectives] are top-down, some are bottom-up. The latest three-year strategic plan involved a process whereby all the managers went away for a weekend and drafted some ideas, then prepared a whole college working day to present those draft ideas and develop them in multi-disciplinary and sectional teams. The teams reported their ideas and observations to a co-ordinator who then worked with senior management to put together the formal strategic plan. But at the time the corporation and the senior management would be developing ideas that fed into the planning cycle. So 'cycle' is the appropriate description of the process.
>
> *Andrew Smith, HR manager*

A major food manufacturer sets objectives for individuals at the beginning of the year, and ties them closely to business-planning. Individuals' objectives are set in four areas:

☐ contribution to achieving the year's annual plan – in quantifiable, measurable terms

☐ long-term contribution ie contribution during the year to moving the business one year nearer achieving the strategic plan (this is seen as very important for the long-term health of the business)

☐ personal development

☐ people development (those without direct reports are still expected to be involved in developing the people around them).

The approach at **Great Ormond Street Hospital for Sick Children** was described by Sarah Bonham, training and development manager, as follows:

Objectives have to be relevant to the job, fair and equitable, clear and agreed and contribute to the trust and directorate objectives. In reality, therefore, most objectives are set in a cascade down approach emanating from the business plan. Objectives are intended to be open, with managers sharing their own objectives with staff and agreeing the links.

At the **NSPCC**, as explained by Ruth Spelman, director of personnel, the emphasis in monitoring and evaluation is geared towards quality. There are no quantitative targets for child protection staff. A balanced scorecard approach is used to measure the outputs and performance of the organisation. They are therefore able to use a mix of qualitative and quantitative criteria that they believe gives them better-quality information and reflects their particular type of organisation.

At **NatWest**, assessment is based on objectives, which are set in January, and reviewed four times over the course of the year. A performance assessment is given by the line manager at the end of the year. There is no 'tick-box' self-assessment, but individuals are invited to make comments about their performance, which are commented on by managers. At **3M Healthcare**, objectives are set by individuals, although managers may intervene. Objectives are not just cascaded down from corporate goals; they also tend to reflect what suits the unit. At the individual level, people are encouraged to take an interest in things that are not day-to-day priorities.

Focus on development

The most significant development in the management of performance since the (then) Institute of Personnel Management's study in 1991 was the shift in emphasis from pay to development. Although pay was a feature in a significant number of performance-management schemes we studied, the overwhelming majority said that their processes were development-led and that a key issue was to identify and fill development needs.

Jose Pottinger, director – personnel at **Cummins Engines**, told us that performance management can encourage a reflective conversation about performance and development. Performance management should not be seen as an end in itself: it is simply one of the dimensions that can be used in improving the performance of the organisation. 'Performance management should address the needs of both the organisation and individuals. They want feedback on how they are doing. The direction performance management should take is to move from a controlling/critical process to an enabling process.' Managers have to answer the question: 'How can we help individuals to realise their potential and thus contribute most effectively to business improvement?' They have to be involved in helping individuals to understand what skills they need and in providing the opportunity for them to develop these skills. Coaching is critical. Performance management may not lead organisational development, but it can support it. For example, it can play a part in the development of teamworking approaches.

At **Control Risks Group** one of the key objectives of the scheme is to create better career structures to get people moving between the business units and develop better cross-functional expertise. At **3M Healthcare**, the move towards a focus on development in the performance review means that it is vitally important to integrate this with career management. Mike Grocott, HR director, commented:

> If you're talking to people about their personal development needs, those are obviously influenced by what you see happening to them career-wise, as well as by how they are doing in their present job.

3M had experienced a need to shift the emphasis of performance management towards development. There was growing discomfort with the emphasis on backwards perspectives in appraisal, and the potential conflict between assessment and development that rating-driven and pay-related performance-assessment processes create. People tended to be preoccupied with their rating and its implications for pay, with development in second place. A performance-management instrument was needed to help people take responsibility for their development-planning.

Performance-related pay

Despite the strong focus on development we found in almost

all of the examples, 82 per cent of the organisations visited still operated some form of performance- or competence-related pay. This was much bigger than the proportion of those with PRP responding to the questionnaire (43 per cent). The discrepancy may be partly attributable to sampling differences. Overall, the experience of PRP was mixed, but one strong theme emerged, in that most organisations felt that, the weaker the link between performance management and PRP, the better it was for both processes, and the more likely they were to have a positive impact.

At **Abbey National** John King, human resources director, commented on the introduction of PRP 10 years previously:

> At the time it captured a mood ... Staff felt that if they worked harder they should be paid more. One supposed advantage of linking pay to appraisal is that managers *had* to appraise their staff – they had to commit themselves to what they really believed about someone's performance.

He went on to say that 'What is important about PRP is that staff should feel better about it at the end of the day – they should not be short-changed.'

At **Assidoman Packaging**, there is no question of linking the performance-review process with reward, because of negative feeling about the previous process, in which pay became the sole focus of the appraisal meeting. Joy Lysenko, HR manager, commented:

> Basically people wanted to know what they'd got, and when they knew they'd not got it, there was then an argument trying to justify why they should have got it. If they knew they had got it, then there was no interest in anything else. We found people covered up and didn't want to admit to any weaknesses, any need for improvement, any need for training because it might suggest that they shouldn't get the performance reward.

Les Davies, director of human resources at **Bro Taf Health Authority**, felt that PRP depends on subjective judgements and is therefore open to abuse concerning such grey areas as whether managers have performed or not. He said, 'It is often difficult to establish realistic and attainable targets. PRP increases may motivate for a time but will soon be accepted as the norm.' He went on to say that PRP 'does not act as a motivator and can act as a demotivator. Once you introduce pay into performance management the relationship between managers and their subordinates changes – sometimes for the worse.'

However, some of the people we talked to were more positive about linking pay to performance management. One personnel manager commented:

> A lot of text books say, don't link [performance management and pay], don't use the same schemes. In practice, I can't see us having the organisational capacity to separate the schemes because of the time involved and the falseness, if you like, of separating them.

Another felt even more positive about the link, and said, 'We've got all the tools we need to make fair judgements around performance in order to link it to pay. The issue is execution.'

Line-manager ownership of performance management

The prevailing ethos in the case-study organisations appeared to be that performance management is essentially a manifestation of good management practice, and is therefore a tool that can be provided by personnel professionals to enable line managers to manage their teams better. This was in line with the 1991 research that concluded that best practice in performance management equated with good management practice generally. It was therefore not surprising that a majority of our interviewees said that performance-management data was not kept by the personnel department, that personnel people only needed to have the information to enable them to budget for training requirements, and that the outcome of appraisals and performance reviews was for employees and managers only.

At **Great Ormond Street Hospital for Sick Children**, the review process is not compulsory, although it is actively encouraged, and reliance is placed on managers being or wanting to become good managers and therefore using the process. At **NatWest UK**, the objective is to develop systems to reward staff who perform and deliver. Managers have a reward pot, which they can allocate to individuals, based on the performance of the branch or unit against a 'balanced business score card'. It is the responsibility of the manager to ensure individuals buy into the plan for their business unit, and managers cannot receive higher personal reward ratings than their units. At **Vauxhall Motor Company**, line managers own performance management. Meetings identify things deemed to be important, and people are encouraged to decide and communicate the things chosen as performance measures. Tony Lines, personnel manager, believes that the process of performance management is heavily underpinned by measurable items and this makes it more relevant to everyone.

Rejection of bureaucracy

The final trend we were able to identify from our interviews and case-study visits was a move away from bureaucratic form-filling and ratings to something much more informal, which was about improving the quality of conversations between managers and their subordinates rather than generating data. The issue of ratings was a rather controversial topic. One HR director commented:

> A rating system is a tag which is, by its nature, inevitably totally simplistic. How can you take everything that somebody has done and all the strengths and weaknesses they may be exhibiting and boil it down to a single letter on a piece of paper? Clearly in itself it doesn't mean very much, except where you need a rating for a secondary purpose. But then, if you really begin to look at how valid that is, you begin to doubt it. In organisations like ours the scope for individual contributions is ... well, it's still there, but the implications of teams and achievement at team level is much more obvious.

There was a general move away from ratings. Where they are still used, organisations tend to use descriptive phrases (rather than just numbers or letters) and simpler systems, and to put less emphasis on the whole process. One senior manager commented, 'In the old system, one number was your life. Every other HR process was locked in behind the appraisal.' Hence the need to move to something more flexible and less formal.

Other organisations were trying to minimise the paperwork – in at least one instance to a completely computerised system, and in other cases the aim was for one single piece of A4 paper to be generated with learning objectives summarised on it. Joy Lysenko at **Assidoman Packaging** commented that it is the communication that matters, not the paperwork. She said:

> I've tried to emphasise to everybody that the performance review is not the piece of paper. The performance review is the meeting you have with the manager. The piece of paper is simply the record you make of it.

Organisational culture can also be a powerful force in determining the nature of the performance-management process. One HR director remarked:

> The culture of the firm and the nature of its work affected the reaction of managers to performance management. Because professional services people deal with form-filling on a daily basis, they tend to see paperwork as something that has to be done to conform with compliance regulations and to go through the motions of filling in forms without attention to what the process is trying to achieve.

Another pointed out:

> Bureaucracy is a failing of the scheme, in that it tends to be managed and delivered in a fairly bureaucratic way with adherence to the setting and reviewing of numerical objectives. However, the organisation exhibits a strong performance culture and there is strong support within it for a performance management system which identifies and rewards high performance.

Conclusions

Generally, it was believed that performance management could and did make a positive impact. However, few of the organisations visited had, as yet, put in place any formal procedures to evaluate the impact of their performance-management processes. Where evaluation was taking place, it tended to revolve around the perceptions of manager and staff as to whether performance management enabled them to do a better job.

As described above, the process of managing performance is varied, ranging from formal procedures based on hard, identifiable measures to informal processes supported by philosophy rather than paperwork. However, in general the same sort of pressures were driving organisations to revise or implement performance management, pressures that revolved around the changing nature of the market, the need for a focused approach to the development of staff, the need to establish clarity about what the organisation expected from its people, and the need to improve communication between managers and their staff.

8 CASE-STUDIES IN PERFORMANCE MANAGEMENT

This chapter details the experiences of eight best-practice organisations chosen to reflect a range of concepts and approaches to performance management. The **Automobile Association** (AA) operates a comprehensive objectives- and competency-based approach accompanied by 180-degree feedback for managers. In AA Insurance the scheme is geared to the special context of a company in the financial sector. Ratings are incorporated, and there is a strong emphasis on performance development planning. The scheme is supported by extensive and focused training. Performance management at **Bass Brewers** emphasises developing people to increase the added value they can provide for the business, focuses on competencies, incorporates a powerful personal development planning process and is linked to a broadbanded pay structure. **BP Exploration** (BPX) provides a good example of an organisation in which the management of performance is more a way of life than a distinct stand-alone system, and of a fully integrated approach to managing performance as a fundamental part of the management ethos which can be adopted in running a business. The **Corporation of London** case-study is an example of performance management introduced to further and support culture change. Consequently there is considerable emphasis on corporate values, missions and strategies, and the development of performance management was closely associated with the development of strategic-planning processes.

New Forest District Council provides an impressive example of an organisation that integrates performance management with corporate-planning processes. A primary aim is to achieve clear and identifiable links between what people do and what the Council wants to achieve. Performance management is seen as an important tool in bringing about organisational development. The **United Distillers** approach to performance management is another excellent example of the management of performance as a way of life rather than a separate 'system'. The emphasis is on strategic integration and on the improvement of the ways in which managers and individuals can work together to improve performance and personal development. The **Victoria and Albert Museum** provides interesting information about how performance-management processes can be developed and introduced in the special context of a major museum. This included considerable emphasis in all aspects of the process of performance management as a dialogue rather than as a top-down and judgemental appraisal system, with attention to the strong influence of the context on process design – the Museum's culture and ethos, the type of people working there and the type of work they carry out. The most significant aspect of the **Zeneca Pharmaceuticals'** approach is that it is a well-established and sophisticated scheme with the emphasis on employee development; it is also linked to reward, although not on a formulaic basis, and there is as much (if not more) emphasis on non-financial rewards. Both objectives/targets and competency elements are incorporated in the process, and there is no requirement for ratings. In addition, line managers are used as performance-management coaches, and individuals can initiate the process with their managers.

The Automobile Association (AA)

The AA employs about 12,500 staff, a large proportion of whom are 'on the road' or carrying out administrative/clerical duties. There are about 800 managers to whom performance management applies throughout the organisation. In AA Insurance there are about 1,750 staff, all of whom are included in the performance-management process, which has been specially adapted for that division.

Basis

The process is based on 'a disciplined roll-out of objectives'.

As Peter Stemp, group personnel director, commented, it is 'as near to management by objectives as you can get without being in a state of rigor mortis'.

Business/personal objective-setting

The business-planning sequence consists of a five-year strategic plan, a three-year tactical plan and a one-year budget. It is the objectives and critical success factors contained in the budget that initiate the performance-management process. These start with the director general's objectives and are cascaded down through the managing directors of the three AA businesses and the function directors.

Sequence

The performance-management sequence is:

1   January–February: agreement of objectives
2   Mid-year: a 'stock-check' review of the personal development plan, but no rating
3   End-year: full review and a rating
4   The following April: salary review.

The personal performance review

The personal performance review covers the following areas:

☐   what was achieved against the personal objectives set for the period
☐   an overall view of performance, including strengths and weaknesses
☐   performance rating based on a five-point scale (1 to 5) where a three-rating is seen as commendable and the benchmark for an experienced, capable performer
☐   a competence rating based on a five-point scale (A to E), where C is seen as commendable and the benchmark for a competent individual who matches the requirements of the role
☐   what needs to be done to improve performance and competence, together with the help and support that will be provided (both training and development)
☐   direction and objectives for the period ahead.

Competence

Generic competencies developed within the AA are used. They comprise:

Capability: readiness and capacity to perform
Motivation: drive, commitment and willingness
Efficiency: management of self and other resources
Effectiveness: approach to delivering results
Presence: impact and influence on others.

Benefits

It was stated by Peter Stemp that the main benefits have been that the process:

☐ integrates objectives – 'We were deeply concerned that they should integrate'

☐ focuses managers on critical success factors

☐ gains commitment to objectives and provides a basis for reviewing progress on a one-to-one basis

☐ encourages managers to think more systematically about what they are doing and what they are trying to achieve

☐ encourages managers to 'think in the round' about their staff.

Issues

The two issues raised by Peter Stemp were that:

☐ he was not really convinced that rating is desirable – 'a simplistic rating denigrates the comprehensive review process'

☐ the biggest difficulty is getting people to prepare worth-while personal development plans.

180-degree feedback

A 180-degree feedback process has been introduced for managers as part of a campaign called 'Management Standards We Can Trust'. This concentrates on the factors that make a good manager ie the approach used to managing people.

The process involves completing a management standards questionnaire. This is analysed by an external agency which feeds back aggregated (and therefore anonymous) summaries to the managers concerned of the views of their staff about how they (the managers) manage.

This is an entirely self-developmental process: the reports are for the managers' use only. It started at the top, using trained facilitators as coaches. There was some resistance – feelings that it was unnecessary, fear that it would distract managers from their business-generating activities. But these fears have largely been overcome for the 270 managers so far involved.

AA Insurance

A new performance-management process (the personal performance review) was launched in September 1996 to cover all staff. It took about a year to design. The process was developed from the manager's scheme. The design of the process was strongly influenced by Investors In People (IIP) principles.

The process is broadly similar to the AA management scheme incorporating a review and rating of performance against agreed objectives, a review and rating of 'personal competence' (using the same headings as the senior management scheme), and a personal development review and plan.

The process was developed in consultation with focus groups and the relevant trade union. The union is apparently satisfied with the scheme itself, but still dislikes the PRP element. An important element in the process, as for managers, is the integration of objectives. Considerable efforts are made to ensure that individual objectives are linked to AA Insurance critical success factors by the use of such devices as posters, 'icons' setting out the main headings and 'mystery shopping' – ringing staff to ask what their objectives were and how they were linked to the critical success factors (with financial prizes for those who provided good answers).

In line with IIP requirements, the process is 'rigorously evaluated' by ensuring that reviews take place and by examining the quality of review data. But there is still a central tendency in ratings, so to help overcome this a unit in which the distribution of ratings was more acceptable was used as a model to underline the need to be more discriminatory.

The forms used by AA Insurance are set out in Appendix C (pages 409–14).

Bass Brewers

Background to the development of performance management

The performance-management system was developed after a survey of best practice and the translation of that into a relevant Bass Brewers approach. The previous system had been a typically mechanistic appraisal scheme which fed ratings into PRP decisions, with development needs a secondary factor.

The two basic aims have been to enhance performance and to develop individuals in order to increase the added value they can provide for the business. Training and development is an important part of the process, especially the personal development plan. Potential is also assessed as a basis for succession- and career-planning.

Initially the scheme concentrated on outputs (objectives), but competence assessments were introduced three years ago. The 'driver' for this was a recognition that managers needed to develop a set of competences – core, managerial and technical.

New competence frameworks are now being developed, based on an analysis of Bass plc's purpose and values. The aim is to develop a competence framework that will match and support these values.

The performance-management process

The main features of the process are these:

☐ Targets are agreed for development in a maximum of five areas, with at least one from each of the main competence groups – core, management and technical.

☐ Personal business objectives are agreed for managers in the shape of individual output-based performance targets, for which achievements can be readily measured – no more than five.

☐ The core competences are putting the customer first,

teamwork, dedication to quality, bias towards action, commercial focus, fairness and decency, and communication.

☐ The managerial competences are problem-solving, focus on results, interpersonal skills, managing people.

☐ Technical competences relate to specific role requirements.

☐ For each core and managerial competence there are 'range statements' – improvable, on-target and superior – setting out levels of competence.

☐ Reviewers are encouraged to record levels of competence for each area, but are not required to rate them all separately.

☐ An overall competence rating is made which is informed, but not governed, by the individual competence assessments. The rating is on a five-point scale (superior, on-target, improvable, unacceptable and too early to rate).

☐ There are no range statements for personal business objectives – they are either achieved or not achieved.

☐ A career development potential rating is made for managers, indicating the perceived level of potential that the employee currently displays – eg two or one organisational levels within a five-year time horizon; subsequent potential job moves are captured for succession-planning purposes.

☐ A personal development plan is agreed by the reviewer and the reviewee.

Link to pay

Bass Brewers has a broadbanded pay structure in which position in the band depends on market rates for roles and competence ratings of individuals. An incentivised bonus scheme for senior managers has just been introduced, related to the achievement of business objectives.

BP Exploration (BPX)

Context

BP Exploration employs about 2,600 UK staff in the business of finding and extracting oil and gas. It produces 16 per cent of the UK's oil and 13 per cent of its gas, and operates 18 producing fields, with equity interests in a further 13.

Over the last few years the organisation has become much flatter (from 22 levels of management to, for example, only four levels between the technicians on oil platforms and the chief executive at BPX). The number of employees has also diminished significantly.

BPX is organised as a 'federation' of assets or business units. In the nature of things, oil and gas fields have a distinct life-cycle from discovery and growth to decline and abandonment. Performance issues and priorities will differ according to the position of the asset in its life-cycle.

Networking is an important feature of the company. This is facilitated by networks such as the Global Networks linking people in related functions world-wide and by the peer-group processes linking assets at similar stages in their life-cycle.

The contextual issues that affect the management of performance processes at BPX are:

☐ the business BPX does

☐ the way BPX does business

☐ the shape BPX is in.

These are changing rapidly, and the processes are expected to facilitate these changes and adapt to them.

The overall approach to managing performance

In one sense, BPX does not have a distinct performance-management 'system'. Instead, it has a number of aligned processes that reflect the principle that 'BPX will not grow unless its people grow'. The management of performance is therefore not about going through the motions. It is seen as a natural part of the leadership role, which is to:

☐ define 'boundaries' eg health and safety and cost absolutes

☐ provide directions – defining performance expectations, getting people to understand where their part of BPX is going

☐ provide space for the individual to perform and therefore to grow

□ provide support for the individual and, in the case of managers, asking their staff, 'What can I do for you as your manager to help you get there?'

Managing performance processes

The managing performance processes at BPX are:

□ performance contracting
□ personal development planning
□ one-to-one performance appraisal
□ upward 360-degree feedback
□ competency and skills reviews
□ use of the 'People Management Assurance Standards'.

The performance contract process

This process starts with the agreement between an asset manager and Exco (executive committee) on an annual performance contract which spells out expectations on net income production-lifting costs, health and safety and environmental performance and, importantly, people management.

A quarterly performance review is carried out, which takes the form of a 'face to face' meeting between the asset manager and his or her team with an Exco member.

Peer groups of asset managers are set up to review and, where necessary, challenge each other on how they manage their performance and develop their asset. Peer groups are formed from assets that are at a similar stage in the field life-cycle, so that they are operating within the context of the same challenges or problems. Thus the management of performance is a horizontal as well as a vertical process. These peer groups play the lead role in determining how capital projects are prioritised.

Individuals have their own performance agreements incorporating personal objectives that set out how they are expected to support the achievement of their asset's overall performance agreement. This is how alignment is achieved between individual, asset and corporate objectives.

Although all will emphasise delivery of performance to the asset targets, performance agreements are to a degree stratified; those for technicians may largely be concerned with tasks and those for middle managers may focus more on medium-term deliveries and objectives, whereas those for senior managers may be more concerned with process and leadership.

How the process works at asset level

This is how one of the asset managers described the process of developing performance agreements:

> We have the Asset Manager, reporting into the Executive Committee, then we have these various resource groups: engineering, the business team, well engineering, sub surface, HSA, IT – the list goes on. Then, at the point of delivery, where we actually produce oil, deliver safe performance and look after the environment, we have five platforms. This is where we actually deliver. Each of the resource groups has its own performance contract with me, but these are agreed and signed off by the platforms. To me, having a list of top-level measures on capital, how we're going to manage people, production, the in-fill programme and all that for the entire field is fine, but it doesn't mean much to the people on Charlie. What's Charlie platform going to do? What's their piece of delivery? So, you've got to go from the Asset agreement to the platform/support agreements and agree how these folks support delivery.
>
> We get direction and steer from the Executive Committee, but also from our own peer group. That's a collection of the Asset Managers and some of the resource team leaders getting together and looking at the whole portfolio and what the peer group can deliver to Exploration, then setting a realistic challenge on sustaining oil production. So we provide challenges at this level and we complement that in the Asset by benchmarking – third parties who roll up costs for the whole North Sea. They tell us where the gaps are.

How the process works at individual level

The following is the way in which a member of the commercial department described the process:

> My perception of how it works is that it's a nesting process, starting at the very top level – the asset performance contract. Beneath that are the team performance contracts, and then there will be sub-team performance contracts. And by the time

it gets down to team or sub-team performance contracts, instead of it saying 'Team X will do this' it becomes personal and you get initialled against the headings. Then it finally becomes crystallised as part of your individual objectives. And it's action-orientated – 'This is what will happen'.

Personal development planning

BPX philosophy and process emphasise the accountability for development rests primarily with individuals in partnership with their line manager or team leader. Support is provided by the company in the form of staff-development processes, networks and the personal development plan. The latter is described as a way of structuring the skills, experience, interests and aspirations of individuals into possibilities they can commit themselves to with respect to their career. It is for those who want to get more out of their current job, as well as those who wish to change jobs or the direction of their careers.

The completion of a personal development plan is a matter of individual choice, but the company believes that it undoubtedly enhances and structures input into other supporting processes such as career-counselling from mentors, or as part of the staff development and deployment process. Frequently, the production of a personal development plan is an outcome from the staff development process in instances where an individual is unsure of possible career directions, where to move next or how to make his or her current role more interesting. Equally, an individual may produce a personal development plan following a staff development meeting where a developmental move into another business is actively being sought. This is what a member of staff had to say about personal development planning:

> I've found the personal development planning process good. We did go through a phase several years ago when we tried to be very prescriptive about PDPs and about skills, and we abandoned that and left it as a more free-form process. And now most people have their own personal development plan, sometimes committed to paper, sometimes carried around in their head. But the actual discipline of writing it down on paper – where you want to get to and the various steps you want to

take to get there – is a powerful process. It allows you to think about where the major gaps are, where you need to be trained up – skills development on the job – and also major courses to build towards your ultimate goal. So I think that's a good process, and it's actually better for being more free-form than prescriptive.

The development map

Guidance on developing skills and improving performance is provided by the Development Map. This is based on the BP competencies model under the headings of technical and professional skills, behaviours, business skills and knowledge, and BP leadership competencies. The guide covers the ways in which individuals can analyse their development needs, and lists the everyday learning opportunities and other options for training, as well as recommending training courses that match the competencies model.

One-to-one performance appraisal

As defined by BPX, performance appraisal is the ongoing process of setting objectives and assessing individual and collective behaviour and achievements during a finite period of time. It is regarded as being primarily about counselling and feedback on ways to improve performance at an individual and team level, and the quality of working relationships.

It is suggested that performance improvement results from people being clear about priorities and objectives, what skills need to be enhanced, and which types of behaviour can help to this end. This comes from open, positive and constructive discussion between supervisors, individuals and teams, and from agreement on how to focus on doing the job better. It is concluded that 'What really delivers performance improvement is a process of continual dialogue throughout the year.'

The key elements are:

□ *agreed objectives*, which are related to the performance-agreement process described above

□ *the performance review*, which involves individuals in appraising themselves against the agreed objectives and seeking comment from their supervisors

□ *the essential behaviours 'check-list'*, which is an aid to assessing strengths and weaknesses and to focusing on areas for improvement

□ *the personal improvement and development plan*, which is used to help develop personal growth, record views on the future, and plan for action to enhance contribution and develop skills and abilities.

Objectives are agreed towards the end of the current appraisal year, or very early in the New Year. Both the manager/team leader and the individual are expected to prepare for the performance review meeting as soon as possible after the end of the appraisal year. The personal improvement and development plan meeting is held separately from the performance review meeting. This is how two members of staff commented on the process:

> 1 My general experience in BPX is that it has been a good process. There have been none, or perhaps only one, I've been unhappy with. There has been the right element of looking back and the right element of looking forward. This year in my new job my manager has been keen every three or four months to have a mini-appraisal – 'How are things going?' I would ask if the Asset is getting out of me what it expects, my manager would ask if I was getting out of the job what I expected to get out of it. And we would build that up to think about in what areas are there still deficiencies and in what areas can I say 'Been there, done that' and move on to something else. So instead of it being kind of a once-a-year cataclysmic process, it's every quarter or every four months. And in between that, I'll often go in and have a chat with my manager on a number of issues and get a sense from him how things are progressing. So, between the appraisals, lots of conversations.

> 2 I find meetings a good opportunity to get your message across about where you want to go. It's a good time to get the feedback as to whether your aspirations are realistic and get agreement on levels of training and on where you want to be, whether it's a grade upwards or a move into another job.

Upward feedback

Upward feedback to team leaders and managers (and the increasing use of 360-degree feedback) is an important part of the appraisal process. It is based on the leadership competencies. The manager, the individual and team members complete the profile by scoring from one to ten on competencies grouped under the following nine headings:

☐ respected player
☐ acts wisely and decisively
☐ leads change
☐ strategic influencer
☐ builds best teams
☐ shapes performance
☐ strategic conceptualiser
☐ environmentally astute
☐ ensures alignment.

Feedback is anonymous and goes to the individual who normally discusses the outcome with team members. A facilitator is usually present. As one senior manager commented: 'This is a way of benchmarking myself – big gap, smaller gap, a gap that doesn't matter.' The same manager replied as follows to a question on how he thought the next meeting with his team members would go:

> They will probably give me ten or twelve things I need to work on. I am going to say: 'OK, can't fix everything for everybody, but what are the headlines up there that I ought to really focus on?' Maybe it will end up with three or four. And I think they'll go away feeling pretty good, and I'll at least have an awareness of what the problems are.

Competencies and skills

Competency is defined in two ways by BPX:

☐ the attainment of performance against a standard
☐ that which distinguishes superior performance.

The second aspect of competence is regarded as the more important.

Competence profiles highlight the core ('spike') competencies, but also define the 'buttress' skills (eg interactive skills) needed to achieve success. A leadership competence profile is used for managers, which provides for them to be rated by themselves, their manager and members of their team (ie upward appraisal as described above).

A set of business skills has been developed for the Global Business Network defining nine key skills such as business-planning, business-negotiating, business environment and business review. The wording aims to describe attributes that can be observed, measured and objectively verified. There are four levels for each skill, which are described as follows:

- □ basic – knows where the book is and can refer to it
- □ developing competence – has read and fully digested the book
- □ fully conversant – teaches or coaches from the book
- □ expert – the author!

Business skill leaders have been identified for each area, and courses are listed supporting the acquisition and application of each skill. Supporting skills in such areas as finance, tax and legal have also been identified, as have behavioural skills eg networking, communication, teamwork and decision-making.

A senior manager described how this works as follows:

> So you have those four skill levels, then you can say to some-one: 'What skill levels do you wish to get to? What skills would be appropriate for your plans, your aspirations in economic evaluation or in business negotiation?' Then you can say: 'Well, you want to get to level three, how are you going to do it?'

People-management assurance standards

Mike Conway, head of human resources for the UK assets, pointed out that 'The management of people is part of managing the business but we need assurance that managers are actually delivering to well-defined standards.' The People Management Assurance Standards set out principles and expectations covering leadership, resourcing, development, reward and risk management. These support the following commitments, which are designed to enhance business per-formance:

- ensuring that people know where they stand and have a realistic sense of their future
- helping people develop so they can realise that future
- taking decisions about people fairly and equitably
- recognising and rewarding people's success and their willingness to take appropriate risks
- communicating openly, honestly and in a timely manner between managers and staff
- rewarding those who manage people effectively.

The standards set out the way in which BPX wants its managers to behave. They are therefore effectively performance management standards. Managers interpret and apply them in line with their own context. HR is there alongside asset management supporting delivery at the asset level and leadership on the broader federal people agenda. The standards are not used formally as the basis for performance appraisal, but they provide a clear indication of the behaviour expected and therefore, broadly, the criteria used for assessing the people-management capabilities of managers.

Link to pay

Performance and competence levels influence the position of individuals in their pay ranges. But there is no formula for linking the appraisal to pay ie there are no ratings.

This was one of the most impressive examples we met of a fully integrated approach to managing performance as a fundamental and effective way of running a business.

Corporation of London

Context

The Corporation of London is the local authority for the City of London, providing the full range of such services as housing, education, social services and town-planning. In addition, however, the Corporation performs a number of special functions, many of which extend beyond the City's boundaries. These relate to open spaces such as Epping Forest and Hampstead Heath, the Port Health Authority for the Thames

Tidal estuary, three wholesale food markets, the Central Criminal Court, the Old Bailey, and the Barbican Centre.

The administration for the corporation is carried out by 32 separate departments, each headed by a chief officer. Overall authority is exercised by the Lord Mayor, the Aldermen and the 150 members of the Court of Common Council. There are many committees.

The Corporation is a highly complex organisation with a long-established and strong culture. Achieving change is therefore difficult. As Gary Annels (director, personnel and management services) commented: 'Departments have to be picked off one by one.'

There is a staff association (CoLSA), and manual workers are represented by the GMB.

Reasons for introducing performance management

The existing arrangements for staff appraisal were not satisfactory, so Gary Annels impressed upon his colleagues the fact that a comprehensive performance-management process could play a key role in the programme for change then being developed called 'The Health of the Corporation'.

It was noted that within the Corporation the changes needed to respond to external pressures included the requirement for high levels of competence in managers in planning work, focusing effort on key objectives, setting standards and monitoring performance, and communicating.

Development of performance management

A working party was set up that produced a list of actions required to build on positive forces of change in the Corporation. These included reviewing and updating mission statements and objectives for the Corporation and each department, carrying out SWOT (strengths, weaknesses, opportunities, threats) analyses, formulating human resource plans, establishing performance-management processes, and setting up change teams in departments to develop and implement initiatives in support of the mission, objectives and human resource plan.

Another working party was set up in 1993 to develop performance management. It consisted of senior officers from key departments, and met eight times. Its terms of reference were these:

> To report to the Strategic Management Support Group on steps which might be taken to encourage and facilitate the successful establishment of comprehensive performance management processes supporting the business strategies of all departments of the Corporation with particular reference to the introduction of performance review and development review schemes for all staff.

Their report covered the points summarised below. It was considered by members of the chief officers' group who supported it – with the proviso that there should be flexibility to tailor the model schemes and documentation to the needs of their department if this was felt to be necessary.

The overall approach to performance management

The working party defined performance management as follows:

> Performance management is a systematic approach to the creation of a shared vision of the purpose and aims of the organisation, helping each individual to understand and recognise their part in contributing to them and thereby managing and enhancing the performance of both individuals and the organisation. It involves the agreeing and continuous review of corporate, service, team and individual objectives and the use of targets and relevant performance indicators against which performance is appraised and staff development needs identified. The outcomes must match the objectives and policies of the Corporation, reinforce a high performance culture and optimise quality of services to customers.

Criteria for performance management

The working party recommended that for performance management to be effective it would be important to ensure that all employees in the organisation:

☐ understand the Corporation and department's mission, strategy and business objectives

- □ understand the key business indicators and current business performance
- □ receive feedback on internal and external customers' perceptions and concerns
- □ have a clear definition of their individual roles and accountabilities
- □ are working towards the achievement of specific departmental and individual objectives
- □ understand how their individual performance will be monitored and assessed
- □ understand what the organisation values, particularly in relation to working and management styles
- □ have their performance monitored continuously both in terms of achievement of objectives and job behaviour (ie the way in which they carry out their work)
- □ are coached in and counselled about their job performance, attitude and behaviour
- □ are given the appropriate job experience, knowledge and skills training for their current job and for succession to future jobs
- □ have the necessary equipment and working environment to be able to do their job effectively
- □ have their performance monitored continuously both in terms of achievement of objectives and job behaviour.

The working party stated that:

> The main mechanism for meeting these criteria is an annual appraisal scheme supplemented by the continuous review of progress with objectives and feedback on job behaviour which becomes established as the way managers manage. For most managers what is being proposed is not something new which creates an additional burden, but rather it builds on current good practice and is the essence of the managerial role. The scheme will however improve on the quality of objective setting, feedback on performance given to staff and their development. In short, it will improve individual and departmental performance.

The working party's proposals were accepted subject to the

implementation of the guiding principles as set out below. The scheme has been successfully introduced progressively for staff. Manual workers will be incorporated in a scheme designed for them later. Only two departments employing mainly manual workers have not yet started to introduce performance management.

The secret of success was an intensive programme of communication, consultation and training backed up by comprehensive documentation. As Gary Annels commented: 'We aimed to get success stories on board and then encourage the doubters to make the leap.'

The performance-management process

The following guiding principles were drawn up on the operation of performance management:

- ☐ If there is no commitment from the head of department, don't do it!
- ☐ Clearly stated work objectives or tasks should be subject to regular review and updating.
- ☐ Standards of performance should be clearly stated.
- ☐ There should be feedback on job behaviour.
- ☐ Comments rather than performance ratings are desired.
- ☐ Development needs should be identified.
- ☐ There should be an agreed training plan.
- ☐ Parties should reach agreement through a two-way process.
- ☐ An appeals procedure should be incorporated.
- ☐ It should be used as a day-to-day management tool.
- ☐ There should be no link to pay.

Performance management is seen as an integrated process flowing from statements of values and missions, and Corporation and departmental strategies.

Performance appraisal is at the heart of the process, and is concerned with:

- ☐ objective-setting and performance reviews for project-type objectives
- ☐ objective-setting and performance reviews for routine tasks

- job behaviour reviews (assessing competence under a number of different behaviour headings)
- performance summaries (objectives and job behaviour)
- development reviews – training plan.

There are no ratings because, as Gary Annels pointed out, 'People will focus on the ratings rather than the process, and it is the process which is important.'

The purposes of appraisal are to:

- provide staff with an overview of the objectives of the department
- give staff a clear understanding of the organisational values and the desired organisational culture and work behaviour
- review, agree and update the principal accountabilities of the job
- agree with staff clear individual objectives and stretching but achievable targets linked to the principal accountabilities of the job
- agree plans to ensure the successful achievement of the objectives
- encourage staff to undertake self-evaluation of performance, work behaviour and competence
- examine in detail the reasons targets have not been met or conversely have been exceeded
- feedback to staff on how their level of performance is perceived both in terms of achievement of objectives and work behaviour
- give clear messages to those whose performance is inadequate and afford a chance to agree remedial action
- assess and agree the inputs or competence needed to ensure successful achievement of objectives
- assess and agree the level of competence of the individual relative to the needs of the job
- determine in a rigorous manner the true training and development needs of staff
- agree and plan training over the forthcoming year

- identify potential among employees and focus succession-planning and development resources on those most likely to respond positively and effectively
- encourage managers to seek feedback from their staff on their own management style and any matters of concern
- demonstrate proper management interest in staff needs and development, hence raising motivation
- ensure two-way communications within the department
- develop a more open, efficient and effective style of management.

Link to pay

The purpose of performance management is primarily to integrate corporate and departmental objectives, provide a means of improving performance, assess development needs and contribute towards meeting them. It is not linked to rewards.

Benefits

Gary Annels believes that, overall, the two major benefits are:

- 'a very clear focus on what the department is trying to do, which is communicated to everybody'
- 'the ability of the process to clearly identify the development needs of staff so that the resources devoted to training and development can be put to good use.'

A major communication and training exercise was conducted to introduce performance management.

New Forest District Council

Context

New Forest District Council is a major, high-status local employer paying in the upper quartile. As a result they experience very little staff turnover and successfully attract the best people in the area to work for them.

Their system for managing performance has evolved since 1990, but has recently undergone a fundamental review because an unacceptable level of dissatisfaction with the process had become evident. Managers did not like 'marking' people, considering it was somewhat akin to being back at school. The organisation also wanted to ensure that the process was as simple and flexible as possible to ensure maximum effectiveness.

New Forest District Council is well-known for its progressive and innovative HR policies. However, we were informed that they do not aim to follow 'best practice': they just want to identify and do whatever works best for them. However, much of their well-publicised work in changing the culture and introducing organisational values is undoubtedly translated into the organisation's philosophy with regard to performance.

The performance-management process

The performance-management process has three core elements:

- *corporate planning*. A corporate planner oversees the co-ordination of the Council's performance-management systems and the link with organisational needs both in the short and long terms. Hence, the organisation will be able to identify what skills they need to develop for the future and what sort of people they need to be attracting to provide a good-quality service.
- *training and development strategy.*
- *performance and development interviews*. These are carried out against corporate aims and objectives through the business plan and a set of competencies or skills.

The aim is to set up a framework for use by each directorate of the Council. The ethos of the approach is that individual and team objectives will be linked with corporate aims. However, they do not want the system to be too rigid or dogmatic, and will therefore leave directorates free to fill the framework with their own priorities, objectives and goals. The system has moved away from a scoring approach, and appraisers are instead given a set of range statements to describe progress.

What they do want is clear and identifiable links between what people do and what the organisation needs to achieve. For this reason the performance-management process contains a work plan intended as a rolling document reviewed on a regular basis in monthly meetings with managers. The work plan will be assessed on an annual basis as part of the performance and development interviews. Within the work plan, individual targets or objectives are set and training and development needs identified.

The training and development part of the performance-management system is linked with a personal development plan that is work- rather than life-focused, although life events are moving onto the agenda. Training is also high on the organisational agenda, and is seen as an important tool in achieving organisational development. The Council has achieved the IIP standard, which is seen as an expression of their own high standards and their desire to invest in their people.

Link to pay

The link between performance management and pay has become considerably weaker since 1990. However, the organisation believes it would be unrealistic to break the link entirely. They intend to introduce a non-consolidated bonus that will reflect performance, paid at any time during the year. This will be at the discretion of managers and enable them to give individuals immediate reward for outstanding achievements.

In addition to this, directors have the ability to move people up the pay scales if they consider their performance warrants this.

Keith Ireland, the head of HR, believes that New Forest District Council is a performance-oriented organisation, and therefore people have little difficulty with the concept of performance management. He believes that performance management can be an important tool in bringing about organisational development, which is the criterion against which the Council will monitor the effectiveness of their activities.

United Distillers
Context

United Distillers is the spirits division of the Guinness

Group. It employs about 9,000 people, of whom over half are outside the UK.

The performance-management process

As Chris Bones, HR director international, said in a presentation to the Institute of Personnel and Development's annual conference (October 1996):

> Performance does not automatically imply delivery, let alone strategically aligned delivery. Those elements of HRM processes that support the management and improvement of performance have to be aligned and integrated with the strategy of the business. A discussion on performance management is not, therefore, a discussion on performance management systems. If anything, the system is the least important element in successful performance management. The whole organisational environment must enable performance to happen and to be measured against key strategic measures.

The Guinness Performance Review (GPR) process is used to manage the performance of the top 25 per cent of personnel, people who manage other people, those who report directly to a general manager, and graduate trainee high-fliers. The performance of all other staff is managed using local adaptations of GPR, but everyone uses the GPR objectives to set their goals.

Currently, United Distillers is in the process of linking GPR much more closely to business plans and the vision which it has for the future of the business. The result is a system less about processes and more about improving the quality of performance discussions between managers and their subordinates. Chris Bones said he was working towards a situation where forms are unnecessary and that people 'do performance management' automatically as a best-practice way of managing their staff.

Overall, the management of performance is central to management strategy; Chris Bones described it as the only way of communicating the business plan in the operating/business units.

Performance management is dominated by the use of objectives that stem from business needs. Formal objectives are set and reviewed bi-annually; however, the company is encouraging the use of the objectives and assessment against them in monthly review meetings so that they will simply become 'a way of managing'.

In addition, performance management at United Distillers provides for the rating of individuals against a number of critical competencies. These were developed by interviewing people at the top of the organisation to identify the valued and effective qualities. United Distillers' international businesses have also developed their own key competencies, which match with their 'operation entrepreneur' vision and which, they believe, are necessary to develop the future of the organisation. The operation entrepreneur vision requires all employees to operate as entrepreneurs, reacting quickly to emerging markets and being world-class in sales and marketing. It incorporates many characteristics of the classic learning organisation, such as high trust and the ability to learn from mistakes.

Chris Bones argues that objective-setting has changed in recent years from an activity to an output. In the past, objectives tended to be set around an activity (such as writing a report) without considering the output or effect of that activity.

An overall rating of performance is given that is directly related to the bonus scheme determining the award of individual bonuses.

Every appraiser at United Distillers has been given training in performance management, and the company intends to extend training to all appraisees in the near future. Much of the training tends to be done in a coaching model, depending on the demands of managers, rather than as a training course that people are required to attend.

One of the objectives set for each individual has to be about personal development. Chris Bones operates the '10 per cent rule', requiring managers to provide detailed plans for improving the performance of the bottom 10 per cent of their staff. Development is carried out in two parts: the need to develop individuals in their current job, and the need to develop their experience for the next job. This means closing skills gaps by training and developing people through coaching, mentoring or exposure to different sets of experience.

The effectiveness of performance management at United Distillers is measured against a number of key performance indicators linked to the strategy and operating plan. Performance-management processes are also evaluated against achievement of business targets. However, the organisation recognises that performance-management processes are so closely integrated with other aspects of managing the business that it is impossible to separate out their individual effect.

United Distillers operate 360-degree appraisal separately from the Guinness Performance Review. It is optional whether people do this or not, and the outcomes are not linked to pay. However, the output from the process is fed into objectives, particularly development objectives.

Victoria and Albert Museum

Context

The Victoria and Albert Museum (the V & A) is a multicultural organisation with eight different collections and 800 (mainly unionised) staff. There is a great diversity of objectives and activities, and there are issues at senior-management level concerning, for example, the balance between scholarship and public access. Within the Museum there are many different entities, and any HR system has to recognise this diversity and help to achieve a 'one-nation' environment.

Development of performance management

When the head of personnel, Gillian Henchley, joined the V & A in 1990, the standard Civil Service appraisal system was in place but was little or badly used. The Government insisted that, although the responsibility for pay was delegated to the V & A, there had to be some form of PRP.

A staff opinion survey was conducted in 1995, with 362 responses out of 800 forms sent out. The questions were concerned with what people felt about the existing pay and grading scheme and what they wanted in the future to achieve a fair pay system. A wide range of views was expressed.

It was therefore decided to run focus groups facilitated by a management consultant. The groups discussed reward philosophy, the ways in which rewards were provided and the overall climate. A report was produced by the consultant and fed back to the groups. The reactions were positive; people felt they had been consulted. The importance of developing some form of performance management to replace the existing scheme was recognised. As a result, as Gillian Henchley said, 'There were now people who had got an engagement with the issue' and who would be ready to participate in the development of performance management.

A number of performance-management groups gave initial consideration to the approach, considering such aspects as setting objectives, performance standards and the link to pay (the latter was a 'given' because of the Government requirement).

A cross-functional working party (largely volunteers) was then set up to devise the system, which was launched in 1996. There was an overall felt need to 'edge forward'.

The performance-management process

Performance management is defined at the V & A as:

> a continuous process involving: agreeing standards and objectives, giving and receiving constructive feedback on performance; and identifying appropriate training and development opportunities in order to contribute to the success of the organisation.

Performance management aims to help in the improvement of performance and the motivation of staff at work, and to encourage dialogue between the assessor and the assessed by:

☐ self-assessment, where the assessed is required to review his or her performance against agreed performance standards and objectives and make an objective assessment

☐ encouraging openness between the assessor and the assessed through discussions about achievements expected from the assessed and regular progress reviews

☐ identifying training and development opportunities to support the assessed in the job

☐ using the document to record changing circumstances and priorities when they arise

Figure 7
PERFORMANCE MANAGEMENT AT THE V & A

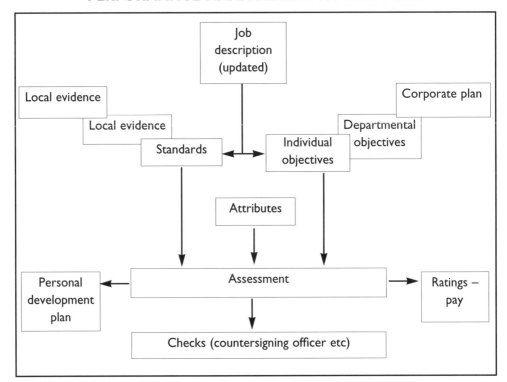

☐ the assessed's retaining the completed document (the only part of the document returned to personnel is a copy of the personal development plan).

The overall process is described in Figure 7.

The performance plan consists of the following sections, as set out in the performance management document:

☐ *Key standards and objectives.* These consist of brief, fairly broad-brush statements of standards of performance drawn from the main responsibilities of the job or objectives. The latter relate to the achievement of activities at work, but they can be personal objectives that give rise to training and development needs. A standard is defined as a statement of the conditions that exist when the job is being done effectively, and are long term, often ongoing. An objective is defined as a 'task to be completed by a specific date'. The proportion of standards to objectives varies. At the support staff level (eg security), the emphasis is on standards. Objectives become increasingly important at higher levels.

☐ *critical steps.* These are the actions that individuals have to take to achieve key standards or objectives. Each is illustrated by a number of brief points indicating what needs to be done and by when.

☐ *success criteria.* These concern the way in which individuals demonstrate achievement. This is critical to the assessment process. Clear examples are required of success which can be used when reviewing performance.

☐ *development needs.* A yes or no answer is obtained against each standard or objective as to whether there is a development need. This forms the basis for the personal development plan (see below).

☐ *self-assessment.* This provides examples of achievements relating to specific standards or objectives. The state of play is noted and, if applicable, the reasons and constraints for non-achievement are stated. In some instances, milestone targets that have been reached are noted, because they contribute to the achievement of an objective.

☐ *line-manager assessment.* These are comments by the line manager on achievements.

Both parties are expected to prepare for the review meeting, and it is recommended that they should think about:

☐ performance since the last meeting
☐ examples of work carried out well and areas for improvement
☐ how results were obtained
☐ constraints that prevented work from being achieved
☐ the way that problems may be resolved in future, and improvements made
☐ any amendments to the performance plan that may be required
☐ how performance should be rated
☐ feedback from clients and colleagues
☐ management style adopted by the assessor.

The suggested structure for a review meeting is:

☐ views of the assessed on their own performance and development

☐ achievements and areas for improvement, with specific examples

☐ new or amended performance standards and examples

☐ follow-up action if required.

Assessors are expected to make their own assessment of the assesseds' achievements. More often than not this is likely to be 'agreed'. The assessor may add fuller comments after the meeting, but it is stressed that 'It is important that the assessed sees a draft of the comments before they are formally written into the performance plan.'

Where the assessed needs to improve performance, the assessed and the assessor are expected to agree an action plan detailing expected standards of achievement, a timescale and any assistance or training that might help the assessed to improve their performance.

There is an overall rating on the following three-point scale that provides the link to performance pay:

1   Outstanding performance

2   Good performance

3   Performance improvement required.

Gillian Henchley would like to remove the ratings 'so that we can concentrate on development', and feels that 'the performance process would be very much better if it did not feed into pay'.

Competency assessment

Competencies or attributes (the latter term is preferred at the V & A) have been developed for senior management in consultation with them. The key attributes are:

☐ *museum* – vision, leadership and organisational skills, awareness

☐ *team* – team/people management, decision-making, communications

☐ *self* – drive, adaptability, self-management and development, expertise.

Senior managers assess themselves under these headings.

Personal development plans

Personal development is defined as being all about individuals' acquiring skills, knowledge and experience to carry out their job effectively and to prepare for future jobs and for their careers.

It is emphasised that personal development is not simply about training courses. Training and development opportunities can be provided by a variety of means, but they should be realistic for both the individual and the organisation, taking into account operational requirements, costs etc.

Opportunities may include:

- on-the-job coaching
- mentoring
- shadowing other staff
- taking on new responsibilities
- project work or contributing to working parties
- attachment to other departments or organisations
- visits to other collections
- professional updating
- conferences, seminars and symposia
- training courses and workshops.

Training arrangements

A comprehensive training programme played an important part in introducing the scheme. This included a self-study programme that is a model of its kind.

Key factors

Gillian Henchley has no doubt that the keys to designing a successful performance-management process are:

- being clear about what is meant by 'performance'
- understanding where the organisation is – and needs to be – in its 'performance culture'
- being very focused on how individual employees will benefit and play their part in the process.

Zeneca Pharmaceuticals

Context

Zeneca Pharmaceuticals has about 15,500 employees world-wide, 5,000 of whom are in the UK.

Background to performance management

Performance management is well established, having been introduced as a formal process in 1990. Its development took place as part of a 'Development of People, Work and Reward' initiative. This contained eight guiding principles and, in summary, the key aims were these:

- All staff, irrespective of hierarchy, will see themselves as a business team, working towards a common goal.
- All jobs will be constructed in relation to business objectives and evaluated by the same method.
- Reward systems will have more scope to reward individual contribution.
- Line managers will be responsible for the development, motivation and performance of each member of their staff.

Developments since 1990

The performance-management process as it operates currently is described below. The main developments since its introduction in 1990 have been:

- the use of performance management in an international, project-based organisation
- the greater part taken by individuals in the processes – they can lead review sessions using their line manager as a resource
- an emphasis on *agreeing* rather than *setting* targets
- a more thorough application of competencies
- the linking of financial rewards to performance
- the introduction of 360-degree feedback in some areas on a voluntary basis – 'where the energy is'

The objective of performance management

The primary objective of performance management is defined as 'To improve business performance by raising each individual's effectiveness.'

From the start, performance management focused on individual development and improving performance. It was and is perceived as being 'about how we manage people'; it is *not* regarded as a system. The emphasis is on line-manager ownership. Acting as performance-management coaches, a selection of line managers played a major part in the introduction of performance management and in its further application and development with HR support. The 'PM coaches' have annual seminars to share best practice and help each other with any issues.

Definition of performance management

As defined by Zeneca:

> Performance management is a continuous cycle of discussions between you and your manager to plan and review your work and your development. By sharing with your manager the responsibility for managing your work, performance management is designed to encourage you and help you increase your capabilities. It is based on best management practice and is the core way we manage people in the International Pharmaceuticals Business. Performance management helps people both individually and in teams to grow their skills, improve their performance continuously and be rewarded fairly and according to business performance. It also therefore helps to strengthen and grow the business.

It is a process that:

☐ relates individual job objectives to those of the work group and the business

☐ ensures that individuals concentrate on the results expected from their jobs

☐ objectively measures performance

☐ rewards consistent performance

☐ assists in planning ways to improve the abilities necessary to do the job and for the individual to develop

☐ provides for regular reviews of performance.

Figure 8
PERFORMANCE MANAGEMENT AT ZENECA

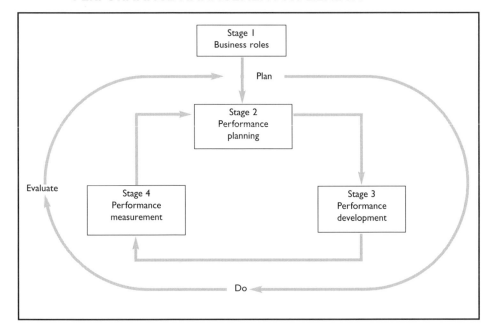

It is emphasised that 'The performance-management process offers a structure within which the day-to-day management of work may take place through the agreement, monitoring and assessment of targets: it is not a separate activity.'

The four stages of performance management

These are:

☐ business-role clarification
☐ performance-planning
☐ performance development
☐ performance measurement.

These stages are illustrated in Figure 8.

Stage 1   Role clarification

The aim of this stage is to ensure that each employee has a clear statement of his or her business role, and that they understand and are committed to the objectives of their work group which, in turn, are derived from, and contribute to, overall business objectives. The objective-setting process is not just a top-down, one-way flow. Zeneca's project-oriented environment means that a horizontal flow is required to ensure that the complete matrix is represented in the process.

The guiding principles for objective-setting are to:

☐ focus on a limited number of critical issues and avoid the trap of chasing comprehensive detail to the extent that the main thrust gets lost

☐ state the issues as succinctly as possible, with every word carefully weighed – this should trigger the right sort of discussion in the next stage of the process

☐ ensure that the statements are framed in such a way that they indicate a relevant measure of performance

☐ determine, on scanning the full set of objectives, whether its balance and emphasis best reflect your perception of priorities.

Stage 2   Performance-planning

The aim here is for the individual and the line manager to agree targets for the individual for a set period. (The term 'target' means individual objectives, in order to differentiate them from the more strategic 'objectives'.) This stage also encompasses the results of planning ie the 'doing' and 'evaluating' by the individual and line manager in a continuous way – the 'plan-do-evaluate' elements of managing performance.

The process at this stage involves another meeting between the individual and the line manager. The outcome should be that the individual has a set of targets for a defined period, (which may be quarterly, half yearly or annual), derived from his or her job accountabilities, project responsibilities and work-group objectives. A monitoring and review process is agreed between the individual and the line manager and, where appropriate, the project manager. The guidance notes on this meeting state that:

☐ individual targets should be set within the context of business objectives. The best targets are those that combine both business objectives and personal-development needs.

The most motivating targets are those set by the individual. The line manager's responsibility is to make sure that individual targets are in line with business objectives. Targets for the individual should be supportive of the manager's targets and complementary with his or her peers' targets.

☐ individual targets should incorporate both line and project activity. Line and project managers should work together to ensure the correct balance within an individual's targets.

☐ a set of targets for an individual should be critical to performance in the job. This does not mean that targets will relate only to task goals but also to work processes eg relationships with other people.

☐ targets should be about the 'what' rather than the 'how'. It is the individual's responsibility to decide how he or she meets the achievement level. Motivation and commitment are obtained if the individual and the manager are satisfied that the targets are achievable and realistic and if the individual has autonomy on 'how to get there'. Ideally, targets should have priorities assigned.

☐ a good target is one in respect of which both manager and individual can monitor progress and achievements. Thus targets must be specific and measurable and have a time-scale.

☐ individuals should be able to monitor their own progress. Target-setting will stimulate individuals to appraise critically their own performance and to identify both where they should focus their efforts and where they could benefit from development. Targets should be stretching and encourage performance beyond the target.

☐ there should be a satisfactory process in place for progress review. The more critical the target, or the less experienced the performer, the higher the frequency with which reviews should take place. Individuals' performance should be reviewed with a focus on future improvement, not fault-finding.

Stage 3   Performance development
The aim of this stage is to help the individual achieve the

agreed targets by defining and developing the relevant skills. As with performance-planning, there is a 'plan-do-evaluate' cycle associated with performance development. The 'plan' phase involves the definition of the skills/knowledge/competencies needed by the individual to meet the performance targets. The 'do' phase involves primarily the manager in coaching (or arranging coaching for) the individual in the defined skills/competencies/knowledge areas of the job, although this may be supported by more formal off-the-job training programmes. The 'evaluate' phase involves monitoring by the individual and the manager of the individual's developing performance and ability, the manager giving feedback to the individual and, where appropriate, modifying aspects of the performance and development plans in the light of experience.

This is also a meeting between the individual and the line manager. The outcome should be that the individual has a personal development plan derived from his or her level of ability in the relevant skills to meet present and perhaps future job requirements. The guidance notes state that:

- all employees must have an individual development plan jointly agreed with their managers, and that the plan should be progressed and regularly reviewed and updated

- each individual development plan should be derived from the personal targets for the coming period, along with any expected future needs. An analysis of skills, knowledge and experience required to do a particular job (the job or role profile) provides the basis for defining the development needs of the individual job-holder.

- as the purpose of agreeing and working on development goals is to improve performance, primarily in the current job, it is essential that development needs are expressed in behavioural terms ie what would individuals be doing better than now, how would they be handling new situations, what would be different?

- individuals should be invited to assess their own development needs before any feedback from the manager is offered

- no more than two or three development needs should be

agreed between the line manager and the individual at any one time

- □ the next stage is to identify options for working on the development needs. It is important that work is seen as a learning opportunity as well as a productive task, and so the line manager is to help the individual to identify work situations that can be development opportunities
- □ the formulation of the individual development plan is only the start of the process.

Stage 4 Performance measurement
This stage has two distinct aims:

- □ to provide ongoing feedback during the 'plan-do-evaluate' cycles already described
- □ to provide an annual summary of an employee's perform-ance to be used as the basis for decisions on financial or non-financial reward.

When assessing performance, not only the achievement of targets but also the way in which the individual has worked towards the targets have to be taken into account ie the 'what' *and* the 'how'.
  The stage involves two meetings:

- □ a review meeting between the individual and the line man-ager in which targets may be reviewed and modified, and in which the individual obtains objective feedback on per-formance towards targets
- □ a review meeting between the individual and the line man-ager first, then the line manager with peer and more senior managers, the outcome of which is agreement within the department of the appropriate levels of reward.

No overall ratings of performance are given.
  The Performance Summary Statement requires a precise summary of the individual's agreed contribution to business performance for the year and is used as a basis for decisions on annual reward made to individuals within departments. Although this is the 'formal' part of performance manage-ment, it is emphasised that there should be no surprises

during the discussion about the assessment. The purpose of this particular part of performance management is a review of the past year. As with the whole of the performance-management process, the emphasis is on shared responsibility and two-way problem-solving, and therefore it is not viewed as an end-of-term report. Ultimately, its most important purpose is to be developmental – to assist in the improvement of performance.

The competency framework

The competency framework is based on groups of behaviours associated with successful performance identified from extensive external and internal studies. These have been classified into five categories:

☐ *thinking competencies* – the ability to carry out effective analysis, interpret and model complex information, generate new ideas and develop strategic objectives

☐ *self-managing competencies* – the ability to learn, develop and be in control of both self and situation

☐ *influencing competencies* – the ability to gain the commitment of others, anticipating and properly taking account of their interests and concerns

☐ *achieving competencies* – the desire and ability to get things done and to perform to high standards

☐ *managing people competencies* – the ability to gain the commitment of others and develop the potential of people, thus providing a focus for individual development discussions.

Competencies may be 'threshold' for effective performance, or may additionally be 'distinguishing' for outstanding performance.

The link with pay

The reward-management approach aims to reinforce performance management ie its successful application should help to raise performance standards. Each department develops an annual reward plan reflecting its business goals and priorities;

the implementation of this is managed locally within a defined budget over the year. Included in each departmental reward plan are details of the type of contribution the department wants to reward or reinforce, and the range and type of reward options likely to be relevant.

Managers have at their disposal a portfolio of reward options for use in their departments, and it is likely that the emphasis on various options may differ both between and within functions and also over time.

In the application of reward distribution it is regarded as imperative that clear links between performance and reward are established and maintained although the link is not governed by a formula, because there are no ratings.

Flexibility in the system can be used to make sure that there are not long gaps between the reward and the valued performance. Smaller cash awards given rapidly after achievement of key results or outstanding effort during the year are believed to be more motivational than bonuses given at the end of the year.

In considering the type and range of options used to reward people, it is emphasised that the use of money and other tangible or extrinsic rewards needs to be balanced with intrinsic rewards such as praise, recognition and greater involvement of individuals, which can all have an equal, if not greater, impact on motivation, and thus improve performance.

Evaluation

An attitude survey is conducted every three years that includes questions on performance management. Individual departments conduct more frequent reviews as part of their approach to the continuous improvement of performance management and its application.

Benefits

The main benefits are believed to be:

□ alignment of business, function, department, project, team and individual objectives

□ people are clearer about what is expected of them, where they fit in and what the organisation is setting out to do

☐ a critical contribution has been made to the implementation of several major change programmes, bearing in mind that 'the unit of change in the organisation is the individual'.

9 WHAT PEOPLE FEEL ABOUT PERFORMANCE MANAGEMENT: FOCUS GROUPS AND INTERVIEWS

Introduction: the nature of the research

One of the main objectives of the research was to get people 'to tell us how it is'. Previous research projects into performance appraisal and performance management have relied on questionnaires, interviews with HR managers and, additionally, in the 1991 IPM survey, the use of attitude surveys. Some academic researchers, as mentioned in Chapter 6, have made contacts with individuals, but there has until now been no systematic attempt to find out from those who experience performance management what they actually think about it. The present research included one interview with a chief executive, three interviews with line managers or team leaders and 12 focus groups. The latter were held in six organisations: two in financial services, two in (broadly) the manufacturing sector, one was a local authority and one a charity. We also conducted attitude surveys in six organisations, the outcomes of which are described in Chapter 10. In addition, we talked to three trade unions about their views on performance management.

The focus groups

In each of the organisations in which focus-group meetings were held a sophisticated form of performance management had been introduced within the previous year or two, accompanied by comprehensive communication and training for those concerned. They had all taken deliberate steps to increase line-management and employee ownership of the processes. Two organisations had performance-related pay (PRP) for managers and staff, although in one example the aim had been to distance pay from performance management. One had PRP for managers only, and two did not have it at all. Another had team pay and pay influenced by performance and competence achievements, but generally pay was not directly geared to a rating system.

We asked for the focus groups to be composed of volunteers, which was the case (with the exception of two groups for managers to which the whole management team had been invited). We used a standard check-list for all focus groups but, inevitably, the discussion often veered away from the check-list points.

In analysing the results of the focus groups we are fully aware of the fact that these are simply snapshots taken of a small and selected sample of organisations. We are also aware that any inferences (we hesitate to use the word conclusions) must be qualitative.

There are two other factors that we took into account in our analysis of focus-group discussions. The first is that the members are responding to questions put by a facilitator. With the best will in the world, facilitators sometimes set the tone of the meeting, however hard they work at not asking leading questions and however much they sit back and let the discussion flow, with only an occasional prompt or grunt. The second factor is that any focus group can be dominated by forceful or articulate members, so there is always a possibility that other members simply follow their leader in response to the dynamics of the group situation they find themselves in. So far as we could judge, although there were indeed some highly articulate participants, they did not suppress other people's views, and there was usually sufficient diversity of opinion to lead to the conclusion that group cohesion factors had not overwhelmed individuality. Our observations, however, were necessarily superficial. Forces affecting the contribution of individual members, leading to choruses of approval or disapproval joined in by all, may have been at work below the surface.

For all these reasons we are cautious about offering any firm and final conclusions from the focus groups. They were simply indicative of the *sort of reactions* people can have to performance management. The fact that in some organisations these reactions were more favourable than might be expected may be coincidental. Reactions in other organisations with a much less sophisticated approach to performance management may have been much more hostile. But at least these were real people telling us, as far as we could judge, what they really thought (all contributions were recorded anonymously). In our view, this does provide some insight into possible reactions to particular aspects of performance management that are well worth considering by all those involved in the design, development and operation of performance-management processes.

The focus groups were held for managers and team leaders or staff to obtain different perspectives in all the organisations – with the exception of the charity, which had a mix of team leaders and support staff. The analysis in the first part of this chapter deals separately with these categories in each of the organisations in which focus groups were held. The quotations are verbatim but we have included only a selection that seemed to us to represent a significant point of view. We have attempted to include a balanced set of quotations to represent different opinions. Quotations immediately following another quotation are from different people. We have provided brief comments at the end of each focus-group discussion summary. These comments attempt to capture the general tone and direction of the discussion, but they are inevitably impressionistic.

Focus groups: Organisation A

Managers' group

The rating system

- ☐ Subjectivity is inevitable. The art is to take subjectivity out through cross-team benchmarking and training.
- ☐ Numbers are more important to individuals than the amount of money they get.
- ☐ How do you get consistency? How do you make sure that the effort that's put into getting a grade 3 is consistent across the business?

☐ What doesn't seem to be clear is what the top executives think is the difference between a 3 and a 4. What do Audit or what do Finance have to do to get a 4, and what do they have to do to get a 3?

Objective-setting

☐ You shouldn't need to wait until the year end to decide how someone is performing. You should be reviewing objectives at least monthly.

☐ People have their objectives on a piece of paper and they know their money is based on these objectives. And, as a result of that, they compromise other areas (of the organisation) in terms of the whole picture to meet those objectives, because they are not actually measured on whether they have messed somebody else up.

☐ It's short-termism. I've seen it where different departments are actually messing each other up consciously to achieve their individual objectives, and that's a real problem for me.

Developing staff

☐ It's a joint thing between them and us. Helping people identify what they should be focusing on – nothing to do with performance.

☐ We've got to develop people to move on to something without really knowing what they are moving on to. Therefore you can only give general advice because no career progression advice is available.

☐ We don't manage underperformers. We just like to push it under the carpet because we want to avoid conflict. We're not very good, perhaps, at developing people who need to be developed.

Link to pay

☐ The whole process is an absolute nightmare.

Comments on managers' focus group

These comments and other unquoted contributions were almost wholly hostile, with the focus on the managers' perceptions of the unfairness of the reward system. Objective-setting and rating and pay systems issues dominated the discussion. Relatively few comments, favourable or unfavourable, were made about other aspects of performance management.

Staff focus group

Comments on performance management

□ You need appraisal to get the best out of people and develop them.

□ What we've moved away from is people's perceptions – just marking someone depending on how they felt about them. Now there's evidence.

□ It's subjective between the manager and the appraisee. It's OK if you are doing your objectives, but if your manager doesn't agree there's nothing you can do about it.

□ The managers aren't managing the performance of the individual. You've got to look at each individual and their targets and objectives within the team and, if they are not coming up to scratch, you need to counsel them and get them back to a satisfactory level.

□ If you've got an underperformer, people are not dealing with these people in the correct way. They are moving on somewhere else and people are not being addressed properly.

Comments on rating

□ Performance management, if it worked right, would be good. But there's too much inconsistency. You've got different managers marking in different ways.

□ Wherever you move, people are going to manage, motivate and mark you in different ways. And that's something that we all need to be aware of.

Comment on objective-setting

□ Everybody's individual plans go towards the big team plan, but sometimes that isn't communicated as it should be, because we all should be working for one big goal. All our little bits and pieces should add up.

Link to pay

☐ Performance and money, different things. People link their level to the percentages all the time; they have to come away from that, don't they?

☐ That's what I'm saying about the performance culture: it just doesn't happen. The idea is there and we've kind of got halfway there, but having got only halfway, it could possibly be more destructive than doing good ... It's not the truth that if you perform well you'll be rewarded.

☐ The system might be right but the implementation is absolutely terrible.

Comment on the ability of managers to manage pay

☐ Line managers are used to being told what to do, and we are trying to move away from that and give them free rein. They can't actually deal with that; they can't cope with that.

Comments on the staff focus group

Although some of the comments welcomed the concept of performance pay, quite a lot of dissatisfaction was expressed about the way it was administered.

Focus groups: Organisation B

Summary of points made by the group (comprised of managers and team leaders)

☐ Self-analysis by staff was realistic – *Manager*: 'They didn't differ from me with what they came up with.'

☐ Meetings were realistic – *Manager*: 'Because they were comfortable where they were, knowing their role.'

☐ Review meeting went well – *Manager and team leader*: 'Because we work well together and it's easier to communicate the information across.'

- *Team leader*: 'Providing the dialogue flows and it's open, everything falls into place.'
- *Manager:* 'When I first started in management, you would get an overall view of someone – they're good or they're not so good – but it is difficult to say what they are not so good at. You've got nothing to measure it against. Now I have, and that's what it's about for me.'
- *Manager*: 'It gives you the opportunity to provide focus – to look into a particular area and to be able to say more development is needed in that area.'
- *Team leader*: 'So it's actually tying it down and saying, OK, let's focus on these three points for the next six months. Once they're developing, then we'll pull in a few more.'
- *Team leader*: 'It takes the vagueness away and puts the specifics in.'

Observations

This organisation had taken considerable pains with the development of a competence framework as a basis for performance management. Extensive training had also taken place that contributed to the generally favourable response. The single comment about ratings was echoed by other people, and ratings have since been discontinued.

Focus groups: Organisation C

Managers

General comments on the performance-review process

- It gives our staff a sense of direction and feedback.
- It focuses your attention on the fact that you should be spending some quality time with your staff.
- It gives me something to aim for, short-term and long-term.
- I think it's an opportunity to consolidate all the feedback you've given on a more informal basis.
- When you have six-monthly reviews it formalises and

pulls together everything else that has been on an ongoing basis.

☐ You give continuing attention to your team members one way and another so they don't get any surprises at the review.

☐ It is an ideal management discipline to have in place, because it does ensure that you have a structured discussion between yourself and your manager or whomever.

☐ It gives staff the chance to discuss with their managers any problems they've got which they can't discuss at any other time.

☐ My staff falls into two categories. Some are very keen, look forward to the review and are well prepared. Then you get the other group who will listen to what the line manager has to say to them, and they will have a little input, but will not have prepared in advance. About 40 per cent are well prepared, 20 per cent reasonably well prepared and 40 per cent not really prepared.

☐ I think it is right that there should be some form of appraisal, but I have some problems with the content, and I have heaps of problems managing to cope with it because of the volumes of paper etc.

☐ The potential problem is that you are asking some managers to conduct 20 or 30 reviews. And staff feel it is something they should have but the manager is not paying enough attention to it because of other pressures.

☐ The time involved for managers is definitely an issue.

Comments on objective-setting

☐ We do link individual objectives with business objectives, so that staff can quite clearly see their impact on what the business is doing – we are all working in the same direction.

☐ It depends where you are. It's more difficult to tie the two things together (business and personal objectives) if you are pushing a trolley around the building. But it is much easier where people can say that, if I increase my volume and if I can get my quality right, then I can see what I am doing towards the business objectives.

☐ The gap remains of trying to translate these generic objectives to the individual who has to achieve X, Y and Z. They may be small cogs in a big machine.

Observations

These managers were generally supportive. A crude measure of the degree of support can be obtained by an analysis of the number of favourable comments (the meetings were recorded in full). In this case, 71 per cent of the remarks supported the process because, essentially, those present thought it provided 'quality time' and the opportunity to consolidate feedback and 'pull everything together'. This organisation has well-developed competency frameworks, and the favourable comment about their use is interesting. There were some complaints about the time taken for reviews, and doubts were expressed about the possibility of cascading objectives.

Team leaders
General comments on the performance-review process

☐ It gives you a structure for where you're going. You agree where you need to pick up on. It's a two-way discussion. And you're responsible for setting these objectives with your line manager. You're not just told what to do. And you go through and decide on which you want to concentrate in the next six months. It gives you a sense of responsibility for your own future.

☐ I think you get quality time with your manager. And it's very difficult to get that time in the working environment.

☐ The majority of my staff like the performance review. They like to know how they are doing and where they are going in the future. The ones who don't like it are those who want to do the minimum of what they can get away with.

☐ People like feedback. They like to know how they are doing. They like to discuss their development. Even if they are not performing up to standard, they want to know how they can progress.

☐ If you have a member of staff who is not doing so well and you sit down to talk about it, at first they say, 'Well, I don't know about that.' But when you give them particular instances and you talk it through, at the end of it they do say, 'Well, yes, you're right, I did do that.' It makes them reflect positively on the negative aspects as well.

☐ What my staff get out of it is communication. Someone is interested in what they are saying, just for once.

Comments on ratings

☐ For me, the rating is something to work for.

☐ It makes it a lot better when someone says, 'If you do this or that, you can have that.'

☐ If you are being subjective you have to justify the rating. And it leaves you as an assessor wide open when someone asks, 'Why has someone got that when I've got this?'

☐ The only time that rating helps is when it comes to pay.

☐ Different managers have different expectations. Even when my performance remains just the same, one manager may not like my style, and another manager might. So it's subjective.

Comment on objective-setting

☐ The generic objectives were fine for us, but when they were applied to the staff – cascaded down to everybody – there was a lot they couldn't do or accomplish.

Comments on development

☐ It makes you realise where your areas of improvement lie.

☐ The performance review process makes you think, 'I have all these individuals, and some like to do this and some like to do that', and you tailor-make the training to what they want to do.

Comment on pay

☐ If anything, PRP is the negative side of the scenario.

Observations

As in the case of their managers, the team leaders generally approved of performance management: 61 per cent of the comments were favourable. They liked the structure it provided for discussions on performance and development, the 'quality time' it provided and the opportunity it gave for them and their staff to get to know each other better. But some concern was expressed about the problems of achieving objectivity. Doubts were also cast about the rating and objective-setting processes. If reactions to the review meeting are isolated, the proportion of favourable comments increases from 61 per cent to 84 per cent.

Staff
General comments on the performance-review process

- They can tell us what they want, just as we can tell them what we want!
- In a one-to-one meeting, people can bring things out to their supervisors who say, 'I've never been aware of that; why didn't you tell us before?' That's definitely an advantage.
- If you want to go ahead, if you want to work yourself up, then it's good, because you find out what your needs are. You can discuss the issues, rather than being told, 'This is what you need to do.' You can then go away happy, thinking, 'I know what I want to know about that.'
- I think my team leader carries out the review very well. You get everything across, and she listens to it, and then she tells me what I've got to do to get where I want to get.
- Some do the job well; others just do the job to get it over.
- Our line manager has 20 or 30 people to look after, and that's an awful lot of people.

Comments on rating

- I go in prepared to do battle. I always know what mark I'm going to get before I go in, so I go in and I'm going to say exactly what I want to say.

- ☐ The principle is good – if you do a good job you get rewarded. But the fact is that it's your immediate superior. It's their interpretation – how they class your work, good or bad – that determines how much you get paid.
- ☐ My team leader doesn't know us. And he marks us down on things. But he doesn't speak to anyone on the section. So how can he mark you personally when he doesn't know you?

Comments on objective-setting and review

- ☐ I think it's fine to define the critical success factors broadly: 'This is what we want to achieve'. And everybody's job links into the whole lot, really.
- ☐ You've got to have your own targets, and every individual has them and knows what they have to do. But there has to be one target for the company. Everything is linked.
- ☐ I know what my job is, but I couldn't tell you what my objectives are.
- ☐ I don't think anyone here could really link their objectives to the critical success factors.
- ☐ If anything goes wrong in my area, it's always not 'How shall we fix it?' but 'Who did it?'

Comments about development

- ☐ If the personal development plans are done properly, they are probably the greatest benefit of the performance review process – you get your say about your career.
- ☐ It helps you to understand where you want to get to and how you're going to get there.
- ☐ I'd rather do my training at work than going out of the office and with a pen and paper writing it down. I'd rather be there, doing it, learning from my mistakes.

Comments on pay

- ☐ It's more crucial when performance review is related to your pay.
- ☐ I know it isn't fair.

Observations

Staff were not so well disposed to performance management as their team leaders and managers. There were quite a few favourable comments on the advantages of one-to-one performance review meetings, but fewer than half the overall comments were favourable. The negative reactions were, however, focused more on rating and pay issues, and the feeling that ratings were likely to be unfair. If the rating and pay comments are excluded, the proportion of supportive comments goes up to 61 per cent. One factor that may have influenced the overall reactions may be that staff had received less training in performance processes than their superiors.

Focus groups: Organisation D

Professional staff

General comments on the performance-review process

- There has been a general maturing of the performance-contracting process here over the last three or four years. We're pretty good at getting some of the business issues 'contracted', so to speak, but the cascading of those into personal objectives is sometimes a wee bit hit-and-miss.
- From my point of view, as someone on the receiving end, I have yet to see it integrated into the real business.
- It makes you sit down and think, 'Why am I here? And how do I add value? Do I fit into the business objectives of the people I work for?'
- For me, the real strength of the process lies in the continuing dialogue and negotiation as the year goes on (*general agreement*).
- For me, it creates a sense of reality.
- The conversation assists the attainment of good performance. It's good for you, it's good for the company.
- It's tough giving negative feedback. But it is very important – a continuing dialogue with staff. It's a matter of finding the time to do it.
- I suppose one of the feelings I have is one of frustration. I am trying to be very careful here. It's not a personal thing.

If you have one issue which you want discussed, and it doesn't get resolved satisfactorily, then that becomes your negative perception of the way it worked.

☐ I find meetings a good opportunity to get your message across about where you want to go. It's a good time to get the feedback as to whether your aspirations are realistic and get agreement on levels of training and on where you want to be.

Comments on objective-setting

☐ The performance contracts of senior managers flow downwards and are directed as they go down through different layers in the organisation. There's nothing worse than when you're doing something which is of zero relevance to what the company's trying to do.

☐ It's the foundation of the company's success over the last few years: being able to articulate performance, particularly the hard edge side of it – financial and cost performance. The softer issues – the right-hand side of the performance contract – we're still learning about, in my opinion.

☐ It is very clear that the team has to develop its objectives and get agreement with whomever sits above them that it's the right thing to do. It cannot be imposed.

☐ There are certain things where you know you'll be encouraged and challenged as part of the conversation. But, fundamentally, they're a bottom-up process, and I think that's absolutely vital.

☐ We're not a command-and-control organisation. I hope we're a leadership organisation – space, direction and support. So management creates the space and direction into which we fit our performance aspirations. If we were just told from the top what has to happen, it would be dreadful.

☐ [the performance-contracting process] works reasonably well. It is not passed down from the top. It's a dialogue about one's performance, upwards as well as down.

Comments on development

☐ It's very much up to the individual to manage their own career.

☐ We have deconstructed where we were five or six years ago, and are building something quite new. And it is a fledgling, but I fully support it.

☐ The development plan is personal to yourself. It's my understanding that the content is almost like an agreement with the company and your boss about how you are going to develop over the next few years – what your career is going to look like.

Observations

The feedback was generally positive (73 per cent of the comments were favourable). The professional staff liked the way that the process made them focus on performance and created a sense of reality. One participant saw it as 'a necessary evil', and there were some doubts relating to the integration of objectives.

Team leaders

Comments on the overall process

☐ Performance contracts contribute quite well; they provide a framework to work within; they provide areas for measurement, quantitative or qualitative.

☐ One of the keys is to complete the loop. It's a case of 'Go and deliver this; this is what I expect you to do.' Yet by the time you've gone a certain way down the road, things might be different. So somehow you have to complete the loop.

☐ People tend to regard quarterly meetings, reviews of your performance and the annual appraisal as second priorities. It's difficult to find the time and it's difficult to get the entire attention of your manager because he's working on something more important, which is business, and this isn't business.

☐ But circumstances don't count, that's the point. They say, 'Look, we appreciate that these things are not entirely within your control, but it's up to you to manage that piece of business.'

Comments on objective-setting

☐ A lot of it is about measuring quality and how well you did things, and this tends to be extremely difficult in a marketing or service-type function.

☐ How does it work for me? Not very well.

☐ You can't move objectives down to the individual except in exceptional circumstances, such as the sales force.

☐ You have to have sophisticated measures to avoid the danger of putting wrong signals and drivers on people to do things that end up being bad for the business.

☐ I always try to make it an individual thing, such that if someone only wants to spend 15 minutes on it I didn't expect to spend 50 minutes. And if they wanted to spend two hours, we'd spend it.

☐ My performance appraisals with my line manager have been very good. They have been pretty honest.

Comments on development

☐ It's very much a personal responsibility, especially with line managers' having such broad spans of control. You identify where you see gaps in your skills base, gaps in your competencies and where you see the need to learn.

☐ You can't expect managers to give you more than general guidance in these matters. They generally like to be guided by you on what you would like to do to develop your skills.

Observations

The team leaders were not so enthusiastic as the professional staff (55 per cent of the comments were favourable, compared with 73 per cent of the comments made by the professionals). They liked some aspects of the process but were worried about the time it takes in relation to the benefits, and about objective-setting.

Focus groups: Organisation E

Senior managers
General comments on the review process

- I've found it very beneficial from my point of view – being able to focus more clearly on what our ultimate aims and goals should be in the medium to short-term. And my relationship with my manager has benefited.
- For me and my people, it works – on the basis of all the feedback I am getting from the appraisal meetings so far. There was an element of scepticism initially but, after two appraisals, my staff are beginning to realise that it's not just a management tool to use as a whip but there is an opportunity for real communication and for targets and objectives to be agreed.
- One thing this has led to is better communication.
- Both my meetings have been difficult in the extreme, in that they had to be deferred because they started to become a little heated. I felt I was being asked to do things which I couldn't achieve and therefore responded accordingly.

Comments on objective-setting

- Targets used to be set top-down. There was a chance to discuss them, but that wasn't formalised. The appraisal system bolted onto performance management and it formalised target-setting and it allowed a measure of negotiation between the appraisee and the manager.
- The theory of cascading objectives is great, in that you can see a task that the department has to do and then somehow break it down into project and individual objectives. And then you can cascade it down further and further until, at the lowest level, it's about an individual member of staff – that they have got to do this activity within a timescale. But we are not yet very good at it. We're still learning.

Comment on development

- I think performance management is helpful because it

gives the individual a chance to speak to you in a semi-formal setting about what they perceive to be their training needs.

Observations

The comments by senior managers were very favourable (89 per cent). They liked every aspect of the process itself, and their objections were relatively minor. They were, however, critical of their chief executive, who they felt was not taking part in performance management, leaving it entirely to his deputy. As one of them commented, 'I do resent the fact that it is very much middle-organisation-centred at the moment. I don't see any commitment from the top towards it. And my immediate subordinates are having a great deal of difficulty in generating enthusiasm to the people below them, because they can see what is happening above.' This is the classic situation of an HR process being prejudiced because of lack of support from the top.

Middle managers

General comments on the review process

- ☐ I came out of my meeting feeling as if I had met my boss for the first time. I knew more about him by the end than when I went in, and we had a really good chat. And it changed our working relationship for the better.
- ☐ It's a good way to air things. It's a good forum to discuss things that could be improved and it's a relaxed interview. I think we've all tried to make it that way.
- ☐ I think it opens up discussion.
- ☐ Certainly I learnt more about individual members of my staff, and I've been with them for years.
- ☐ Appraisal must be the positive end of personnel management.
- ☐ It makes [my staff] feel they are valued. You spend time talking to them and give them time to talk to you, and that is a positive thing.
- ☐ I don't think anything new comes up at the appraisal. You're further away from the occasion and the discussion

is more diluted. There shouldn't be that many surprises. You should be aware of what's happened. Appraisals are just a formality.

□ I think it's sad that managers should need this kind of feedback from a meeting. They should be in touch with their staff already and be aware of the situation.

□ Because it is a fairly informal, relaxed environment, people are prepared to raise issues themselves. If it's out in the open, you can then do something about it.

□ If we have a problem at work, people come to me. So when we get into a performance appraisal situation there's nothing to be said.

Comment on objective-setting

□ You are not just setting targets, telling people – 'you've got to do it' – you do it by agreement.

Comment on development

□ At the time, all the talk about training and development goes well and people feel motivated. But when you come up against budgetary constraints, then people think, 'What's the point? Why did you do it?'

Observations

On the whole, middle managers supported performance management (56 per cent of the comments were favourable). They liked the fact that it opened up discussion, but some felt it was a bit of a waste of time, and there were quite a few unfavourable comments about training, to the effect that because of budgetary constraints, it did not happen.

Administrative and support staff
General comments on the review process

□ I thought it was very helpful. We were relaxed over it. You could talk to him.

□ You're one to one with your boss. You chatted, and it wasn't as if it was your boss. It was more relaxed. He would listen and then you'd chat about it. I enjoyed it.

☐ My manager handled the meeting very well. His manner was friendly and open and it was more like a chance to have a conversation than a formal meeting. I felt quite pleased at the end. Before that, I never got the opportunity to be in the know.

☐ I felt it was very positive.

☐ I think I dreaded my first meeting. But after the meeting I felt very positive about it.

☐ I think it gives you the opportunity to state how you feel you might be able to improve your job, and make the job run smoother.

☐ You've just done your job ordinarily and you don't think twice about it. You don't need praise.

☐ I don't really get negative feedback. My boss tells me about areas where he feels I could improve. And this is constructive.

Comments on objective-setting

☐ I thought it was beneficial, in that you see eye to eye with your boss. But it was a bit like one-way traffic. It was about how *they* think your work should be done, rather than taking up matters that are personal to you.

☐ It's very good. You can agree your targets there and then, and you know where you are going.

Observations

The staff were remarkably positive about performance management: 84 per cent of their comments were favourable. They particularly liked the opportunity to talk to their managers, and generally felt that the meetings went well.

Focus groups: organisation F

Managers
General comments about the process

- ☐ It tries to appraise and reward people at the same time. This is a fundamental mistake.
- ☐ It is quite useful, but it depends on how well it is connected with the operating plans of the department. Without a planning network in your own area, it is just words, without any substance.
- ☐ I find the best part of this appraisal is that it puts a clear focus on when you are going to talk to somebody.
- ☐ Your normal management skills involve interacting with employees – actively following up and discussing things. That is part of the process, and the appraisal meeting is not a substitute for it.

Comment on objective-setting

- ☐ We sit down and think what, in the context of what we want, is best for that person to do. There is no opportunity for that person to contribute. It's top down.

Link with pay

- ☐ The appraisals are leading to PRP – the score on the door leads to money in your pocket.
- ☐ PRP is perceived by many as a possible problem, because it will get back to what we had prior to the grading system – favouritism.

Comment on rating

- ☐ I don't like the rating. You can't sum up someone in three numbers.

Observations

The feelings about performance management were mixed, only 55 per cent of the comments being favourable. Concern was expressed about the objective-setting process, rating and the link to pay, and some group members expressed doubts about the value of the performance review meetings.

Staff
General comments about the performance-review process

- ☐ I definitely think it is worthwhile. It's useful to have a chat – you can discuss any issues on either side.
- ☐ The old reviews were just about someone giving you their opinions of what they thought of you, rather than you giving feedback on what you think about it all.
- ☐ I have no problems with the process.
- ☐ Initially, I thought it was a worthwhile exercise, but I now think it's just total repetition. I know before I go in what conversation I'm going to have.
- ☐ If things do go wrong for reasons beyond your control, you should raise them along the way. But I suspect that many people wait until the review process to tell their managers what's gone wrong. And that's not the way to do it.

Comment on objective-setting

- ☐ The targets you are asked to achieve can be very subjective and very difficult. We have this thing called 'stretch', which means that you think of a number and treble it. And that puts the fear of God into some people: 'How am I going to achieve those targets?'

Observations

There were quite a few negative comments: only 35 per cent were favourable. There was a fairly general feeling in the group that the meetings were not productive, and they disliked the objective-setting process.

Overall comments on the focus-group findings

Overall, and taking account of the caveats mentioned at the beginning of this chapter, there was a fairly high, sometimes very high, proportion of favourable comments from all the groups, except those from organisation A (which were largely influenced by very negative feelings about PRP) and the staff in organisation F. What particularly appealed to many people, managers and staff alike, was the opportunity that performance management gave both parties to have a worthwhile discussion about work. There was no real evidence that either managers or staff disliked the process. The number who thought it a waste of time were in a tiny minority.

This finding is completely at variance with the assumptions made by many commentators about the inadequacies – iniquities, according to some academics – of the process. If managements in these organisations were using performance management solely to get compliance to their commands, this fact had certainly escaped the people who attended the focus-group meetings. And the sturdy way in which other criticisms were expressed about, for example, rating and PRP (or, in one case, the lack of support at the top) indicated that the group members would not have hesitated to express their distrust, if they had any, of their managements' motives.

In general, the main messages that these groups delivered were that they:

□ liked the performance-review process itself
□ disliked rating – often vehemently
□ disliked the way in which PRP was operated
□ sometimes had problems with objective-setting, especially if they were at the bottom of a cascade
□ wholeheartedly approved of the developmental aspects of performance management as it affected them, although in some cases their enthusiasm was modified by a perceived inability or unwillingness to spend money on training.

Of course, the conclusion cannot be drawn from this small and unrepresentative sample that all is well with performance management elsewhere. But it does indicate that some organisations can get it right on the whole and, if they can, so can others. Furthermore, getting it right is not about using 'best-practice' systems but a question of a determination from the top to explain why performance management is worthwhile, and to make it work. This belief was shared with managers, team leaders and staff in these organisations by example, through communications, comprehensive training, and continuing support, encouragement and guidance to all concerned. That is the secret of their success.

What individuals feel about performance management

We carried out a number of individual interviews. These are some of the more interesting answers to our questions.

Organisation B

How do you see the changes you have made fitting the needs of the organisation?

What we do is completely service-delivery-oriented. It's people working with people. And, to measure that, there are financial measures and other performance measures. This system will help by putting more flexibility into their pay but, more importantly, it is going to have a very structured personal and staff-development and training focus from the minute that people are recruited until the moment they leave the organisation.

What contribution do you think the programme has made to this culture change?

It's been quite fundamental to it, because it is at the heart of why we exist. If you focus on people's skills and personal development, and you focus on these in a structured and organised way, it does not become additional to what they do but an integral part of it. Then ultimately this will affect how well individuals perform, how competent they are and how well they work with other people. And because people are the business this organisation is in, ultimately this will be better for the organisation as a whole.

What about your middle managers and practice leaders?

The practice leaders are probably the less hesitant. The people just above them are the most hesitant. My senior managers are not hesitant at all. The practice-side look at it as validating the things they do.

Chief executive

Organisation E

How well does the performance-agreement process go?

Brilliantly – and what is the evidence of that? Look at the performance of the company over the last five years. I could go back to 20 May 1989, when our chief executive arrived. He insisted on so much clarity to the discussion that everyone was aligned to the same way of thinking. He set targets, he made sure they fitted the market, he set business targets. Each part of the business has a set of targets. He involved the team leaders – they have targets. Everyone sees how they are contributing to the business, with clarity.

What do your staff gain from the process?

Structure, and of course that very natural human reaction of having someone interested in them, their development … What people get is feedback – 'Someone's interested in what I'm doing.'

Senior commercial executive

Is your time on performance management well spent?

You know why it's time well spent? I find with 22 reports I have very little time to really get to know people. I have a handful of people – five or six – I know well. With the others, because of geography or differences in personal style, I don't have that much of a personal relationship. This is a chance to sit down and talk things through with them – to let them air their views on how they are being developed, where the problems might be, what I could be doing differently. Actually, I would have told you a couple of years ago 'not time well spent'. I now find the mid-year appraisal, because it doesn't link to salary or advancement, invaluable. I got feedback because I made a point of writing down on one piece of A4 those developmental things for them and then what I ought to be doing. I gave it back to them and said, 'Use this to start our annual appraisal.' And not directly, but through other channels, I got a lot of positive feedback. It takes an hour or an hour-and-a-half times 22, and if you squeeze that in over a month it chews up half the month, but it's time very well spent.

Senior production executive

How well does the process work?

Overall, it's working well to very well. A lot of it, particularly competency-mapping and skills, depends on your discipline. The skills side of things has been taken very seriously in the area in which I work. They have been at great pains to competency-map all the commercial staff. So we understand what level of skills we are at. I was really impressed by that process. It was good to have conversations with yourself [the interviewer] around the various competency areas, and that helped me very much as a newcomer. That side of things is really impressive.

What about personal-development-planning?

I've found the personal-development-planning process good. We did go through a phase several years ago when we tried to be very prescriptive about PDPs and about skills, but we abandoned that and left it as a more free-form process. But now most people have their own PDP, sometimes committed to paper, sometimes carried around in their heads. But the actual discipline of writing it down on paper – where you want to get to and the various steps you want to take to get there – is a powerful process.

Team leader

Trade-union views

We sought views from the Trades Union Congress, the General Municipal and Boilermakers' Union, and the Manufacturing, Science and Finance Union.

The Trades Union Congress (TUC)

Perhaps the most important step being taken by the TUC is to provide training for trade-union representatives to enable them to contribute more effectively to discussions on people-management issues, especially training and development. It is recognised that the willingness of employers to work in partnership is often affected by the quality of the contribution that can be made by trade-union officials.

In general, it is the partnership approach that is advocated by the TUC. Their research tells them that what people most want from their jobs is employment security and interesting work. Therefore the TUC is keen for unions to broaden the bargaining agenda beyond pay and conditions.

David Coates of the TUC stresses that it is important for employers and unions to achieve a shared understanding about business objectives. Unions must be involved in discussions about the business plan, and should have some influence over policy and strategy issues. The aim should be an agreed framework for the improvement of productivity and the re-organisation of work so that employers can manage performance in a context that is seen as fair by employees. He believes that trade unions can add value to the business by negotiating on training and skills and by raising the capacity of workplace representatives to cope with change. He pointed out that unions adopt a pragmatic approach to PRP and will seek to ensure that the criteria are objective, benchmarked externally and part of a negotiated process. The TUC does not believe, however, that individual performance pay is particularly efficient. Team-based or competency-based approaches are more likely to produce results.

The General Municipal and Boilermakers' Union (GMB)

The discussion with GMB mostly revolved round PRP rather than the broader issues of performance management. In general, the GMB is sceptical about the value of PRP. As Steve Pickering of the GMB argued, PRP can be detrimental to women, who often have less access to education and training. If people focus too much on targets they can neglect such non-productive factors as maintenance. But he emphasises that they are not totally opposed to PRP as long as it is negotiated with regard to fairness and the above issues.

The Manufacturing, Science and Finance Union (MSF)

Chris Ball of MSF told us that the union is in favour of policies to improve performance, as long as they are balanced with fairness and a positive view of training and development. He argued that badly handled performance management could be a significant cause of stress. For example, this could arise when people are encouraged to behave unethically to achieve targets, or when areas that are a significant source of job satisfaction are sacrificed as non-productive.

MSF takes the view that the best course of action is the pragmatic one, securing the best possible deal for the largest number of people and agreeing a framework in which fair and equitable decisions can be made about performance.

10 WHAT PEOPLE FEEL ABOUT PERFORMANCE MANAGEMENT: ATTITUDE SURVEYS

In addition to the focus groups and interviews covered in the last chapter, surveys on attitudes to performance management were conducted in six organisations. These comprised two public-sector organisations, one management services company, an NHS Trust, a manufacturing company and a business in the financial services sector. A total of 140 people responded to the surveys. The questionnaire is reproduced in Appendix B.

We summarise the outcomes of the survey under the following broad headings (the 'not stated' responses are not recorded):

☐ general responses

☐ responses from individuals

☐ responses from line managers.

Our observations on the findings are set out at the end of this chapter (see page 203).

General responses

Understanding of what performance management means

Table 7 shows what people understood by the term 'performance management'.

Table 7

UNDERSTANDING OF PERFORMANCE MANAGEMENT

Regular meetings with boss	80%
Performance appraisal or review	77%
Setting objectives	75%
Assess training needs	72%
Personal development plans	67%
Pay based on performance ratings	37%

The general understanding conforms to most organisations' views about performance management, with a strong emphasis on reviews and development. The perception of pay as a key element was much less evident.

Completion of requirements

It was claimed by 73 per cent of the respondents that all their organisations' requirements for performance management had been carried out in the previous year. If this were really the case, it is not too bad a proportion. In answer to the question why the requirements had not been complied with, 42 per cent said that they were too busy – the usual excuse.

Actions following the review meeting

The actions following a review meeting are shown in Table 8.

Table 8
ACTIONS FOLLOWING A REVIEW MEETING

Received a pay rise		44%
Attended a training course		44%
Implemented self development		44%
Identified career development		42%
Agreed work improvements		38%

Pay and development actions are fairly common. Work improvements are slightly less frequent.

Feelings about the organisation and colleagues

Table 9 sets out the views of respondents about their organisations and colleagues.

On the whole respondents felt that they had good employers who, however, did not communicate all that well. Relationships with colleagues were quite good.

Attitudes to performance management

Attitudes to performance management are set out in Table 10. Answers to these questions revealed a strong measure of

Table 9
VIEWS ON ORGANISATION AND COLLEAGUES

Statement	Strongly agree	Slightly agree	Slightly disagree	Strongly disagree
My organisation is a good employer	22%	54%	22%	2%
My organisation communicates well	13%	34%	34%	19%
People in my work group are committed to the organisation	27%	43%	21%	9%
My colleagues and I work as a team	37%	46%	11%	6%
My colleagues and I respect one another	50%	37%	9%	4%

Table 10
ATTITUDES TO PERFORMANCE MANAGEMENT (PM)

Statement	Strongly agree	Slightly agree	Slightly disagree	Strongly disagree
PM is a way for people to discuss their progress openly and honestly	46%	37%	11%	6%
PM motivates people and makes them feel part of the organisation	24%	46%	19%	11%
PM helps people to do a better job	47%	43%	9%	1%
PM values the contribution of the team	30%	39%	22%	9%
PM is about getting people to work harder	9%	50%	34%	7%
PM is about individuals and their long-term development	39%	46%	9%	6%
PM is a two-way process, with both parties expressing their views	64%	28%	7%	1%
PM is a way of keeping a record of an individual's progress and performance	47%	46%	6%	1%

agreement with most of the fundamental precepts of performance management. There is no evidence here of any hostility or even indifference.

Negative questions about attitudes to performance management

Table 11 gives the answers to somewhat negative questions on opinions about performance management. On the whole the replies were fairly positive. Even the statement that performance management is about controlling people was only agreed with 32 per cent of respondents. This is a much lower response than the hostile academics quoted in Chapter 6 might have expected. And at least in these organisations,

Table 11

REPLIES TO NEGATIVE QUESTIONS ABOUT PERFORMANCE MANAGEMENT (PM)

Statement	Strongly agree	Slightly agree	Slightly disagree	Strongly disagree
PM has no value for individuals, only for organisations	7%	11%	41%	41%
PM is about managers controlling people	6%	26%	36%	32%
PM does not develop careers; it only improves work performance	9%	26%	37%	28%
PM is of use only to personnel people	4%	6%	22%	68%

personnel seems to have got the message across that it does not own performance management.

Opinions about objectives, work and feedback

Opinions about objectives, work and feedback as set down in Table 12 indicate a strong measure of belief that objectives and expectations are understood and that respondents have authority to determine their work objectives, which are themselves not unrealistic. They feel that they have a reasonable degree of autonomy, and have little difficulty in discussing work problems with their manager. They are only moderately happy about feedback, thus confirming that this is one of the more difficult areas of performance management.

Views on pay

Views on pay, as shown in Table 13, are mixed. A majority of respondents (57 per cent) did not wholly agree that pay was the most important part of their jobs. Most people felt that their organisation valued their contribution but, inconsistently, a large proportion felt that hard work is not necessarily recognised or rewarded.

Responses from individuals

Responses from individuals are shown in Table 14. There is a reasonable degree of support for the statements that performance management 'helps me to do my job better' and 'helps

Table 12
OPINIONS ABOUT OBJECTIVES AND WORK

Statement	Strongly agree	Slightly agree	Slightly disagree	Strongly disagree
I fully understand my organisation's business goals and objectives	51%	42%	4%	3%
I know what is expected of me by my organisation	37%	53%	7%	1%
My work objectives are unrealistic and difficult to achieve	6%	18%	36%	40%
I have authority to determine my work objectives	39%	45%	11%	5%
I have authority over the way I perform my work	37%	49%	9%	5%
I find it difficult to discuss work problems with my line manager	5%	14%	31%	50%
I receive a lot of feedback about my performance	21%	37%	27%	15%

Table 13
VIEWS ON PAY

Statement	Strongly agree	Slightly agree	Slightly disagree	Strongly disagree
The most important thing about my job is the pay	13%	30%	31%	26%
The people who get the best pay rises are those who ask for them	4%	19%	26%	46%
My organisation values my contribution	12%	53%	23%	12%
Hard work is not necessarily recognised or rewarded	36%	45%	12%	7%

me to develop my skill and potential'. Quite a large proportion felt that they got useful feedback, and people were reasonably satisfied with the way the review was conducted. Assessments were felt to be quite fair, and the majority strongly or slightly agreed that they felt motivated after a review meeting (although a substantial minority, 38 per cent, did not). Most respondents felt that they understood how assessments were made but many believed that the best ratings are given by managers to the people they like. A large proportion believe that time spent on performance manage-

Table 14

VIEWS OF INDIVIDUALS ON PERFORMANCE MANAGEMENT (PM)

Statement	Strongly agree	Slightly agree	Slightly disagree	Strongly disagree
PM helps me to do my job better	24%	44%	25%	7%
PM helps me to develop my skills and potential	29%	39%	30%	12%
I get useful feedback from my PM review	25%	42%	13%	18%
I am not satisfied with the way my manager conducts my performance review	11%	17%	35%	36%
Assessments of my performance are consistently fair and unbiased	24%	46%	18%	2%
I feel motivated after a review meeting	21%	37%	27%	11%
Time spent on PM is worthwhile	46%	36%	9%	8%
I do not understand how my manager decides my rating/assessment	5%	21%	34%	37%
Managers give their best ratings to people they like	14%	39%	21%	26%
PM works well here and does not need to change	4%	23%	41%	31%
I have received adequate training in PM	19%	36%	23%	21%

ment is worthwhile, but quite a few would like to change the system. Only 55 per cent of the respondents strongly or slightly agreed with the statement that they had received adequate training in performance management.

Responses from line managers

Responses, as set out in Table 15, were received from 95 people expressing opinions on performance management from the point of view of line managers or team leaders. So far as the performance review meetings are concerned, the responses are reasonably favourable. For example, managers or team leaders are quite comfortable conducting meetings, think that it is time well spent and are convinced that they rate staff fairly. They believe performance management helps them to manage and motivate their teams better. Half of the respondents felt that they could have been better trained, and they were somewhat doubtful about the documentation. Quite a few want changes made to the process.

Table 15

VIEWS OF LINE MANAGERS/TEAM LEADERS ON PERFORMANCE MANAGEMENT (PM)

Statement	Strongly agree	Slightly agree	Slightly disagree	Strongly disagree
It helps me to communicate to my team what is expected of them	50%	40%	7%	3%
I have no difficulty in agreeing objectives	37%	41%	17%	5%
PM helps me to manage my team better	36%	49%	11%	4%
PM helps me to motivate my team	34%	49%	9%	8%
The time I spend on performance reviews could be spent more productively elsewhere	5%	5%	35%	55%
The information gained from performance reviews is of no value	4%	8%	30%	58%
I am not comfortable with conducting performance reviews	5%	15%	32%	48%
I give consistent and fair ratings to the members of my team	55%	38%	5%	2%
I have not been adequately trained in PM processes	13%	37%	26%	24%
The documentation is unclear and unhelpful	12%	31%	30%	27%
The current PM process works well and does not need to change	6%	26%	43%	25%

Observations

The attitude surveys were of course conducted in a small number of organisations, and the views expressed by the participants cannot be assumed to be representative. But the impression from this (admittedly) limited sample is certainly that the people involved did not think that performance management was a 'dishonest annual ritual'. Many people in these organisations believe that it is worthwhile, and they appear generally to be comfortable with the processes involved.

11 THE IMPACT OF PERFORMANCE MANAGEMENT

The report on the 1991 IPM research stated that:

> One positive theme which can be traced throughout the research
> is the extent to which performance management raises aware-
> ness of the pressures on the organisation to perform.
>
> IPM (1992)

Our research confirmed that this type of impact was still
being made in 1997–98. This was reflected in the continuing
concern with identifying and establishing agreed objectives to
ensure that everyone is aware of what is expected of them and
can relate their own efforts to organisational performance.

A more detailed definition of what performance management *should* contribute was defined by Jones *et al* (1995).
They argue that it should:

☐ communicate a shared vision throughout the organisation
to help to establish and support appropriate leadership and
management styles

☐ define individual requirements and expectations of all
employees in terms of the inputs and outputs expected
from them, thus reducing confusion and ambiguity

☐ provide a framework and environment for teams to
develop and succeed

☐ provide the climate and systems that support reward and
communicate how people and the organisation can
achieve improved performance

☐ achieve improved performance

☐ help people manage ambiguity.

Our analysis of the case-study data reveals that organisations are also concerned to identify and fill training needs more effectively and efficiently, to direct their energy towards developing the skills the organisation will need in the future, to manage careers more successfully and to target reward strategy so that they are offering employees things they value.

Measuring contribution and impact

It is notoriously difficult to establish causation when investigating the relationship between an HR (and indeed any other) initiative and organisational performance. There are too many other factors that get in the way. Indeed, it is often easier to prove reverse causation: 'We know that you cannot prove that X produces Y, but neither can you prove that it did not.' For example, when research projects such as the McDonald and Smith (1991) study claimed to establish that there is a proven connection between performance management and measures of organisational performance, it is a matter of speculation as to whether the results in the most effective companies were created by performance management or whether the most effective companies were the ones most likely to introduce performance management. They conducted research covering 437 publicly quoted US companies, 205 with performance management and 232 without. The findings were that the 205 respondents with performance management as opposed to the others without demonstrated:

- □ higher profits, better cash flows, stronger stockmarket performance and higher stock value
- □ significant gains over three years in financial performance and productivity
- □ higher sales growth per employee
- □ lower real growth in number of employees.

The researchers commented that 'In the successful companies the difference in managing employee performance seems to be that it is regarded as a mainstream business issue, not an isolated "personal problem".'

Beliefs that performance management will contribute to

organisational effectiveness are to an extent acts of faith based on the notion that certain actions are likely to produce certain results, although the conviction that approaches to motivating people based on goal and expectancy theories are likely to have a positive impact on performance has been supported by research, such as that conducted by Latham and Locke (1979). One of the aims of our survey was therefore to investigate whether it is possible to establish a relationship between the use of certain performance-management tools and organisational effectiveness.

The relationship between performance management and organisational performance

Our survey provided usable responses from 388 organisations with formal performance-management processes, and it is these responses that formed the basis of our analysis. Background information was obtained about the major elements of their present business strategy and how the participants compared the performance of their organisation with that of other organisations operating in the same industrial sector. Opinions were also collected about the criteria used in the measurement of individual performance. The data obtained is summarised below in Tables 16, 17 and 18.

The organisations concerned are confident that they are largely in the upper quartile, or at least the top 75 per cent, compared with others, especially with regard to quality of goods and service and the workforce.

Table 16
PERCENTAGE OF ORGANISATIONS RANKING ELEMENTS OF BUSINESS STRATEGY FIRST IN ORDER OF IMPORTANCE (PUBLIC-SECTOR REPLIES IN BRACKETS)

Expand/develop markets	24 (8) %
Reduce costs	17 (23) %
Increase efficiency	14 (24) %
Improve quality	12 (14) %
Develop skills	6 (9) %
Increase productivity	6 (2) %
Develop new products/services	5 (5) %
Reduce head count	0.7 (0.5) %
(base all organisations)	

Table 17
RATING OF OVERALL PERFORMANCE OF ORGANISATION AGAINST THE REST OF UK ORGANISATIONS OPERATING IN THE SAME SECTOR (PERCENTAGE OF ORGANISATIONS IN EACH CATEGORY)

	Top 25%	Middle 50%	Bottom 25%
Quality of goods and services	57	28	0.5
Quality of workforce	41	41	3
Cost	36	43	3
Innovative capacity	36	35	9
Market share	34	24	8
Efficiency	27	50	7
Return on investment	23	29	7
Profitability	23	27	9

Table 18
PERCENTAGE OF RESPONDENTS RANKING THE FOLLOWING CRITERIA VERY IMPORTANT AS A MEASURE OF INDIVIDUAL PERFORMANCE

Achievement of objectives	57%
Quality	53%
Customer care	51%
Competence	48%
Contribution to team	42%
Working relationships	35%
Aligning personal objectives with business goals	34%
Flexibility	30%
Productivity	27%
Skills/learning targets	23%
Business awareness	20%
Financial awareness	13%

The opinions of organisations about the effectiveness of their performance-management processes in improving overall performance are in Table 19.

The IPD survey results were analysed by Professor David Guest and colleagues at Birkbeck College using multivariate analysis to explore the coherence of performance management, to identify determinants of its effectiveness, and to assess its impact on organisational performance. This revealed that respondents rated performance-management

Table 19
IMPACT ON PERFORMANCE – PERCENTAGE OF ORGANISATIONS

Very effective	7%
Moderately effective	41%
Slightly effective	29%
Ineffective	8%
Don't know/not stated	13%

effectiveness very positively, less than 10 per cent rating it less than effective. The key criteria used for determining the effectiveness of performance management were the achievement of financial targets, development of skills, development of competence, improved customer care and improved quality. Personnel managers, who in the main were the ones who responded to the survey, believed that others (more particularly senior managers) are even more positive in their evaluation. Many also believe that the overall performance of their organisation, judged by internal criteria such as quality, productivity and cost and by external criteria such as market share and profitability, is at least as good as, and is often better than, that of their main competitors.

The features of the performance-management process likely to determine whether performance management is rated as more or less effective include the use of more innovative practices (eg 360-degree feedback), the presence of a formal evaluation system, a focus on employee contribution and achievement of individual objectives, and line-management responsibility for keeping documentation.

The Birkbeck analysis also reveals that performance-management practice falls into six broad areas: innovative approaches, career development, concern for the timing of appraisal, continuous assessment, competence assessment and self-appraisal *versus* support systems. It also found that beliefs about what performance management should be fall into the following five distinct categories:

☐ an integrative, ongoing developmental process
☐ PRP
☐ bureaucracy

□ goal-based motivation
□ success criteria.

These beliefs are strongly held, except in the case of performance management as bureaucracy, and there are mixed feelings about the role of PRP (but they tend to be negative).

These findings are encouraging, because they demonstrate
that there is a cohesive belief in the UK about what the practice of performance management actually is, and should be,
achieving. However, the Birkbeck researchers were still
unable to find any apparent difference in effectiveness
between organisations that use performance management and
those that do not. This is not so surprising in view of the fact
that we found very little evidence of any attempts to evaluate
systematically the impact of performance management.

Despite these findings, it is apparent that the majority of
people concerned with the management of performance
believe that it is worth the considerable effort and expense.
Beliefs in the benefits of performance management to organisations are based on the assumption that people are more likely
to respond positively and are more likely to work to improve
their performance and develop their capabilities if they share
in the processes of defining expectations and reviewing performance and competence against those expectations, and are
involved in creating and implementing plans for developing
their skills and competencies. If this happens generally (admittedly often a big if), and if the organisation provides the managerial and systems support necessary, than the assumption
that this will contribute to overall performance improvement
is not unreasonable, even if it cannot be proved. Certainly,
other aspects of our research, such as the focus groups and attitude surveys, revealed a generally positive attitude to performance management by those who are actually involved.
This seems to indicate that, properly carried out, performance
management can help to improve individual and team performance, and it is reasonable to assume, even if it cannot be
proved by statistical evidence, that improvements in organisational performance should follow.

Other contributions from performance management

Performance management can make a positive contribution to various other aspects of people management, particularly in the areas of motivation, developing a learning organisation, total quality management, employee relations and culture.

Motivating people

Performance management can motivate people by:

- [ ] clarifying goals and expectations
- [ ] providing reinforcement through feedback
- [ ] providing opportunities for people to use and develop their skills
- [ ] facilitating job enlargement, empowerment and job enrichment
- [ ] helping people to increase their self-esteem through their work achievements and growth (intrinsic motivation)
- [ ] providing opportunities for people to feel that they are valued through recognition and praise – extrinsic non-financial motivation
- [ ] rewarding people financially – extrinsic motivation.

Developing the business as a learning organisation

Performance management can help to develop the business as a learning organisation by:

- [ ] aligning the learning that takes place at team and individual level with the learning that should take place at organisational level
- [ ] focusing attention on continuous improvement and continuous development
- [ ] recognising that every project or task tackled by an individual or a team provides a learning opportunity
- [ ] ensuring that the analysis of performance and behaviour, which continues throughout the year as well as during formal reviews, is a means of identifying learning needs and making plans to meet them
- [ ] providing opportunities for people to discuss and reflect on what effective behaviour looks like and then to take steps

to learn how to modify their behaviour

☐ continually emphasising to people as part of the development process that 'if you are good you can grow and we shall help you'

☐ providing communication channels for identifying and transmitting learning needs at organisational, team and individual levels, and the means of integrating these needs with programmes for development at each of the levels.

Total quality management

Performance management can support total quality management processes and initiatives by:

☐ recognising that everyone in the organisation is an internal customer to the performance-management processes and should therefore be involved in the design and operation of these processes

☐ emphasising the importance of continuous improvement

☐ providing a basis for the systematic measurement and evaluation of the impact of the organisation's systems or work processes on team and individual performance and what can be done to improve those systems

☐ getting things improved through a partnership between managers, their teams and the individuals in those teams – this requires mutual trust and respect, and managers' adopting the attitude that individuals in their teams are colleagues, not subordinates (that in fact they are the internal customers of the processes of leadership)

☐ ensuring that, as 'internal customers', people know what the organisation is setting out to do, how well it is doing it and the part they can play as team members or individual contributors

☐ ensuring that the expectations of customers, not job descriptions, generate the performance expectations of individuals and teams

☐ spelling out the values of quality performance and total customer satisfaction that everyone is expected to uphold, and reviewing performance in the light of these values

☐ ensuring performance expectations include behavioural

skills that make the real difference in achieving high-quality performance and total customer satisfaction

☐ providing for employees to be active participants in the process, not merely 'drawn in' to management's actions.

As Guin (1992) has explained:

> The process of performance management actually reinforces total quality management. Because it gives managers the skills and tools to carry out 'the management part' of TQM, performance management can enable managers to sustain TQM as a vital part of the organisation's culture. To be most effective, senior managers should make sure performance management is integral to the way they do business.

Employee relations

Performance management can help to build positive employee relations by:

☐ helping to define the employment relationship (the psychological contract)

☐ improving the quality of communication between managers and staff

☐ establishing clarity of objectives

☐ enabling people to have a clear understanding about what is expected and what actions and behaviours are valued by the organisation

☐ developing channels for upward communication and feedback

☐ developing frameworks to enable empowerment to occur and give individuals real responsibility over how they carry out their work

☐ establishing a framework that ensures that what management actually does is consistent with what it says

☐ treating employees as stakeholders

Culture management

Performance management can have an impact on culture by:

☐ reinforcing the values of the organisation

☐ ensuring consistency between what the organisation says it values and what is measured in performance terms

- communicating the understanding that everyone is responsible for performance, and that managers and their teams are mutually dependent on one another to attain this purpose
- establishing that the needs of the individual as well as the organisation must be recognised and respected
- giving individuals the right to obtain feedback on their performance
- putting the focus on developing performance rather than just measuring it.

Conclusions

The preceding chapters summarise the considerable amount of research we have conducted into the practice and impact of performance management in the UK. We can conclude that organisations have come a long way over the years towards establishing integrated processes that have a real impact on the management of people, their development and hence the overall quality of the workforce. There are areas in which less progress has been made, significantly in the areas of evaluation and in the debate over the positive and negative effects of PRP. However, the overriding consensus is that performance management is an activity well worth the effort and pain. At its best, it can significantly enhance people-management processes and help to establish good working practices. But it is also apparent that experiences differ considerably, according to organisational context and history. In the following chapters we shall discuss some of the practical implications of establishing good performance-management practices in the reality of the workplace.

PART III

THE APPLICATION OF PERFORMANCE MANAGEMENT

12 PERFORMANCE MANAGEMENT AND DEVELOPMENT

Overwhelmingly, performance-management processes in the organisations covered by our survey focused on employee development as the route to improved organisational performance. This was generally interpreted as increasing the capabilities and potential of individuals to perform more effectively now and in the future, and the development of transferable skills to enhance career and employability prospects. Respondents were concerned with organisational learning and the creation and maintenance of a learning organisation, but they tended to follow the line taken by Senge (1990):

> Organisations learn only through individuals who learn. Individual learning does not guarantee organisational learning. But without it no organisational learning occurs.

The conceptual framework

Performance management is about learning at the organisational, team and individual levels. For individuals, learning is concerned with self-knowledge, understanding and development, and what needs to be known and how things can best be done to improve effectiveness and potential.

But individual and team learning takes place within the context of the organisation, and the concept of the learning organisation as described in the next section underpins much of the developmental aspects of performance management. But this concept is nebulous unless backed up with an understanding of the processes of organisational learning, single- and double-loop learning, individual learning, self-managed or self-directed learning, and continuous development, which are also considered below.

The learning organisation

A 'learning organisation' has been defined by Wick and Leon (1995) as one that 'continually improves by rapidly creating and refining the capabilities required for future success'. It has been described by Pedler *et al* (1986) as 'an organisation which facilitates the learning of all its members and continually transforms itself'. As defined by Garvin (1993), it is one that is 'skilled at creating, acquiring, and transferring knowledge, and at modifying its behaviour to reflect new knowledge and insights'. He has suggested that learning organisations are good at doing five things:

1 systematic problem-solving that rests heavily on the philosophy and methods of the quality movement. Its underlying ideas include:

   □ relying on scientific method, rather than guesswork, for diagnosing problems – what Deming (1986) calls the 'plan-do-check-act' cycle, and others refer to as 'hypothesis-generating, hypothesis-testing' techniques
   □ insisting on data rather than assumptions as the background to decision-making – what quality practitioners call 'fact-based management'
   □ using simple statistical tools such as histograms, Pareto charts and cause-and-effect diagrams to organise data and draw inferences.

2 experimentation – involving the systematic search for and testing of new knowledge. Continuous improvement programmes – 'kaizen' – are an important feature in a learning organisation.

3 learning from past experience – learning organisations review their successes and failures, assess them systematically and record the lessons learned in a way that employees find open and accessible. This process has been called the 'Santayana principle', quoting the philosopher George Santayana who coined the phrase 'Those who cannot remember the past are condemned to repeat it.'

4 learning from others – sometimes the most powerful insights come from looking outside one's immediate

environment to gain a new perspective. This process has been called SIS, which stands for 'steal ideas shamelessly'. Another, more acceptable, word for it is benchmarking – a disciplined process of identifying best-practice organisations and analysing the extent to which what they are doing can be transferred, with suitable modifications, to one's own environment.

5   transferring knowledge quickly and efficiently throughout the organisation by seconding people with new expertise, or by education and training programmes, as long as the latter are linked explicitly with implementation.

As Burgoyne (1994) has pointed out, learning organisations have to be able to adapt to their context and develop their people to match the context.

One approach, as advocated by Senge (1990), is to focus on collective problem-solving within an organisation. This is achieved using team learning and a 'soft systems' methodology, whereby all the possible causes of a problem are considered in order to define more clearly those that can be dealt with and those that are insoluble.

As Harrison (1997) emphasises, there are inconsistencies and ambiguities in the concept of the learning organisation. There is lack of clarity about 'what is or could be their specific impact on organisational capabilities and how they can be managed'. But Harrison does accept that the concept focuses attention on crucial tasks for organisations: 'to develop knowledge, to unlearn and relearn as well as learn, to distinguish between the capability to survive in the short term and the capacity and skills required to innovate for long-term profitability.' Thus, practical responses can be stimulated that benefit individuals and organisations, but there have to be effective processes linking individual and organisational learning.

The idea of the learning organisation may be surrounded by rhetoric, but performance-management processes can promote organisational learning.

Organisational learning

Organisations can be described (Harrison 1992) as continuous learning systems. The contribution of performance management to the development of organisations and people can be enhanced in the light of a better understanding of how organisations and people learn. This understanding will also help to make practical use of the learning organisation concept.

Organisational learning has been defined by Marsick (1994, quoted in Harrison 1997) as a process of:

> co-ordinated systems change, with mechanisms built in for individuals and groups to access, build and use organisational memory, structure and culture to develop long-term organisational capacity.

Organisational learning aims to develop a firm's resource-based capability which, as defined by Harrison (1997), is:

> based on what the firm knows and can do, vested primarily in the legacy of knowledge, strategic assets, networks and reputation bestowed by its past human resources, and in the skills, values and performance of its current people.

Argyris (1993) makes the point that:

> Learning is not simply having a new insight or a new idea. Learning occurs when we take effective action, when we detect and correct error. How do you know when you know something? When you can produce what it is you claim to know.

Harrison (1997) has defined five principles of organisational learning:

1   The need for a powerful and cohering vision of the organisation to be communicated and maintained across the workforce in order to promote awareness of the need for strategic thinking at all levels.
2   The need to develop strategy in the context of a vision that is not only powerful but also open-ended and unambiguous. This will encourage a search for a wide, rather than narrow, range of strategic options, will promote lateral thinking and will orient the knowledge-creating activities of employees.
3   Within the framework of vision and goals, frequent dialogue, communication and conversations are major facilitators of organisational learning.

4   It is essential continuously to challenge people to re-examine what they take for granted.

5   It is essential to develop a conducive learning and innovation climate.

These principles could be applied equally well to performance management as one of the processes that can help to promote organisational learning. This will be especially the case if the focus is on strategy, vision, communication and challenge, and if it is understood that an important aim of performance management is to help in the development of a learning culture.

The way in which a business can operate as a learning organisation was described by Armstrong (1992). The business was Book Club Associates, where he was director of human resources and strategic planning. In this case, the leadership came from the top. Stan Remington, as chief executive, had a clear vision of what the business was and what he wanted it to become. He also knew that learning was taking place all the time, and frequently said, 'A business is the totality of its knowledge.' For example, an operational research department was set up, the purpose of which was to analyse performance and draw conclusions for future development. If a new book club was created, discounted cash-flow techniques were used to project returns on investment. Every time an advertisement was placed for that club (or any of the clubs), an analysis took place of the buying performance of the new members recruited by this advertisement, so that a return on the investment in the advertisement could be calculated and compared with the target return. At board meetings, marketing meetings and the annual management conference, the chief executive encouraged, cajoled and sometimes compelled people to think about the outcomes of that research, to analyse the lessons they had learned and to discuss and decide what changes and improvements ought to be made to get higher returns in the future. The learning could be generalised in terms of the choice of media, or down to such details as 'Was yellow the best background colour for an advertisement?' The point Remington insisted on making was that everyone was learning all the time and that learning had to be captured, published and put to good use. Meetings and conferences therefore always ended with learning points and action plans, which were followed up. The company was highly profitable, and this approach undoubtedly created a climate of innovation, professionalism and concern for excellence.

Single- and double-loop learning

Argyris (1993) suggests that learning occurs under two conditions: first, when an organisation achieves what is intended and, second, when a mismatch between intentions and outcomes is identified and corrected. But organisations do not perform the actions that produce the learning: it is individual members of the organisation who behave in ways that lead to it, although organisations can create conditions that facilitate such learning.

Argyris distinguishes between single-loop and double-loop learning. Single-loop learning organisations define the 'governing variables' ie what they expect to achieve in terms of targets and standards. They then monitor and review achievements, and take corrective action as necessary, thus completing the loop. Double-loop learning occurs when the monitoring process initiates action to redefine the 'governing variables' to meet the new situation, which may be imposed by the external environment. The organisation has learned something new about what has to be achieved in the light of changed circumstances, and can then decide how this should be achieved. This learning is converted into action. The process is illustrated in Figure 9.

Argyris believes that single-loop learning is appropriate for routine, repetitive issues: 'It helps get the everyday job done.' Double-loop learning is more relevant for complex, non-programmable issues. As Pickard (1997) points out, double-loop learning questions why the problem occurred in the first place, and tackles its root cause rather than simply addressing its surface symptoms, as happens with single-loop learning.

Individual learning

Individuals learn for themselves and from other people. They

Figure 9
SINGLE- AND DOUBLE-LOOP LEARNING

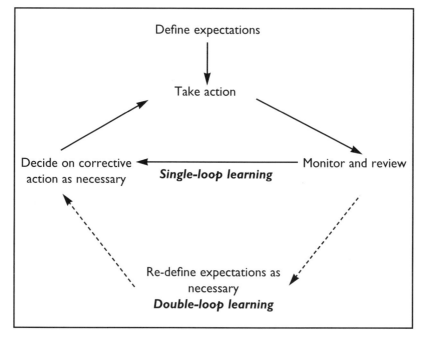

learn as members of teams and by interaction with their managers, co-workers and people outside the organisation. In the words of Birchall and Lyons (1995):

> For effective learning to take place at the individual level it is essential to foster an environment where individuals are encouraged to take risks and experiment, where mistakes are tolerated, but where means exist for those involved to learn from their experiences.

This is a blueprint for those aspects of performance management designed to create and maintain a learning culture that encourages and supports personal development.

Learning can best be seen as a continuous process, which is described by Kolb *et al* (1974) as a learning cycle consisting of four stages, as shown in Figure 10. He defines these stages as follows:

1 *concrete experience* – this can be planned or accidental
2 *reflective observation* – this involves actively thinking about the experience and its significance

Figure 10
THE KOLB LEARNING CYCLE

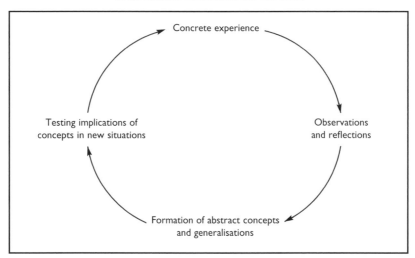

3   *abstract conceptualising* – generalising from experience
in order to develop various concepts and ideas that can be
applied when similar situations are encountered

4   *active experimentation* – testing the concepts or ideas in
new situations. This gives rise to a new concrete experience, and the cycle begins again.

The key to Kolb's model is that it is a simple description of
how experience is translated into concepts, which are then
used to guide individuals on how to deal with new experiences. Performance management can enhance the learning
process by providing people with opportunities to reflect on
their experiences, to learn from them, and to develop their
capacity to handle new experiences. Organisations such as
Hay Management Consultants use the Kolb model in their
performance-management training programmes.

But it is not the case that everyone learns in the same way.
We each have our own learning style. Honey and Mumford
(1986) have identified four styles:

1   *activists*, who involve themselves fully without bias in
new experiences and revel in new challenges

2   *reflectors*, who stand back and observe new experiences

from different angles – they collect data, reflect on it and then come to a conclusion

3   *theorists*, who adapt and apply their observations in the form of logical theories – they tend to be perfectionists

4   *pragmatists*, who are keen to try out new ideas, approaches and concepts to see whether they work.

However, none of these four learning styles is exclusive. It is quite possible, for example, that one person could be both a reflector and a theorist, and that someone else could be an activist/pragmatist, or a reflector/pragmatist. This learning style model is used by such companies as ICL and Littlewoods as a guide for people in preparing their personal development plans.

Self-managed learning

Self-managed or self-directed learning means that individuals take responsibility for satisfying their own learning needs to improve performance, to support the achievement of career aspirations, or to enhance their employability, within and beyond their present organisation. It can be based on processes that enable individuals to identify what they need to learn by reflecting on their experience and analysing what they need to know, so that they can perform better and progress their careers.

It has been argued by Knowles (1989) as reported by Tamkin *et al* (1995) that all individuals are naturally self-directed learners, even if they may need some help initially to get started. As Harrison (1997) has noted, 'No new learning will occur unless there is a stimulus to activate the learning process'.

The case for encouraging self-managed learning is that people learn and retain more if they find things out for themselves. But they may still need to be helped to identify what they should look for. Self-managed learning is about self-development, and this will be furthered by self-assessment, which leads to better self-understanding. Pedler *et al* (1978) recommended the following four-stage approach:

1   *self-assessment* based on analysis by individuals of their work and life situations

2   *diagnosis* derived from the analysis of learning needs and priorities

3   *action-planning* to identify objectives, helps and hindrances, resources required (including people) and timescales

4   *monitoring and review* to assess progress in achieving action plans.

Mumford (1994) suggests that self-managed learning can be carried out as follows:

☐ Identify the individuals' learning styles.

☐ Review how far their learning is encouraged or restricted by their learning styles.

☐ Review their core learning skills of observation and reflection, analysis, creativity, decision-making and evaluation, and consider how to use them more effectively.

☐ Review the work and other experiences in which they are involved in terms of the kind of learning opportunities they offer.

☐ Look for potential helpers in the self-development process: managers, colleagues, trainers, or mentors (ie individuals other than the manager or a trainer who provide guidance and advice).

☐ Draw up learning objectives and a plan of action – a personal development plan or learning contract.

☐ Set aside some time each day to answer the question, 'What did you learn today?'

Pedler *et al*'s concept of analysis and diagnosis, and Mumford's belief in the value of reviewing work to identify learning opportunities, have contributed to a better understanding of the developmental aspects of performance management. The focus is first on the real work that people do now and might do in the future, and what they need to learn to do it, and on getting them to understand how this learning can be accomplished.

But it is still recognised that there has to be stimulus, and there may well have to be help and guidance. This is where performance management comes in.

Continuous learning and development

As Harrison (1997) comments:

> In organisational life, everyday experience is the most funda-
> mental influence on learning. This experience consists not
> simply of the work that people do, but of the way they interact
> with others in the organisation, and the behaviour, attitudes
> and values of these others.

It follows that, when work is continuous, development can be
continuous as people reflect on and learn from their experience. But this is more likely to happen if reflection and learning are encouraged and, to a reasonable degree, structured
within a performance and development framework. The
(then) IPM commented as follows in its (now defunct) code of
practice on continuous development:

> As far as practicable, learning and work must be integrated.
> This means that encouragement must be given to all
> employees to learn from the problems, challenges and suc-
> cesses inherent in their day-to-day activities.

This implies double-loop learning as described earlier in this
chapter.

Again, the reflective, analytical and diagnostic aspects of
performance management, in itself a continuous process, all
contribute to continuous development. This is achieved in
two ways: performance and development reviews, and personal development planning.

Performance and development reviews as learning events

Performance and development reviews, whether conducted
formally or informally, can be regarded as learning events.
Learning opportunities are provided before, during and after
formal meetings.

Prior to reviews

Prior to a review, individuals can be encouraged to think
about their work experiences and their futures. They can be
asked to marshal their thoughts about what they feel they
want to learn, and the direction in which they want to

develop. They can also be asked to think about any specific training from which they believe they could benefit. This could be described as a process of reflection.

During the review

During the review, individuals can present to the reviewer their views about what they have learned and what they need to learn. A dialogue between the reviewer and the reviewee can take place in which learning needs can be analysed, and a diagnosis agreed in priority areas. Review meetings may also provide an opportunity for counselling.

After the review

Performance management goes on after the formal review. This is when coaching by the reviewee's manager and further counselling can take place.

Learning also continues informally. When a manager asks an individual or team to do something, a discussion can take place on how it should be done and what help, in the form of guidance or training, may be required. After the event, an informal analysis can take place of what went well, or not so well, and this can identify further learning needs.

Personal development planning

Defined

Personal development planning is carried out by individuals with guidance, encouragement and help from their managers as required. A personal development plan (PDP) sets out the actions people propose to take in order to learn and to develop themselves. They take responsibility for formulating and implementing the plan, but they may receive support from the organisation and their managers in doing so.

Purpose

Personal development planning aims to promote learning and to provide people with the knowledge and portfolio of transferable skills that will help to progress their careers. A distinction can be made between the learning and developmental aspects of PDPs. Pedler *et al* (1986) see learning as being concerned with an increase in knowledge or a higher degree of an existing skill, whereas development is about moving to a different state of being or functioning.

The initial purpose may be to provide what Tamkin *et al* (1995) call a 'self-organised learning framework'. But, as they comment, within that framework:

> Some organisations have interpreted learning widely, encompassing all aspects of self development or included learning activities that have little to do with an individual's current job or even future career.

Others have focused heavily on job-related skills or knowledge, or have laid a heavy emphasis on the user's future career and required experience.

At Guardian Royal Exchange, personal development planning is carried out for two reasons: 'To fit people better for their current job and because they need to improve or the job itself is changing' (Hegarty 1995).

Royal Mail Anglia defines the purpose of the plan as 'the identification of development and training needs which will enhance their personal contribution to the success of Royal Mail'. At BP Chemicals, it is stated in the guidance notes for staff that:

> It's all very well to say that the responsibility for development rests with the individual, but without the means to approach this in an analytical and systematic fashion, this is an empty statement. BP Chemicals is therefore encouraging everyone to produce a Personal Development Plan.

The research conducted for the Institute of Employment Studies (IES) by Tamkin *et al* (1995) into PDPs did not reveal in any of the 14 case-study organisations that the use of such plans had been initiated as a deliberate step towards becoming a learning organisation.

Focus

As the IES research showed, PDPs were most commonly focused on job or career development, or some mix of both. Less frequently, the emphasis was on the whole person. Tamkin *et al* (1995) comment:

Personal development plans which focus solely on skill development for the current job will not be welcomed by many employees. Those which take a broader view of the individual and their future, may be more effective for encouraging flexibility and have a higher impact on employees.

Personal development planning – the overall process

PDPs can be created as an outcome of a development or assessment centre. But these may make only a limited impact, and most of the IES research contacts extended the planning process to all their staff, or were intending to do so.

Personal development planning has become a well-established feature of performance and development management. It was incorporated in performance-management processes by 67 per cent of the organisations responding to the IPD 1997 questionnaire, and 69 per cent of those organisations thought that the planning aspect was very, or mostly, effective.

As described by BP Chemicals, the four stages in preparing a personal development plan are to:

1   assess current position
2   set goals

Figure 11
STAGES IN PREPARING A PERSONAL DEVELOPMENT PLAN

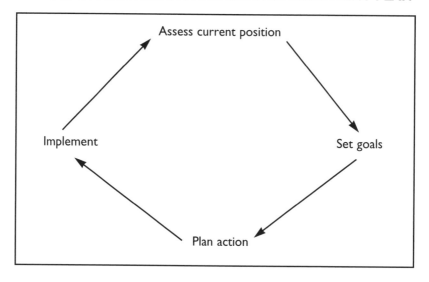

3 plan action

4 implement.

These are illustrated in Figure 11.

These planning stages are in line with those proposed by Gannon (1995):

☐ Analyse current situation and development needs.

☐ Set goals under such headings as improving performance in the current job, improving or acquiring skills, extending relevant knowledge, developing specified areas of competence, moving across or upwards in the organisation, preparing for changes in the current role.

☐ Prepare action plan.

Identifying development needs and wants

Development needs and wants are identified in performance-management processes by individuals on their own or working in conjunction with their managers. This will include reviewing performance against agreed plans, and assessing competence requirements and the capacity of people to achieve them. The analysis is therefore based on an understanding of what people do, what they have achieved, what knowledge and skills they have and what knowledge and skills they need. The analysis is always related to work and the capacity to carry it out effectively.

Individuals can make their own assessment of their personal development needs to get more satisfaction from their work, to advance their careers and to increase their employability.

Identifying the means of satisfying needs

Every organisation we contacted that carries out personal development planning emphasised that it was not just about identifying training needs and suitable courses to satisfy them. Training courses may form part of the development plan, but only a minor part; other learning activities were much more important. As Royal Mail Anglia state in their guidance notes on personal development planning:

Development needs can be met using a wide variety of activities. Do not assume that a conventional training course is the only option. In many instances, activity more finely tuned to the specific need can be more rewarding and appropriate than a generalised training course.

The examples of development activities listed by Royal Mail Anglia include:

□ seeing what others do (best practice)
□ project work
□ adopting a role model (mentor)
□ involvement in other work areas
□ planned use of internal training media (interactive video programmes/learning library)
□ input to policy formulation
□ increased professionalism on the job
□ involvement in the community
□ coaching others
□ training courses.

Other learning activities, which could be mentioned but are not on this list, include guided reading, special assignments, action learning and distance learning.

Action-planning

The action plan sets out what needs to be done, and how it will be done, under such headings as:

□ development needs
□ outcomes expected (learning objectives)
□ development activities to meet the needs
□ responsibility for development – what individuals will do, and what support they will require from their manager, the HR department or other people
□ timing – when the learning activity is expected to start and be completed
□ outcome – what development activities have taken place and how effective they were.

The outcomes may be set out, as at AA Insurance, as SMART objectives ie stretching, measurable, agreed, realistic/relevant, time-related.

Whether or not that formula is used, the aims of the planning process are always to be specific about what is to be achieved and how it is to be achieved, to ensure that the learning needs and actions are relevant, to indicate the timescale, to identify responsibility and, within reason, to ensure that the learning activities stretch those concerned.

As noted by the IES research, the extent to which the development plan is structured varies. A highly structured approach will specify the competency areas to be developed as established in the performance review against each of the competency framework headings used by the organisation. The action plan might also be structured under the headings of the type of development activity proposed. In a semi-structured process, only broad headings would be incorporated in the documentation – for example, the development need and the means by which it will be met. A completely unstructured approach is occasionally used, in effect asking for the plan to be committed to a blank sheet of paper, but with some guidelines on what should be recorded. Most of the organisations covered by our survey adopted the middle-of-the-road approach – some structure, but not too much, on the grounds that they did not want planning to degenerate into a bureaucratic form-filling exercise. The PDP form may be attached to the performance review form or, to emphasise its importance, may be kept separately. The forms we have seen are usually quite simple. At Railtrack there are only four columns, covering:

☐ development objectives and outcome expected
☐ action to be undertaken and when
☐ support required
☐ evidence to demonstrate that a particular activity has been undertaken.

The Guardian Insurance plan has sections for:

☐ *development needs* – what development needs are to be addressed?

☐ *learning objectives* – what knowledge/skills do I intend to gain? What behaviour shall I try to change?

☐ *learning method* – how am I going to achieve my objectives? What tasks/projects/experience will I use?

☐ *learning resources* – what shall I use (books, films, videos, workshops)? What help might I need, and from whom?

☐ *assessment* – what evidence shall I show to assess what I have learned? What criteria shall I use to judge achievement of learning objectives?

☐ *review/completion dates* – when shall I review progress with my appraiser? When do I hope to have achieved my objectives?

Royal Mail Anglia has a simple form for the plan, which sets out the area for action, the supplier and the target date. But this is supplemented by a skills analysis form, which lists 35 skills under the headings professional, communications, interpersonal, managing and personal. An indication is expected of the skills and actions required.

BP Chemicals also has a simple 'personal development review' form, which asks for:

☐ *employee's comments* – 'In order to help you and your team achieve your personal development objectives, what new skills, knowledge and training do you need?'

☐ *supervisor's comments* on personal development

☐ *personal development plan* – agreed between employee and supervisor, including a training plan.

BP Chemicals uses a computer-based system to assist planning.

The ICL approach to personal development planning

The ICL Learning Guide, which is part of the infrastructure that supports Performance Plus, ICL's performance management system, says:

> your continuing personal success depends directly on your skills, knowledge, expertise and attitudes, and the extent to which they add value for those you are working for, whether

Figure 12

THE HONEY AND MUMFORD LEARNING CYCLE MODEL AS USED AT ICL

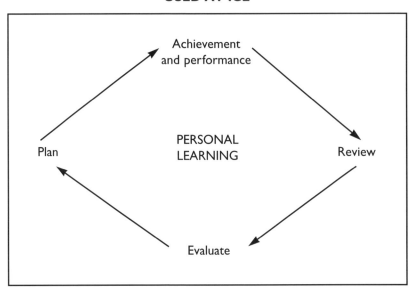

they be employers or clients ... You have to make sure that you have knowledge skills and expertise that are in demand. Continuous personal development through learning is the key.

The Honey and Mumford learning cycle as shown in Figure 12 is adopted by ICL as the model.

The guide specifies how people can increase their personal value by identifying their learning needs through reviews of achievement and performance, assessment, benchmarking, using ICL's assessment and career guidance/development centres and consulting a career counsellor. Guidance is given on learning styles and details are given of 31 learning options. The method of completing a PDP is summarised as follows:

☐ identify your learning needs

☐ identify your learning-style profile

☐ review options available

☐ note down your learning needs under the headings

knowledge, skill, attitudes and experience (the advice is 'Think about what, specifically, you will need to know and do differently')

☐ against each need, note down the specific action chosen, who is responsible for effecting the action and by what date

☐ ensure that your personal learning plan is implemented, reviewed and updated as necessary

☐ ensure that a formal review with your manager takes place at least once a year, preferably twice, to establish that all is going according to plan, or to adapt the plan to meet new needs.

The requirement to prepare PDPs

Most organisations indicate that they expect everyone covered by the planning process to prepare and implement plans. Some, however, take the realistic view that not everyone needs or wants to be involved in elaborate plans, and so they allow a certain amount of flexibility. In other organisations, personal development planning is encouraged and supported but is not obligatory, on the grounds that to insist too strongly on the completion of forms seems to be inconsistent with the principle of self-managed learning. In these organisations, the aim is to help people to understand how they can benefit personally from the process, and to emphasise that their managers and the organisation will help them as much as possible.

Tamkin *et al* (1995) are quite clear on this matter:

> Taking first the issue of whether personal development plans can be compulsory, the simple answer is 'no'. They cannot be and, in any case, should not be.

Responsibility for personal development planning

In most applications, it is emphasised that individuals are primarily responsible for progressing the plan and for ensuring that they play their part in implementing it. But it is generally recognised that, to different degrees, people will need encouragement, guidance and support. Managers are not expected to sit back and let their staff flounder. They have a role to play in helping, as necessary, in the preparation of the plan.

BP Chemicals spells out explicitly what team leaders are expected to do:

- support the individual in his or her efforts to develop
- offer feedback at appropriate stages
- provide information on company activities and requirements
- help produce action plans that are practical and achievable
- assist in implementation.

The HR department also has an important part to play, but it is there to provide support rather than direction. The support will include the provision of learning aids, materials and opportunities, the administration of monitoring processes, advice on methods of learning, and the availability of material and courses (eg distance learning). Some organisations, such as Glaxo Wellcome, have established learning databases from which individuals can access information on PCs about developing competencies, career-planning, and ways of identifying and meeting learning needs.

Introducing personal development planning

The introduction of personal development planning should not be undertaken lightly. It is not just a matter of designing a new back page to the performance review form and telling people to fill it up. Neither is it sufficient just to issue guidance notes and expect people to get on with it.

Managers, team leaders and individuals all need to learn about personal development planning. They should be involved in deciding how the planning process will work and what their roles will be. The benefits to them should be understood and accepted. It has to be recognised that everyone will need time and support to adjust to a culture in which they have to take much more responsibility for their own development. Importantly, all concerned should be given guidance on how to identify learning needs and on the features of the various means of satisfying those needs, and how they can make use of the facilities and opportunities that can be made available to them.

13   PERFORMANCE MANAGEMENT AND PAY

The link between performance management and pay

As the IPD survey demonstrated, performance management is not inevitably associated with pay, although this is often assumed to be the case. Only 43 per cent of respondents to the survey with performance management had performance-related pay (PRP). This figure was not distorted by the number of public-sector organisations that participated in the survey: 46 per cent of such organisations had performance pay, while the proportions in private-sector manufacturing and private-sector service companies were 43 per cent and 46 per cent respectively.

The research, however, showed that contingent or differential pay is still an important element in many performance-management schemes. This is because paying for performance or for competence, or both, is regarded by many organisations as desirable for three reasons:

- It motivates people to perform better or to develop their skills and competences.
- It delivers the message that performance and competence are important.
- It is fair and equitable to reward people differentially according to their performance, competence or contribution.

In this chapter we discuss how the various aspects of performance management and pay work, and how well they work. We consider the basic approaches of PRP, competence-related pay and team pay under the general heading of contingency pay, and examine the new concept of contribution-related pay. Finally, we discuss the relationship between performance management and job evaluation.

Approaches to contingency pay

There are two basic approaches: PRP for individuals or teams and competence-related pay. The distinction between these is not always so clear as it seems, and there is a third approach – a mixed model – that may be called contribution-related pay. These collectively may be referred to as contingency or discretionary pay, because the reward is dependent on the performance of the individual or team, or on individual competence, and the amount awarded is at the discretion of management. This raises a key question about contingency pay and performance management: how can the need to assess performance or competence, usually through ratings, be reconciled with the important developmental aspects of performance management? We address this question first before describing and assessing the general considerations affecting contingency pay on the three approaches referred to above.

Reconciling performance management and pay

The problem of reconciling the developmental aspects of performance management or appraisal and pay has been with us for many years. Two decades ago Armstrong (1976) commented that:

> It is undesirable to have a direct link between the performance review and the reward review. The former must aim primarily at improving performance and, possibly, assessing potential. If this is confused with a salary review, everyone becomes overconcerned about the impact of the assessment on the increment ... It is better to separate the two.

Many people since then have accepted this view in principle, but have found it difficult to apply in practice. As Kessler and Purcell (1993) argue:

> How distinct these processes [performance review and PRP] can ever be or, in managerial terms, should ever be, is perhaps debatable. It is unrealistic to assume that a manager can separate these two processes easily and it could be argued that the evaluations in a broad sense should be congruent.

And Armstrong and Murlis (1994) comment that:

> Some organisations separate entirely performance pay ratings from the performance management review. But there will, of

course, inevitably be a read-across from the performance management review to the pay-for-performance review. The issue is that if you want to pay for performance or competence you have to measure performance or competence. And if you want, as you should do, the process of measurement to be fair, equitable, consistent and transparent, then you cannot make pay decisions, on whatever evidence, behind closed doors. You must convey to individuals or teams how the assessment has been made and how it has been converted into a pay increase.

This is a matter of procedural justice, the rules of which, as expressed by Leventhal (1980), are the:

☐ *consistency rule.* The allocation processes should be consistent between people and over time.

☐ *bias-suppression rule.* Personal (concealed) self-interest and blind allegiance to narrow preconceptions should be excluded at all costs from the allocation process.

☐ *accuracy rule.* It is necessary to base the allocation process on as much good information and informed opinion as possible.

☐ *correctability rule.* Opportunities must exist to modify and reverse decisions made at various points in the allocation process.

☐ *representativeness rule.* All phases of the allocative process should reflect the basic concerns, values and outlook of important subgroups in the population of individuals affected by the process.

☐ *ethicality rule.* Procedures must be compatible with the fundamental moral and ethical values accepted by oneself. Respectful, neutral and trustworthy treatment from authorities must be seen as fair.

Procedural justice therefore demands that there is a system for assessing performance and competence, that the assessment should be based on 'good information and informed opinion', that the person affected should be able to contribute to the process of obtaining evidence to support the assessment, that the person should know how and why the assessment has been made, and that the person should be able to appeal against the assessment.

It therefore seems almost impossible to avoid some sort of assessment or rating in the performance review meeting. The argument that this will not affect the quality of that meeting in terms of its developmental purposes has been dismissed by some people on the grounds that there should be no problem if the reasons for the rating are fully explained (procedural justice), and rating could enhance the developmental aspect of the review meeting if it clearly establishes what people have to do or learn to improve their ratings. This sounds reasonable enough, but the evidence from our focus groups was that rating systems were generally, and in some cases passionately, disliked because they were liable to be unfair and were impossible to understand (or accept). It seems that managers should be good at explaining things, but do not always do it very well.

This is a thorny problem. But it was interesting to note from our research that 24 per cent of the respondents with PRP did not have rating. Two good examples of best-practice companies that do not incorporate obligatory rating in their performance-management and pay processes are BP Exploration and Zeneca. In one of the organisations we contacted, managers propose where people should be placed in the pay range for their grade, taking into account their contribution relative to others in similar jobs and the relationship of their current pay to market rates. This is carried out separately from the performance review, but individuals are given the opportunity to discuss their manager's proposal and to advance reasons why they should be paid more. And managers are expected to respond and to take account of these submissions. This approach has much to commend it. Even if organisations do not want to go as far as that, there are strong arguments for a separate assessment process that could simply place people in a number of broad categories, such as exceptional, consistently good, improvable, and not acceptable. These categories could inform pay decisions.

Some organisations reject the idea of a separate meeting because it imposes an extra burden on line managers. Others believe that the distinction is false, and the fact that there will be an assessment or rating of performance at some time in the future will be obvious, and is just as likely to prejudice the review meeting as if it had taken place at the same time. But the evidence from the focus groups we conducted as part of this research project is that ratings for pay purposes do seriously prejudice the developmental aspects of performance management. Even if there is an inevitable read-across, the case for separating development and pay reviews by a gap of several months is a strong one.

Performance-related pay (PRP)

Individual PRP relates pay progression (increases to base rate) or bonuses to the assessed performance of individuals.

Method of operation

Methods of operating PRP vary considerably, but its typical features are as follows.

Pay structure

This is designed to provide scope for pay progression within pay brackets attached to job grades.

Pay progression and performance

The rate and limits of progression through the pay brackets are determined by performance ratings.

Decelerated progression

Pay progression relating to performance is typically planned to decelerate through the grade because it is argued, in line with learning-curve theory, that pay increases should be higher during the earlier period in a job when learning is at its highest rate.

PRP increases

These may be added cumulatively to basic pay (ie consolidated) until either the maximum rate of pay for the grade or a limit within the grade defined in terms of a level of performance is reached. Increases in PRP typically range from 3 per cent to 10 per cent, with an average of about 5 per cent in times of low inflation. But this can vary considerably between organisations and between different categories of

Chartered Institute of Personnel and Development

Customer Satisfaction Survey

*We would be grateful if you could spend a few minutes answering these questions and return the postcard to CIPD. <u>Please use a black pen to answer.</u> **If you would like to receive a free CIPD pen, please include your name and address.*** IPD MEMBER Y/N

....

1. Title of book ....

2. Date of purchase: month ....   year ....

3. How did you acquire this book?
   ☐Bookshop   ☐Mail order   ☐Exhibition   ☐Gift   ☐Bought from Author

4. If ordered by mail, how long did it take to arrive:
   ☐1 week   ☐2 weeks   ☐more than 2 weeks

5. Name of shop .... Town....................................... Country ....

6. Please grade the following according to their influence on your purchasing decision with 1 as least influential: (please tick)

	1	2	3	4	5
Title					
Publisher					
Author					
Price					
Subject					
Cover					

7. On a scale of 1 to 5 (with 1 as poor & 5 as excellent) please give your impressions of the book in terms of: (please tick)

	1	2	3	4	5
Cover design					
Paper/print quality					
Good value for money					
General level of service					

8. Did you find the book:
   Covers the subject in sufficient depth   ☐Yes   ☐No
   Useful for your work   ☐Yes   ☐No

9. Are you using this book to help:
   ☐In your work ☐Personal study   ☐Both   ☐Other (please state)

Please complete if you are using this as part of a course

10. Name of academic institution...

11. Name of course you are following? ....

12. Did you find this book relevant to the syllabus? ☐Yes ☐No ☐Don't know

Thank you!

To receive regular information about CIPD books and resources call 020 8263 3387.

Any data or information provided to the CIPD for the purposes of membership and other Institute activities will be processed by means of a computer database or otherwise. You may, from time to time, receive business information relevant to your work from the Institute and its other activities. If you do not wish to receive such information please write to the CIPD, giving your full name, address and postcode. The Institute does not make its membership lists available to any outside organisation.

1795/05/00

Publishing Department

Chartered Institute of Personnel and Development

CIPD House

Camp Road

Wimbledon

London

SW19 4BR

people within organisations. Alternatively, they can be paid as non-consolidated lump sum bonuses (variable pay), although this is less common.

Rationale for PRP

Three propositions are most frequently advanced to justify PRP:

1   It is an effective motivator because it provides a financial incentive and rewards people according to the level of performance they achieve. If PRP is based on measuring performance in relation to agreed objectives, is fully transparent (as it should be), and provides worthwhile as well as attainable rewards it will function in accordance with the principle of expectancy theory.

2   It conveys a clear message to employees that the organisation believes in – indeed requires – a high level of performance from everyone, and is prepared to pay for it. PRP can therefore be used as a lever for cultural change – helping to create performance-oriented organisations and individuals.

3   It is right and proper for pay to be related to the contribution made by individuals to achieving organisational objectives. High performers should be paid more than low performers.

Criteria for performance pay

The eight golden rules for paying individuals or teams for their performance, as quoted by Armstrong and Murlis (1994), are these:

1   Individuals and teams should be clear about the targets and standards of performance required, whatever those may be.

2   They should be able to track performance against those targets and standards throughout the period over which the performance is being assessed. They must be able to measure their performance, because if you cannot measure performance you cannot pay for performance.

3   They must be in a position to influence the performance by changing their behaviour or decisions.

4   They should understand what rewards they will receive for achieving the end results – there should be a clear link between effort and reward.

5   The reward should follow as closely as possible the accomplishment that generated it.

6   The reward should be worthwhile.

7   The results required to generate the reward should be attainable, although not too easily.

8   The basis upon which rewards are made should be communicated positively and should be easy to understand.

Number of PRP schemes

The 1998 IPD survey of PRP established that 40 per cent of 1,158 respondents had adopted PRP. Contrary to the popular belief that organisations are becoming disillusioned with PRP, its use is growing. Fifty-nine per cent of the respondents had introduced it during the five years prior to 1998. Twenty-three per cent of respondents who currently do not have performance-pay processes had discontinued them between 1990 and 1998. This represents an annual cessation rate of 3 per cent a year, smaller than the growth experienced over the last five years.

Impact of PRP

The IPD survey established that 74 per cent of respondents believed that PRP improves performance. This is a strong vote of confidence in the system. The only reservation that can be made is that it represents the opinion of the respondents, who were mainly personnel specialists and might be expected to be bullish about PRP. The opinion of employees in receipt of PRP was not sought.

The survey found that respondents largely believed that PRP delivered a clear message about organisational performance (67 per cent), and rewarded people in a way they think is fair (57 per cent), although a minority felt that PRP had worsened perception about fairness (14 per cent).

In the opinion of the survey respondents, PRP schemes made their most positive impact on the behaviour of the high performers (21 per cent compared with 4 per cent of average performers and 4 per cent of poor performers). The writers of the IPD's executive summary commented that 'These high performers may be precisely the type of employee that many employers wish to nurture and develop.' This may be so, except that it could be argued that such high performers may well be motivated by a number of other factors (eg achievement) rather than money. The survey does reveal that 41 per cent of respondents thought there was no real change in average performance as a result of PRP, and 52 per cent believed there was no real change in poor performers. But these are the very people whose performance should be addressed by PRP! Other methods of motivation provided by performance management have to be deployed as well as money.

Advantages of PRP

The advantages claimed for PRP can be summarised as follows:

- It motivates.
- It delivers the right message.
- It is fair to reward people according to their performance.
- It provides a tangible means of rewarding and recognising achievements.

Disadvantages of PRP

The disadvantages of PRP, as pointed out by its many critics, are these:

- It is not a guaranteed motivator; the performance-pay criteria mentioned earlier in this chapter are often difficult, if not impossible, to meet.
- It has to be based on some form of performance assessment, usually a rating, but it may be difficult to produce realistic performance measures. As a result, ratings may be unfair, subjective and inconsistent. If there is undue emphasis on individual performance, teamwork will suffer.
- PRP can lead to pay rising faster than performance (pay drift). In other words, it is not cost-effective.
- PRP schemes are difficult to manage well. They rely upon

effective performance-management processes that many organisations do not have.

☐ PRP can inhibit team work on account of its individualistic nature.

☐ PRP can produce poor-quality performance because people are concentrating on achieving quantitative targets.

☐ PRP can lead to 'short-termism' – the pursuit of quick results rather than paying attention to the achievement of longer-term strategic goals

These disadvantages may appear to be formidable, but the fact remains that in many organisations, as shown by the 1997 IPD survey, the advantages of PRP are perceived as exceeding by far its perceived disadvantages. Perhaps the most compelling reason for taking this view is that it is equitable to give greater rewards to people who perform well than to those who perform badly. And even if PRP is not a powerful direct motivator, it will provide indirect motivation, because achievement will have been recognised by tangible means. It will also deliver the message that high performance is vital and will be rewarded: 'This is what we believe to be important and this is what we will pay for.' But there are a number of stringent criteria for successfully operating PRP, as set out below.

Criteria for installing and monitoring PRP

The following questions should be answered before launching PRP or deciding whether it should be retained:

☐ Will the proposed scheme, or does the existing scheme, motivate people?

☐ Is it possible to devise or maintain fair and consistent methods of measuring performance?

☐ Is there an effective performance-management process in place based on measuring and assessing performance against agreed targets and standards?

☐ Can managers be trained (or are managers properly trained) to rate performance fairly and consistently?

☐ Will rewards be fairly and consistently related to performance?

❑ Will there be – indeed, is there – enough money available to provide worthwhile rewards?

❑ Will the proposed scheme, or does the existing scheme, satisfy the other criteria for an effective performance-pay system – namely, clear targets and standards, ability to track performance, ability to influence performance, clarity on the relationship between effort and reward, the reward following the accomplishment fairly closely?

❑ Will the scheme be, or is the scheme, cost effective?

If an organisation cannot answer these questions satisfactorily, one alternative is not to use PRP as a means of adding performance-related increases to the base rate. It could be replaced with a 'variable pay' system that awards cash bonuses only as and when they are earned for notable and measurable achievements. In addition, cash bonuses could be paid for people who have achieved sustained levels of high performance as demonstrated by exceeding targets and standards over an extended period.

A second alternative to which a number of organisations are turning is competence-related pay.

Competence-related pay
How it works

Competence-related pay provides for pay progression to be linked to assessments of the levels of competence that people have achieved. Typically, the headings in a competence profile or framework are used as the basis for assessment. The level of competence expected from a fully effective individual in a role is defined, and the actual levels achieved are compared with requirements. In some schemes, people are assessed against each competence heading, an overall assessment then being made that may be expressed on a scale such as exceeds level of competence required, fully competent, not yet competent but developing at the expected rate, not yet competent but developing at less than the expected rate. These assessments are then translated into a pay increase.

Measuring competence

The problem with competence-related pay, as Sparrow (1996) pointed out, is that of measuring levels of competence, although Brown and Armstrong (1997) have asserted that measurement and assessment are possible if a well-researched and clearly defined competence framework exists and people are trained how to collect and assess evidence on competence levels. This is easier when hard, work-based competences are used rather than softer, behaviourally-based competences. If competence or capabilities are used, they will have been defined in output terms ie 'In this aspect of the role the person should be capable of ... '. The capability will be described in terms of doing something that produces a result. The measurement of competence therefore starts by reviewing results in each area of capability, and thus assessing how effectively the competence has been used.

If this approach is adopted, competence-related pay begins to look suspiciously like PRP. But if competence is not about performance, what is it about?

Differences between performance- and competence-related pay

However, there are differences between performance- and competence-related pay. These are summarised below:

☐ Competence-related pay is based on an agreed framework of competences or capabilities, some of which are generic (applicable to a number of roles), some of which are specific to particular roles.

☐ Competence-related pay is not based on the achievement of specific results expressed in the form of targets or projects to be completed, although it can be said that it is concerned with the attainment on a continuing basis of agreed standards of performance.

☐ Competence-related pay looks forward in the sense that it implies that, when people have reached a certain level of competence, they will be able to go on using it effectively into the future; conversely, PRP looks backwards – 'This is what you have just achieved, this is your reward for achieving it.'

☐ Competence-related pay is (or should be) based on agreed

definitions of competence requirements expressed in the language of role-holders and on agreements about the evidence that can be used to assess levels of competence. In contrast, PRP is often, although not always, based on managerial judgements that the individuals concerned may find difficult to accept.

Advantages and disadvantages of competence-related pay

The list of differences between competence- and performance-related pay given above summarise a number of the advantages of the former. If the organisation really believes that successful performance depends on raising levels of competence, then some form of competence-related pay makes sense.

But however carefully competences are defined, there may still be problems in measuring them, and translating any measurements into an overall assessment can seem to be an arbitrary process. Competence-related pay also seems to ignore the fact that performance is about delivering *results*. That is why some organisations have introduced hybrid schemes, in which base pay is related to competence, but out-of-the-ordinary achievements are rewarded with cash bonuses. Many people think that this is the best way forward.

Conditions necessary for introducing competence-related pay

An organisation should not contemplate the introduction of competence-related pay lightly. The following demanding criteria need to be met if it is to work:

- Well-researched and analysed competence frameworks must be in place.
- Reliable, fair and consistent methods of assessing competence must be available.
- Managers, team leaders and employees generally should be trained in how the process operates and must be convinced that it is workable and fair.

Competence-related pay is generally more likely to be appropriate for 'knowledge workers' in organisations where the values and processes focus on flexibility, adaptability and continuous development.

Team-based pay

Team-based pay provides rewards to teams or groups of employees carrying out similar and related work linked to the performance of the team. Performance may be measured in terms of outputs or the achievement of service delivery standards, or both. The quality of the output and the opinion of customers about service levels are also often taken into account.

As described by Armstrong and Ryden (1996), team pay is usually paid in the form of a bonus shared among team members in proportion to their base rate of pay. (Much less frequently, it is shared equally.) Individual team members may be eligible for competence-related or skill-based pay, but not for PRP.

Advantages of team pay

Team pay can:

- □ encourage effective teamworking and co-operative behaviour
- □ clarify team goals and priorities
- □ enhance flexible working within teams
- □ encourage multiskilling
- □ provide an incentive for the team collectively to improve performance
- □ encourage less effective team members to improve to meet team standards.

Disadvantages of team pay

The disadvantages of team pay are that:

- □ it works only in cohesive and mature teams
- □ individuals may resent the fact that their own efforts are not rewarded specifically
- □ peer pressure may compel individuals to conform to group norms, which may itself be undesirable.

Conditions suitable for team pay

Team pay is more likely to be appropriate when:

□ teams can be readily identified and defined
□ teams are well-established
□ the work carried out by team members is interrelated – team performance depends on the collective efforts of team members
□ targets and standards of performance can be determined and agreed readily with team members
□ acceptable measurements of team performance compared with targets and standards are available
□ generally, the formula for team pay meets the criteria for PRP.

Contribution-related pay

As discussed earlier in this chapter, it is possible to make a number of distinctions between performance- and competence-related pay. But these can become distinctions without differences – more apparent than real. This happens when competence levels are defined, and competence is assessed against those levels, not just by observing behaviour but by analysing the impact of that behaviour in achieving results and meeting required standards of performance.

The distinction between them becomes even less real if the evidence of competence is based on *what* people have done as well as *how* they have done it. But if one of the definitions of performance given in Chapter 2 covers both what people achieve (outcomes) as well as how they achieve it (competences), then a mixed model becomes appropriate. This could be described as 'contribution-related pay'.

Contribution defined

Contribution is *what people do to bring about a result*. Individuals and teams contribute to the achievement of the purpose of their role. In financial terms, contribution is the difference between the sales revenue for a product and its directly attributable marginal or variable costs. It thus indicates what income a product generates towards achieving profit and covering fixed costs. In the context of performance management and pay, however, contribution is a more general concept which describes the overall part people play in generating results as the basis of the attributes they bring to their roles (skills and competences) and how they use these attributes.

Contribution-related pay defined

In accordance with the definition given above, contribution can be measured in terms of both inputs and outputs – competence and results. Contribution-related pay recognises that performance embraces both these factors. The questions to be answered when assessing levels of pay and pay increases or bonus are these:

- ☐ What impact has the person in this role made on team, departmental or organisational performance?
- ☐ What level of competence has been brought to bear in handling the demands made by the role?
- ☐ How has the contribution made to results been affected by the level of competence displayed and applied?

Contribution-related pay can therefore be defined as a process for making pay decisions that are based on assessments of both the outcomes of the work undertaken by individuals and the levels of skill and competence that have influenced these outcomes.

How contribution-related pay works

Contribution-related pay can work effectively within a broad-banded pay structure in which movement across the bands depends on both competence and performance. It also fits well with a belief that the delivery of pay should be based on performance, competence and career-progression considerations.

Paying for contribution, as suggested by Brown (1998), means paying for results plus competence, and for past performance and future success as illustrated in Figure 13.

Contribution-related pay therefore works by applying the mixed model of performance management – assessing inputs and outputs and coming to a conclusion on the level of pay appropriate for individuals in their roles by looking both at past performance and, importantly, the future.

Figure 13
PAYING FOR CONTRIBUTION MODEL

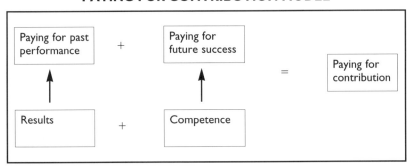

There are two approaches. The first is to take a holistic view of what people have contributed on the basis of information about their competence and what they have delivered. This can be based on a competence framework, so that behaviour can be considered analytically although, ultimately, an overall view will be formed. Similarly, an overview of performance in achieving objectives or meeting standards can take place. The information from the sources is then combined and the level of contribution compared with others in similar roles in order to reach a pay review decision.

The second approach involves rating both results and competence, and taking both these ratings into account in deciding on pay increases. This could be done somewhat mechanistically with the help of a contribution pay matrix, as illustrated in Figure 14.

Figure 14
CONTRIBUTION PAY MATRIX

		Competence			
		a	b	c	d
Results	A	–	–	2%	3%
	B	–	3%	4%	5%
	C	2%	4%	6%	8%
	D	4%	6%	8%	10%

Figure 15

EXAMPLE OF PAYING FOR CONTRIBUTION IN A UK BANK

Past Performance Results	**Client** • Client satisfaction • Change to mix of clients	**Financial** • Meet new business and total income targets • Control direct costs	A P P R A I S A L → Bonus
Competence Future performance	**Internal Processes** • Lead generation • Regulatory requirements	**People** • Team contribution • Personal growth in competence • Referrals	→ Bonus

A model of how contribution pay works in a UK bank has been produced by Brown (1998), as illustrated in Figure 15.

Paying for contribution is appropriate when it is believed that a well-rounded approach is required to make crucial pay decisions related to the criticality of the role now and in the future, and to get the balance of factors affecting pay right in the light of organisational requirements.

Performance management and job evaluation

Job evaluation has been defined by Armstrong and Baron (1995) as 'a systematic process for defining the relative worth of jobs in an organisation'. This definition refers to 'jobs', and one of the dogmas of traditional job evaluation is that it is jobs that should be evaluated, not people. In other words, job evaluators simply decide where a job fits into a hierarchy: they are not concerned with the performance of people in those jobs.

This is a proper and necessary principle in a hierarchical, bureaucratic or mechanistic organisation, where people are slotted into jobs and a rigid approach to job design and work generally means that they have little or no scope to enlarge their roles. But this no longer necessarily applies in today's flexible, flatter and process-based organisations where, especially among knowledge workers, the ability to expand the role as well as to grow in the role is a crucial requirement. In these increasingly common circumstances, the old principle that people should be placed in jobs and be rewarded for non-adaptive behaviour no longer applies. Plachy (1987) comments that 'Jobs are created according to the strengths and limitations of the people who design and fill them'. The result is what has come to be known as people-based, as distinct from job-based, pay. As Hillage (1994) suggests:

> The product of a job is seen as a combination of the skills and attributes a person brings to it (ie supply) and the tasks demanded of them (ie demand)... With the increased interest in workplace behaviours and their impact on performance, evaluation may move even further from its roots in outputs, ie tasks, towards inputs, ie skills and attributes.

Lawler (1986) writes, in connection with this trend towards people-based pay, that 'If an organisation's key assets are its human resources, a system that focuses on people rather than on jobs is the better fit.' The concept of people-based pay suggests that the performance and attributes of individuals will be key factors in determining their rate of pay and how it progresses. Job evaluation may still be necessary in a supporting role to define the boundaries in a broadbanded structure, and to check on internal equity, but performance management, which is concerned with individual contribution, will inform pay decisions rather than job evaluation.

14 PERFORMANCE MANAGEMENT FOR TEAMS

One of the particularly interesting findings of our research was that, although everyone we contacted talked about organisational and individual performance, relatively few organisations made specific arrangements for team performance management (including Assidoman Packaging and Zeneca). This apparent lack of interest in performance management for teams is remarkable because of the attention given in most organisations to improving the quality of teamwork. Of course, there are organisations with team pay, such as those covered by the IPD research (Armstrong and Ryden 1996). These included Dartford Borough Council, Lloyds Bank, Norwich Union, Rank Xerox and Sun Life Assurance. Each of them clearly had to measure team performance as a basis for team pay decisions, so that there was a form of performance management. Their approaches to managing team performance will be described later in this chapter.

It seems to us that performance management for teams deserves more attention. Possible approaches should be reviewed against the background of an understanding of what constitutes team processes, the significance of teamwork, what makes an effective team, the competencies required for teamwork, and a definition of what can be regarded as a team for performance-management purposes. These aspects of teamwork are all discussed in the first section of the chapter. Further consideration in later sections is given to performance measures for teams, and team performance management processes.

Teamworking
The significance of teamwork
Teamwork is important in the new, de-layered and process-

based organisation, in which more work is being organised on a team or project basis. The teams set up under new arrangements can be described as high-performance teams which, as described by Katzenbach and Smith (1993), 'invest much time and effort explaining, shaping and agreeing on a purpose that belongs to them, both collectively and individually. They are characterised by a deep sense of commitment to their growth and success.'

Reservations

The significance of teamwork may seem to be incontrovertible but, when evolving team performance-management processes, it is as well to be aware of certain reservations. These concern the assumptions, first, that teamwork enables people to accomplish more together than they would alone and, second, that if successful, teams can be a source of satisfaction at work. However, research evidence analysed by West and Slater (1995) is:

> consistent in suggesting that the quality of group decision-making generally equals but does not exceed the quality of decision-making of the average member. The quality of the decision-making of the most able members is generally not matched. One of the explanations for this is the so-called 'social loafing' effect. This suggests that when people work in team settings they exert less effort than they would do individually. This claim may be arguable, but what cannot be disputed is that teams are composed of individuals and an over-emphasis on team performance factors may distract attention away from individual contributions and needs.

The IPD research into the lean organisation (Purcell *et al* 1998) produced some interesting findings on teamwork. The authors comment on the impact of teams as follows:

> Although there is clear evidence of an improvement in productivity, the improvements in participation are negligible; indeed, there is some evidence that teamworking reduces the quality of working life.

This, the researchers found, was partly attributable to the greater pressure to achieve tougher performance targets and the closer monitoring of both individual and group performance. As one manager said, work was now a combination of 'fun and surveillance'!

A further reservation may be made about peer pressure as a factor in teamwork. This could have desirable results – 'bringing the slackers up to scratch'. But it could be 'management by stress' applied by co-workers. Is this desirable?

Teams and performance

These reservations suggest that it is possible to focus too much on teamwork but, as Purcell *et al* (1998) point out, teams can provide the 'elusive bridge between the aims of the individual employee and the objectives of the organisation ... teams can provide the medium for linking employee performance targets to the factors critical to the success of the business'. This is an important aspect of performance management and provides further justification for paying more attention to its application to teams. How it is applied will be related to the following factors that affect team performance:

- □ the clarity of the team's goals in terms of expectations and priorities
- □ how work is allocated to the team
- □ how the team is working (its processes) in terms of cohesion, ability to handle internal conflict and pressure, relationships with other teams
- □ the extent to which the team is capable of managing itself – setting goals and priorities, monitoring performance
- □ the quality of leadership – even self-managed teams need a sense of direction which they cannot necessarily generate by themselves
- □ the level of skill possessed by individual team members (including multiskilling)
- □ the systems and resources available to support the team.

Overall, as suggested by Jones (1995), 'Teams need to have a shared purpose. They also need to have the necessary mix of skills and abilities and to be mutually accountable for the outcome.'

The performance of individual team members

Individual team members can influence team performance in three ways:

1   the actual job they are doing and the skills, competences and behaviour they apply to the work
2   the job they perform as team members
3   the team performance as a whole.

Although it is important to consider the performance management of teams as a whole (which is what the rest of this chapter is about), it is also important to consider the levels of performance and competence achieved by individual team members. Obviously, a prime criterion will be the contribution they make to the team in terms of both results and process.

Team competencies

The following is a selection of some of the key competencies for team members as developed by Hay/McBer (Gross 1995):

- *interpersonal understanding* – accurate interpretation of others' concerns, motives and feelings and recognition of their strengths and weaknesses
- *influence* – using appropriate interpersonal styles and logical arguments to convince others to accept ideas or pleas
- *customer-service orientation* – demonstrating concern for meeting the needs of internal and external customers
- *adaptability* – adapting easily to change
- *teamwork and co-operation* – developing collaborative work that generates acceptable solutions
- *oral communication* – expressing ideas in group situations
- *achievement orientation* – setting and meeting challenging objectives
- *organisational commitment* – performing work with broader organisational goals in mind.

Definition of a team

Before embarking on the development of team performance-management processes, it is necessary to define which teams will be involved. There are four basic types of team:

1 *organisational teams*, which consist of people broadly linked together, as in a top management team or departmental heads in an organisation – the team members may be associated with each other by the requirement to achieve an overall objective

2 *work teams*, which consist of self-contained and permanent members who work closely together and interdependently to achieve specified results

3 *project teams*, which consist of people brought together from different functions to complete a task over a period of months or even years

4 *ad hoc teams*, which consist of people brought together from within a department or from a number of functions to tackle an immediate problem.

Performance-management processes are most appropriate in tightly knit work and long-standing project teams. In a general sense, they can play a part in the management of performance in organisational teams. They will be inappropriate on a formal and continuing basis in an *ad hoc* team.

Performance measures for teams

Performance measures for teams will be related to the purpose of the team and its particular objectives and standards of performance. The following are some examples of how performance measures have been established and used by various organisations:

- □ *A service company finance division* – in the processing department, where high-volume and routine tasks have to be performed, the measures are productivity and quality.

- □ *A government agency* – measures are agreed between managers and team members based on task definition, performance standards and timescales.

- □ *A local authority* – measures are related to targets set for tasks suitable for all or most of the team to undertake together, and they are distinct from the tasks set for individual team members.

☐ *A technology company* – 'bid teams' (project teams responsible for developing solutions for customers) have their performance measured by reference to their success in winning contracts.

☐ *A clearing bank* – the performance of branch teams below junior management level is related to two challenges: the 'sales challenge', linked to branch sales against target, and the 'service challenge', based on data obtained from customer questionnaires and mystery shopping.

☐ *An insurance company* – performance measures for the financial planning consultant teams is based on 'net issued business', and criteria for activity levels, appointments attended, questionnaires completed and cases issued.

☐ *Financial services* – the performance measures for policy-processing and claims teams consist of 'hard' measures for speed and accuracy of processing and 'soft' measures for levels of service to internal and external customers.

☐ *A manufacturing company* – the performance measures or 'metrics' for sales teams are based on customer satisfaction, sales revenue and market share.

Types of measure

Team performance measures in this sample are therefore mainly concerned with output, activity levels (eg speed of servicing), customer service and satisfaction, and financial results. Most measures for teams, as for individuals (see Chapter 18), are likely to fall into one or more of these categories.

A distinction is made by Harrington-Mackin (1994) between output/result measures of team performance and input/process measures. The output/results comprise:

☐ the achievement of team goals
☐ customer satisfaction
☐ quantity of work
☐ quality of work
☐ process knowledge
☐ maintenance of technical systems.

The input/process measures comprise:

□ support of team process
□ participation
□ oral and written communication
□ collaboration and collective effort
□ conflict resolution
□ planning and goal-setting
□ participative decision-making
□ problem-solving and analytical skills
□ credibility and trust
□ interdependence
□ interpersonal relations
□ acceptance of change
□ adaptability and flexibility.

Project team measures

Project team measures may be more qualitative. They will refer to the project's goals, which may be staged over a number of intermediate milestones. The measure will primarily be the extent to which the goals, as defined in the terms of reference or brief to the project team, have been achieved, the time taken, the costs incurred, the effectiveness with which team members have worked together, the degree to which internal and external customers or clients are satisfied and, ultimately, the impact the project has made on organisational performance.

Team performance-management processes

Team performance-management activities follow the same sequence as for individual performance management:

□ Agree objectives.
□ Formulate plans to achieve objectives.
□ Implement plans.
□ Monitor progress.
□ Review and assess achievement.
□ Redefine objectives and plans in the light of the review.

The aim should be to give teams with their team leaders the maximum amount of responsibility to carry out all activities. The focus should be on self-management and self-direction.

The key activities of setting work and process objectives and conducting team reviews and individual reviews are described below.

Setting work objectives

Work objectives for teams are set in much the same way as individual objectives (see Chapter 16). They will be based on an analysis of the purpose of the team and its accountabilities for achieving results. Targets and standards of performance should be discussed and agreed by the team as a whole. These may specify what individual members are expected to contribute. Project teams will agree project plans that define what has to be done, who is to do it, the standards expected and the timescale.

Setting process objectives

Process objectives are also best defined by the team's getting together and agreeing how they should conduct themselves as a team under headings related to the list of team competencies and performance measures referred to earlier in this chapter, including:

☐ interpersonal relationships
☐ the quality of participation and collaborative effort and decision-making
☐ the team's relationships with internal and external customers
☐ the capacity of the team to plan and control its activities
☐ the ability of the team and its members to adapt to new demands and situations
☐ the flexibility with which the team operates
☐ the effectiveness with which individual skills are used
☐ the quality of communications within the team and between the team and other teams or individuals.

Team performance reviews

Team performance review meetings analyse and assess feedback and control information on their joint achievements against objectives and project plans. The agenda for such meetings might be as follows:

1 General feedback review:
   □ progress of the team as a whole
   □ problems encountered by the team that have caused difficulties or hampered progress
   □ helps and hindrances to the operation of the team.

2 Work reviews:
   □ how well the team has functioned
   □ review of the individual contribution made by each team member – ie peer review (see below)
   □ discussion of any new problems encountered by individual team members.

3 Group problem-solving:
   □ analysis of reasons for any shortfalls or other problems
   □ agreement of what needs to be done to solve them and prevent their re-occurrence.

4 Update objectives:
   □ review of new requirements, opportunities or threats
   □ amendment and updating of objectives and project plans.

Reviewing the performance of individual team members

Processes for managing team performance should not neglect the needs of team members. As Mohrman and Mohrman (1995) point out: 'Performance among individuals, teams and organisations need to fit, but individual needs must be met at the same time.' They ask how individual needs can be met while still encouraging the sharing required at the group level. Their answer is dual. First, teams have to be managed in a way that enables individuals to feel they can influence group performance. They must provide opportunities for involvement and for team self-management. Second, the team must be managed so that the individual's need for recognition of excellent performance is met.

Individuals should receive feedback on their contribution to the team and also recognition by their team leader and fellow team members of their accomplishments. Special attention should be given to their personal development, not only as members of their existing team, but also for any future roles they may assume in other teams as individual contributors or team leaders.

Individuals should agree their objectives as team members with their team leader, but these can also be discussed at team meetings. Personal objectives and personal development plans can also be formulated for agreement with the team leader. Performance and development reviews between team leaders and individuals can concentrate on the latter's contribution to the team, the level of performance in terms of team-work competencies, and progress in implementing personal development plans.

Peer-review processes can also be used, in which team members assess each other under such headings as:

☐ overall contribution to team performance
☐ contribution to planning, monitoring and team-review activities
☐ maintaining relationships with other team members and internal or external customers
☐ communicating
☐ working flexibly (taking on different roles in the team as necessary)
☐ co-operation with other team members.

Peer reviews can form part of a 360-degree feedback process, as described in Chapter 18, in which the requirements for its successful application are discussed.

PART IV

PERFORMANCE-MANAGEMENT PROCESSES

15 MEASURING PERFORMANCE

Why measure?

There are two well-known sayings about measurement and performance:

☐ What gets measured gets done.
☐ If you can't measure it, you can't manage it.

To improve performance, you have to know what current performance is. As Daniels (1987) comments: 'Anything can be measured and if it can be measured it can be improved.' Agreeing and reviewing objectives is an important aspect of performance management, but there is no point to this process unless all concerned are clear about the performance measures that can be used. It is equally pointless to encourage people to monitor and manage their own performance unless they can measure progress towards their goals.

Oakland (1993) suggests that appropriate performance measurement:

☐ ensures customer requirements have been met
☐ provides standards for establishing comparisons
☐ provides visibility and provides a 'scoreboard' for people to monitor their own performance levels
☐ highlights quality problems and determines which areas require priority attention
☐ gives an indication of the costs of poor quality
☐ justifies the use of resources
☐ provides feedback for driving the improvement effort.

Measurement is an important concept in performance management. It is the basis for providing and generating feedback, it identifies where things are going well to provide the foundations for building further success, and it indicates where things are not going so well, so that corrective action can be taken. In general, it provides the basis for answering two fundamental questions: 'Is what is being done worth doing?' and 'Has it been done well?'

Principles of measurement

Three principles governing the development of performance measures as a means of increasing organisational effectiveness have been advanced by Thor (1994):

1   What to measure is ultimately determined by what the customer considers important.
2   The customers' needs are translated into strategic priorities and a strategic plan indicating what should be measured.
3   Supplying improvement teams with measured results of key strategic priorities contributes to further improvement by providing both team motivation and information on what works and does not work.

Measurement issues

It can be argued that what gets measured is often what is easy to measure. And, in some jobs, what is meaningful is not measurable, and what is measurable is not meaningful. Levinson (1970) asserted that 'The greater the emphasis on measurement and quantification, the more likely the subtle, non-measurable elements of the task will be sacrificed. Quality of performance frequently, therefore, loses out to quantification.' Indeed, there are components in all jobs that are difficult to measure. But all jobs produce results, and these results can be measured.

Boyett and Conn (1995) refer to some of the 'myths of measurement':

☐   'You can't measure creativity or judgement', but you can measure the impact of creativity or judgement.
☐   'Measures fail because they cannot consider things beyond control', but measures only indicate changes in performance levels – they cannot explain changes.

❑ 'Measurement is only possible when results are quantifiable; they cannot be applied when there is nothing to count', but whenever people are expected to do something you can assess the extent to which they do it.

What should be measured

The statement that 'measurement is only concerned with measuring what is important and relevant' is not as obvious as it sounds. It is necessary to be clear about what is important and relevant before defining what measures should be used.

What to measure ultimately depends on what stakeholders and customers believe to be important. In the 'what gets measured gets done' sense, measurements provide the link between customer-oriented strategies and goals and actions. Just as team and individual goals flow from business goals, so do team and individual performance measures flow from the business measures. They provide the basis for reviewing performance at those levels and indicate any actions required. Strategic plans therefore indicate what specifically to measure, and performance measures throughout the organisation should reflect business objectives, plans and policies.

As Hope (1998) points out, businesses should be value-driven, not cost-driven: 'Value-based management is a philosophy of improvement while cost-based management is a philosophy of control.' According to Hope, it is important to understand what creates value in an organisation and then to develop measures aligned to the business strategy. He stresses that 'Every business has a unique value proposition that defines what value it uniquely delivers to its customers', and that 'People cannot focus on value-added work if value-added has not been defined.' He also lists the following measurement problems:

❑ There may be too many measures.
❑ Measures do not relate to strategy.
❑ Measures are results-biased and do not tell managers how the results were achieved – how they got there.
❑ Reward systems are not aligned to performance measures.

□ Measures do not support team-based management structure.

Output and input measures

Measures can be based on outputs in the general sense of the
delivery of service and quality to internal and external customers, and in the particular senses of volume, throughput,
sales etc.

Measures can also be based on inputs – what people bring
to their roles in the shape of knowledge, skills and competencies. A mixed performance management model concerned
with both inputs and outputs will have to be supported by
both input and output measures.

Input measures identify levels of contribution by reference
to observable behaviour. The headings for the measures are
provided by competency frameworks that define organisational core competencies, generic role competencies and role
specific competencies.

Criteria for performance measures

Performance measures should:

□ be related to the strategic goals and measures that are
organisationally significant and drive business performance

□ be relevant to the objectives and accountabilities of the
teams and individuals concerned – they are effective only
if they are derived from statements of accountabilities or
are based on well-researched competence frameworks, or
both

□ focus on measurable outputs and accomplishments and, as
Bailey (1983) puts it, 'ranges of behaviour which can be
precisely and clearly defined' (behaviour is how people act
and how they conduct themselves, which is observable as
it occurs)

□ indicate the data or evidence that will be available as the
basis for measurement

□ be verifiable – provide information that will confirm the
extent to which expectations have been met

□ be as precise as possible in accordance with the purpose of the measurement and the availability of data

□ provide a sound basis for feedback and action

□ be comprehensive, covering all the key aspects of performance so that a family of measures is available, bearing in mind, as stated by Walters (1995), that 'Effective performance is measured not merely by the delivery of results (however outstanding) in one area, but by delivering satisfactory performance across all the measures.'

Although it is important to identify a basket of measures, it might still be appropriate to give some indication of their relative significance.

Classification of measures

There are various types of measures, selected on the basis of the criteria listed above, the most important being that they are relevant, significant and comprehensive. Sun Life, for example, uses the three criteria of work quality, output and timeliness (eg number of cases dealt with over a period of time). It has been suggested by Kane (1996) that the key measures are concerned with quantity, quality and cost effectiveness.

Measures or metrics can be classified under the following headings:

□ *finance* – income, shareholder value, added value, rates of return, costs

□ *output* – units produced or processed, throughput, new accounts

□ *impact* – attainment of a standard (quality, level of service etc), changes in behaviour (internal and external customers), completion of work/project, level of take-up of a service, innovation

□ *reaction* – judgement by others, colleagues, internal and external customers

□ *time* – speed of response or turnaround, achievements compared with timetables, amount of backlog, time to market, delivery times.

The Audit Commission (1987) has recommended that the following indicators be used in local government:

☐ *productivity indicators* that focus on the amount of work completed within a defined length of time

☐ *utilisation rates* that refer to the extent to which available services are used – for example, occupancy rates of school places

☐ *time targets* that refer to the average time taken to carry out defined units of work – for example, the time to process appeals

☐ *volume of service* – for example, the number of housing repairs completed

☐ *demand/service provision*, which refers to such indicators as the number of nursery school places compared with the relevant child population.

Expressing measures

Measures can be expressed in four different ways, as defined by Boyett and Conn (1995):

1   *counts* – the number of times an accomplishment takes place

2   *ratios* – the number of times an accomplishment takes place divided by the number of times it could have taken place

3   *percentages* – the proportion of actual achievement to total available achievement

4   *financial impact* – of achieving or failing to achieve a result.

Focus of performance measures

The focus of performance measures is concerned with the achievement of objectives, levels of competency, standards of performance and work outputs. The emphasis varies for different levels and categories of employees, as illustrated in Figure 16.

Figure 16
FOCUS OF PERFORMANCE MEASURES

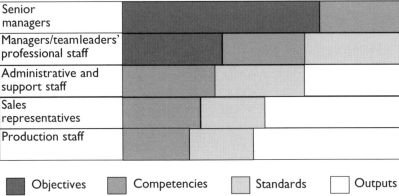

Types of measure: organisational

Jack Welch, CEO of the General Electric Company, believes that the three most important things you need to measure in a business are customer satisfaction, employee satisfaction and cash flow. More specifically, the different approaches to measuring organisational performance are:

☐ a balanced scorecard
☐ the European Foundation for Quality Management (EFQM) model
☐ economic value added
☐ other traditional financial measures.

The balanced scorecard

The concept of the balanced scorecard as originally developed by Kaplan and Norton (1992) addresses this requirement. They take the view that 'what you measure is what you get', and emphasise that 'no single measure can provide a clear performance target or focus attention on the critical areas of the business. Managers want a balanced presentation of both financial and operational measures.'

Kaplan and Norton therefore devised what they call the 'balanced scorecard': a set of measures that gives top managers a fast but comprehensive view of the business. Their scorecard requires managers to answer four basic questions, which means looking at the business from four related perspectives:

☐ How do customers see us (customer perspective)?

☐ What must we excel at (internal perspective)?

☐ Can we continue to improve and create value (innovation and learning perspective)?

☐ How do we look at shareholders (financial perspective)?

Kaplan and Norton emphasise that the balanced scorecard approach 'puts strategy and vision, not control at the centre'. They suggest that although it defines goals, it assumes that people will adopt whatever behaviours and take whatever actions are required to achieve those goals: 'Senior managers may know what the end result should be, but they cannot tell employees exactly how to achieve that result, if only because the conditions in which employees operate are constantly changing.' They claim that this approach to performance management is consistent with new initiatives under way in many companies in such areas as cross-functional integration, continuous improvement, and team rather than individual accountability.

Exponents of the balanced scorecard approach as described by van de Vliet (1997) see it as a way of implementing strategy, linking strategy to action and making strategy understandable to those on the front line as well as to senior managers. David Norton, as quoted by van de Vliet, believes that, although the balanced scorecard is a measuring system, like any such system it cannot live in isolation. Inevitably it becomes tied into budgets, goal-setting programmes, incentives and compensation. He uses the example of Kenyon Stores, a fashion retailer, whose financial objectives were profitable growth, increased penetration and improved productivity, to be measured by operating income growth, sales per store, and expenses as a percentage of sales. Customer objectives of right product, image and ideal shopping experience were measured by average annual purchase growth, premium on branded items, and customer surveys. The internal processes included brand dominance, sourcing and distribution, and shopping experience, measured by market share, out-of-stock incidence, and sales per square foot; and the learning objectives of developing strategic skills, providing strategic information and aligning personal goals with the scorecard were measured accordingly.

Kaplan and Norton (1996a) emphasise that building a scorecard enables a company to link its financial budgets with its strategic goals. They emphasise that the balanced scorecard can help to align employees' individual performance with the overall strategy: 'Scorecard users generally engage in three activities: communicating and educating, setting goals and linking rewards to performance measures.' They quote the exploration group of a large oil company (Shell) that has developed a technique to enable and encourage individuals to set goals for themselves that are consistent with the organisation's. These 'personal scorecards' contain three levels of information: (1) corporate objectives, measures and targets, (2) business unit targets (translated from corporate targets), and (3) team/individual objectives and initiatives. Teams and individuals are expected to define how their objectives are consistent with business-unit and corporate objectives, to indicate what initiatives they propose to take to achieve their objectives, to list up to five performance measures for each objective, and to set targets for each measure.

This personal scorecard is a method of communicating corporate and unit objectives to the people and teams performing the whole. It 'communicates a holistic model that links individual efforts and accomplishments to business unit objectives' (Kaplan and Norton, 1996b). It can therefore be incorporated as a performance-management process at individual, team, unit and corporate levels. To summarise, Kaplan and Norton (1996a) comment that:

> Many people think of measurement as a tool to control behaviour and to evaluate past performance. The measures on a Balanced Scorecard, however, should be used as the cornerstone of a management system that communicates strategy, aligns individuals and teams to the strategy, establishes long-term strategic targets, aligns initiatives, allocates long- and short-term resources and, finally, provides feedback and learning about the strategy.

The NatWest Bank was one of the first large organisations in the UK to adopt the balanced scorecard, using the following headings:

☐ business success
☐ customer service
☐ quality and people
☐ business efficiency.

Wheatley (1996) quotes the head of performance management in the retail banking services arm of NatWest as saying, 'It made us ask ourselves: "What are the 12 or 15 things that really drive our business?" The range of 12 to 15 is critical. Not enough measures and you lose perspective; too many measures and you drown in data.'

The European Foundation for Quality Management (EFQM)

The EFQM model as shown in Figure 17 indicates that customer satisfaction, people (employee) satisfaction and impact on society are achieved through leadership. This drives the policy and strategy, people management, resources and processes leading to excellence in business results.

Figure 17
THE EFQM MODEL

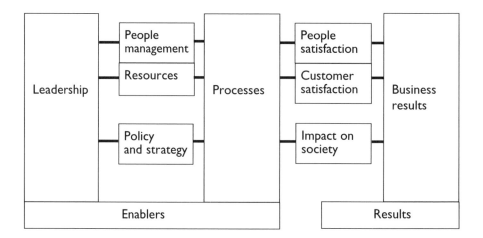

The nine elements in the model are defined as follows:

☐ *Leadership* – how the behaviour and actions of the executive team and all other leaders inspire, support and promote a culture of total quality management.

☐ *Policy and strategy* – how the organisation formulates, deploys and reviews its policy and strategy and turns it into plans and actions.

☐ *People management* – how the organisation realises the full potential of its people.

☐ *Resources* – how the organisation manages resources effectively and efficiently.

☐ *Processes* – how the organisation identifies, manages, reviews and improves its processes.

☐ *Customer satisfaction* – what the organisation is achieving in relation to the satisfaction of its external customers.

☐ *People satisfaction* – what the organisation is achieving in relation to the satisfaction of its people.

☐ *Impact on society* – what the organisation is achieving in satisfying the needs and the expectations of the local, national and international community.

☐ *Business results* – what the organisation is achieving in relation to its planned business objectives and in satisfying the needs and expectations of everyone with a financial interest or stake in the organisation.

As Thomas (1995) comments:

> Organisations who adopt the EFQM model, such as ICL, The Post Office and KLM Dutch Royal Airlines, accept the importance of performance measurement and work all the time to improve the usefulness of their measures, but they also recognise that simply measuring a problem does not improve it. Managers can often devolve their best energies to the analysis, leaving little left for the remedy. The key, they say, is to focus on the enablers and the processes.

He suggests that the EFQM model can help performance management by:

☐ developing a fuller understanding of how business results are achieved and processes continually improved

- ☐ offering mechanisms for tackling systems problems in the workplace
- ☐ promoting performance management as a two-way dialogue
- ☐ providing a positive and universal framework for the description of jobs and roles
- ☐ helping to align individual and business objectives
- ☐ pointing the way to identifying, defining and building the competencies that the organisation needs its people to demonstrate.

Economic value added (EVA)

The EVA measure represents the difference between a company's post-tax operating profit and the cost of the capital invested in the business. The cost of capital includes the cost of equity – what shareholders expect to receive through capital gains. The theory of EVA is that it is not good enough for a company simply to make a profit. It has to justify the cost of its capital, equity included. If it is not covering that, it will not make good returns for investors. Most conventional measures of company performance, such as earnings per share, ignore the cost of capital in a business.

Other economic measures of value

There is much discussion about how best to measure company performance in terms of the value created for its shareholders. This is not simply a debate about metrics theory; how companies measure value strongly influences how they are run and therefore affects all their performance-management processes.

EVA is the current favourite, but other measures include:

- ☐ *added value* – the difference between the market value of a company's output and the costs of its inputs
- ☐ *market value added* – the difference between a company's market capitalisation and the total capital investment; if this is positive, it will indicate the stock market wealth created
- ☐ *cash-flow return on investment (CFROI)* – compares

inflation-adjusted cash flows to inflation-adjusted gross revenues to find cash-flow return on investment

□ *total shareholder return* – what the shareholder actually gets ie changes in capital value plus dividends.

These measures all focus on the creation of shareholder value. They are not concerned with other aspects of corporate performance and take no account of other stakeholders.

Traditional financial ratios

The traditional financial measures include:

□ return on equity
□ return on capital employed
□ earnings per share
□ price/earnings ratio
□ return on sales
□ asset turnover
□ overall overheads/sales ratio
□ profit or sales or added value per employer
□ output per employee (productivity).

Types of measure: team

Team performance measures as described in Chapter 14 can relate to team outputs, team processes, customer relations, quality standards, speed of response or delivery time, project management, financial results and cost control.

As Zigon (1994) proposes, the following steps can be taken to develop team measures:

□ Review and revise organisational and business-unit measures.
□ Review and revise business operating systems measures.
□ Identify team measurement points – process steps (milestones) and final output/outcome.
□ Identify individual accomplishments that support the team's processes by listing the key process steps taken by the team and the accomplishments needed to support each process.

□ Develop team and individual performance measures (quantity, quality, timeliness, cost).

□ Develop team and individual performance objectives.

Types of measure: individual

Team and individual measures are related to key accountabilities and set out under the main criteria headings of quantity, quality, productivity, timeliness and cost-effectiveness. For example, the performance measures for a plant manager might be:

□ *quantity* – unit output, percentage of actual to targeted output

□ *quality* – quality control returns in variances outside limits, number of justifiable complaints

□ *productivity* – output per employee

□ *timeliness* – achievement of delivery deadlines, percentage of units completed on time, backlogs

□ *cost control* – cost per unit of production, direct/indirect labour cost variance.

Defining performance measures

Performance measures should be agreed at the same time as objectives are defined. This provides for the fair assessment of progress and achievements and for individuals and teams. It will provide the best basis for feedback. The following are guidelines for defining performance measures:

□ Measures should relate to results and observable behaviours.

□ The results should be within the control of the team or individual, and be based on agreed targets.

□ Behavioural requirements (competencies) should be defined and agreed.

□ Data must be available for measurement.

□ Measures should be objective.

Obtaining and analysing information for measurement purposes

Information for measurement purposes is obtained from performance data, competence (behaviour) analysis and benchmarking.

Performance data

Performance data is obtained from relevant management information systems, which enable comparisons to be made between what has been achieved and what should have been achieved. They assist in the evaluation of alternative courses of action so that objectives and standards can be set. Performance data is also made available by the direct, often electronic, measurement of activities, quality and output.

Competency levels

Competency levels can be measured only by analysing actual and observable behaviour so that comparisons can be made. If differentiating competencies have been defined (ie the factors that distinguish superior from average performers), scales can be developed. For example, the headings on the scale developed by Spencer and Spencer (1993) for team leadership sets out behavioural descriptions under the following headings:

Abdicates
AO Not applicable
A1 Manages meetings
A2 Informs people
A3 Uses authority fairly
A4 Promotes team effectiveness
A5 Takes care of the group
A6 Positions self as leader
A7 Communicates a compelling vision.

An alternative approach adopted by the New Forest District Council is to produce range statements for each competence heading, as shown in Appendix C. Behaviourally anchored rating scales (BARS) can be used for the same purpose.

In each of these examples a competency rating on the scale

can be made. But this must be based on observable behaviour or evidence agreed by the manager and the individual. It is not essential to rate competence in numerical terms, and it can be argued that a mechanistic rating system is inappropriate when analysing behaviour. At Glaxo Wellcome, the competence base consists of 20 core competencies plus specialist competencies. Competence is not rated numerically, but instead behavioural indicators are used (effective, less effective and very effective), and competency dimensions have been defined that describe the level at which the competency should be performed. But these dimensions refer to the demands of the role rather than the individual's effectiveness. For example, the dimensions for the competency 'establishing a plan' are these:

☐ At the lowest level, you might only be planning your own daily or weekly work; the impact is therefore just on yourself.

☐ At the next level, you may be involved in team plans; your impact therefore is on the whole team plan.

☐ At the next level, you may be involved in planning for a department.

☐ At the next level, you may be involved in company-wide plans that would affect everyone.

These are not, of course, measures, but this sort of approach can provide a framework for deciding what information or evidence is required to establish the degree to which people are performing effectively at each level.

Benchmarking

Benchmarking involves measuring the performance of the organisation, teams or individuals against the best practice for the industry, function or particular activity. Benchmarking for organisations means analysing the performance of comparable businesses under appropriate headings eg productivity, and when the performance of the business is inferior, assessing why this is the case. Benchmarking at this level will look at best practice elsewhere in areas affecting the performance of the organisation as a whole – for example, quality control, manufacturing systems, customer service, employee satisfaction, absenteeism.

At team and individual level, benchmarking involves the systematic collection and analysis of data from other comparable organisations. This data will refer to specific activities or areas of performance such as standards of service delivery, processing times, speed of response and throughput. One of the aims of this type of benchmarking is to establish performance standards and targets based on what can be realistically achieved elsewhere. Naturally, in making such comparisons allowance has to be made for differences in the types of activity, the technology available and resources deployed elsewhere, so that conclusions of what can be achieved within the organisation are not based on invalid evidence.

Benchmarking can also take place within organisations to compare, say, service delivery standards in different divisions or units.

Performance indicators

The terms 'performance measures' and 'performance indicators' are sometimes used interchangeably. Some organisations, however, distinguish between the two by treating performance measures as dealing with results that can be quantified and providing data after the event. Performance indicators are taken to refer to activities that can only be judged more qualitatively on the basis of observable behaviour. Performance indicators may also suggest a prospective rather than retrospective viewpoint, in that they point the way to aspects of performance that will need to be observed.

16 AGREEING OBJECTIVES AND PERFORMANCE STANDARDS

Performance management is concerned with agreeing expectations, making and implementing plans to meet them, and monitoring and reviewing outcomes. This can be described as the process of managing expectations, which is a joint affair, shared between managers, teams and individuals: in other words, management by agreement. Expectations are defined and agreed in the form of objectives, standards of performance and competencies (the latter are discussed in Chapter 17). In this chapter we consider the agreement of objectives and standards, which should be distinguished from one another. Objectives are finite and related to a team or individual. Standards tend to be on-going and longer-term, and are related to the function of the team or the position: they need to be achieved irrespective of the membership of the team or the holder of the position. This distinction is elaborated below.

Objectives

Defined

Objectives describe something to be accomplished – a point to be aimed at. Objectives or goals (the terms are interchangeable) define what organisations, functions, departments and individuals are expected to achieve over a period of time.

Significance

As Williams (1991) has written:

> The setting of objectives is the management process which ensures that every individual employee knows what role they need to play and what results they need to achieve to maximise their contribution to the overall business. In essence, it

enables employees to know what is required of them and on what basis their performance and contribution will be assessed.

The nature of objectives – targets and tasks

Objectives are expressed as:

- *targets* – quantifiable results to be attained that can be measured in such terms as return on capital employed, output, throughput, sales, levels of service delivery, cost reduction, reduction of reject rates
- *tasks/projects* – to be completed by specified dates to achieve defined results.

The nature of objectives – work and personal objectives

Objectives can be:

- *work-related*, referring to the results to be attained or the contribution to be made towards the achievement of organisational, functional or team goals
- *personal*, taking the form of developmental or learning objectives, which are concerned with what individuals should do to develop knowledge, skills and potential and to improve their performance in specified areas – for example, building competencies.

The nature of objectives – levels and integration of work objectives

Work objectives can be defined at:

- *corporate level*, where they are related to the organisation's purpose, values and strategic plans
- *senior management level*, where they define the contribution the senior management team is expected to make to achieving corporate goals
- *business-unit, functional or departmental level*, where they are related to corporate objectives, spelling out the specific targets and projects to be accomplished by the unit, function or department
- *team level*, where they are related to the purpose and accountabilities of the team, and the contribution it is

expected to make to attain unit/departmental and corporate goals

□ *individual level*, where they are related to the principal accountabilities, key-result areas, or main tasks that constitute individuals' jobs and focus on the results they are expected to achieve and their contribution to team, departmental and organisational performance.

The integration of objectives is important in order to achieve a shared understanding of performance requirements throughout the organisation, thus providing opportunities for everyone to make an appropriate contribution to the attainment of team, departmental and corporate goals and to upholding core values.

Integration is achieved by ensuring that everyone is aware of corporate and functional goals, and that the objectives they

Figure 18
INTEGRATION OF GOALS

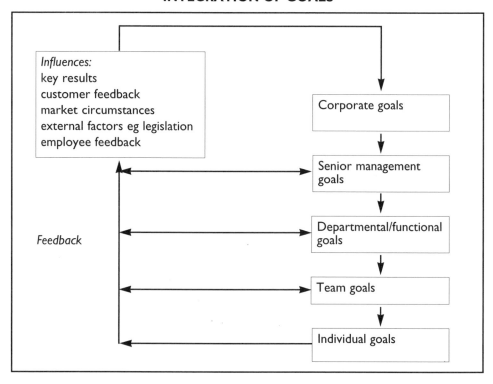

Figure 19
TWO-WAY PROCESS OF AGREEING OBJECTIVES

Level	**Objective**
Corporate	Improve levels of customer service
Functional	Specify aspects of customer service for which function is responsible (eg quality, speed of response, after-sales) and overall functional service improvement targets
Team	Specify team targets within the functional areas of customer service and the improvement targets for the function
Individual	Specify individual targets for contributing to the achievement of team targets

agree for themselves are consistent with those goals and contribute in specified ways to their achievement. This process is illustrated in Figure 18.

An example of how objectives can be integrated in a specific area is given in Figure 19.

The integration process is not just about cascading objectives downwards. As Figures 18 and 19 illustrate, there is also an upward flow that provides for participation in goal-setting and the opportunity for individuals to contribute to the formulation of their own objectives and to the objectives of their teams, functions and, ultimately, the organisation.

Characteristics of good objectives

Objectives are intended to bring about change. They should cover all the key aspects of the job and not focus on one area at the expense of the others. Good objectives are:

☐ *consistent*: with the values of the organisation and with departmental and corporate objectives

☐ *precise*: clear and well-defined, using positive words

☐ *challenging*: to stimulate high standards of performance and to encourage progress

☐ *measurable*: they can be related to quantified or qualitative performance measures

☐ *achievable*: within the capabilities of the individual – account should be taken of any constraints affecting the individual's capacity to achieve the objectives; these may include lack of resources (money, time, equipment, support from other people), lack of experience or training, or external factors beyond the individual's control

☐ *agreed*: by the manager and the individual concerned – the aim is to provide for the ownership, not the imposition, of objectives, although there may be situations where individuals have to be persuaded to accept a higher standard than they believe themselves to be capable of attaining

☐ *time-related*: achievable within a defined timescale

☐ *teamwork-oriented*: emphasise teamwork as well as individual achievement.

Many organisations such as the Victoria and Albert Museum use the SMART check-list as set out below to provide guidance on setting objectives. This states that objectives should be:

S = *Specific*   – clear, unambiguous, straightforward and understandable

M = *Measurable* – quantity, quality, time, money

A = *Agreed* – between individuals and their managers or team leaders

R = *Realistic* – within the control and capability of the individual

T = *Timebound* – to be completed within an agreed timescale.

Some SMART check-lists refer to 'stretching' rather than 'specific' objectives.

Performance measures

Performance measures need to be agreed when setting objectives. It is necessary to define not only what is to be achieved but how those concerned will know that it has been achieved. Performance measures should identity the verifiable evidence on the extent to which the expected result has been achieved and the degree to which the individual or team has contributed to that result. They are discussed in Chapter 18.

Defining and agreeing objectives

Information on objectives can be obtained by asking these questions:

☐ What do you think are the most important things you do?

☐ What do you believe you are expected to achieve in each of these areas?

☐ How will you – or anyone else – know whether or not you have achieved them?

The following steps are required to define and agree objectives:

1 *Define the overall purpose of the job* – what it exists for.

2 *Define performance areas.* These can be expressed in the form of principal accountabilities, key results or main tasks. Together, they spell out all the aspects of the job that contribute to achieving its overall purpose. The number of accountabilities or key-result areas is normally limited to seven or eight. Each definition starts with an active verb and expresses clearly and succinctly *what* has to be done and *why* it has to be done. The definition should point clearly to the performance measures used to

monitor and review progress in attaining objectives.

3 *Define targets/tasks.* These are related to each performance area. Targets should be quantified wherever possible
in such terms as these:

□ Increase sales turnover for the year by 8 per cent in
real terms.

□ Reduce the overhead-to-sales ratio from 22.6 per cent
to 20 per cent over the next 12 months.

□ Increase the ratio of successful conversions (enquiries
to sales) from 40 per cent to 50 per cent.

□ Reduce cost per unit of output by 3 per cent by the end
of the year.

□ Reduce wastage rate to 5 per cent of stock by value.

□ Achieve a 5 per cent improvement in customer ratings
by the end of the year.

□ Reduce the error rate to 1:1,000 by 1 June.

□ Increase market share by 12 per cent within the next
two years.

Short-term projects should be defined in terms of what has to
be done, to what standard and by when. Where it is not possible to determine quantitative targets or specific short-term
tasks, performance standards – which may be quantitative or
qualitative – should be agreed (see below).

Performance standards

A performance standard can be defined as a statement of the
conditions that exist when a job is being performed effectively. Performance standards are used when it is not possible
to set time-based targets. Standards are sometimes described
as standing or continuing objectives, because, as explained
earlier in this chapter, their essential nature may not change
significantly from one review period to the next if the key
task remains unaltered, although they may be modified if
new circumstances arise.

Performance standards should have been broadly defined in
outcome terms in the 'why' part of the accountability/task
definition. But the broad definition should be expanded and,

as far as possible, particularised. They should preferably be quantified in terms, for example, of level of service or speed of response. Where the standard cannot be quantified, a more qualitative approach may have to be adopted, in which case the standard of performance definition would in effect state 'This job or task will have been well done if ... (the following things happen).' Junior or more routine jobs are likely to have a higher proportion of standing objectives to which performance standards are attached than senior and more flexible or output-oriented jobs.

The following are some examples of performance standards that spell out the results required in quantitative terms:

☐ Prepare and distribute management accounts to managers within three working days of the end of the accounting period.

☐ Deal with 90 per cent of customer complaints within 24 hours – the remaining to be acknowledged the same day and answered within five working days.

☐ Hear job evaluation appeals within five working days.

☐ Maintain a level of customer satisfaction in which complaints do not exceed 1:1,000 transactions.

☐ Acknowledge all customer orders within 24 working hours of receipt.

In each of these examples, the figures expressing standards of performance may be changed occasionally, but the underlying objectives (levels of service, customer satisfaction, bad debt control, delivery to time, swift turnaround of customer orders) are standing features of the job.

It may not always be possible to quantify performance standards as in the examples given above. The results required may have to be defined in qualitative terms. But the fact that it is difficult or impossible to set quantifiable objectives for some jobs or segments of jobs does not mean that some form of measurement cannot take place. What *can* be done is to compare the results achieved in factual behavioural terms with the results expected, defined as standards of performance and also expressed in factual or behavioural terms.

It is often assumed that qualitative performance standards

are difficult to define. But all managers make judgements about the standards of performance they expect and obtain from their staff, and most people have some idea of whether or not they are doing a good job. The problem is that these views are often subjective and are seldom articulated. Even if, as often happens, the final definition of a performance standard is somewhat bland and unspecific, the discipline of working through the requirements in itself will lead to greater mutual understanding of performance expectations.

A performance standard definition should take the form of a statement that performance will be up to standard if a desirable, specified and observable result happens. This result could be defined in terms of:

□ achievement of already defined operational norms in such areas as administrative procedures, good employment practices, customer or client satisfaction and public image
□ meeting already defined service-delivery standards
□ proportion of take-up of a service or facility
□ change in the behaviour of employees, customers, clients or other people of importance to the organisation
□ the reaction or opinions of clients, customers (internal and external) and outside bodies to the service provided
□ the degree to which behaviour and performance support core values in such areas as quality, care for people and teamworking
□ speed of activity or response to requests
□ ability to meet deadlines for 'deliverables'
□ existence of a backlog
□ meeting defined standards of accuracy.

The following are some examples of qualitative performance standards:

□ Performance will be up to standard if line managers receive guidance on the interpretation and implementation of inventory policies that is acted upon and makes a significant contribution to the achievement of inventory targets.
□ Performance will be up to standard when callers are dealt

with courteously at all times, even when they are being difficult.

☐ Performance will be up to standard if proposals for new product development are fully supported by data provided from properly conducted product research, market research and product-testing programmes, and are justified by meeting return-on-investment criteria policies.

☐ Performance will be up to standard if the company's business plans are analysed and used to provide the basis for the realistic anticipation of future HR requirements.

☐ Performance will be up to standard if co-operative and productive relationships are maintained with fellow team members.

☐ Performance will be up to standard if there is evidence of a sustained drive to improve quality standards.

☐ Performance will be up to standard if it can be demonstrated that policies and programmes for continuous improvement have been implemented effectively and followed through for members of the department.

17 COMPETENCE AND COMPETENCY ANALYSIS

The performance-planning or performance-agreement aspects of performance management, as described in Chapter 4, may include a discussion on expectations regarding the levels of competence required to achieve or exceed performance standards. This ensures that the agreement covers both *what* should be done (objectives and standards) and *how* it should be done (competence requirements). The continuing performance-management and review aspects of the process refer to these definitions of competence requirements as the basis for assessing the levels achieved under each heading. This indicates any coaching, guidance or support that the individual may need. But as Fletcher and Williams (1992) have pointed out, such agreements and assessments will lack either validity or reliability if the definitions of competence requirements have not been based on empirical research to determine which core competencies are associated with effective performance. It is not enough simply to take down a list of competencies from the shelf. They must fit the culture, context and performance requirements of the organisation, and they must be expressed in language meaningful to those who use them. In this chapter we describe methods of analysing and assessing competencies, but we start with a discussion of what the term means.

Competence and competency defined

The gurus in this field feel very strongly that it is necessary to distinguish between *competence* (hence competenc*es*) and *competency* (hence competenc*ies*). Disaster, they claim, will overtake anyone who confuses the two terms. Whether this is true or not, the received view of the distinction between them should be understood.

Competence defined

Competences describe what people need to be able to do to perform a job well. They are about stripping jobs down into their component parts and linking together the two basic elements of performance – what has to be done, and to what standard. In National Vocational Qualification (NVQ) language, an element of competence is a description of something that people carrying out particular types of work should be capable of doing. The NVQ system assesses people as competent or not yet competent. The accent is on what people *should be able to do* rather than on how they should behave in doing it.

Competences are concerned with effect rather than effort and with output rather than input. Some people adopt what may be called the 'output' model of competence, based on the proposition that the concept of competence is meaningful only when it can be demonstrated that competences have been applied effectively. It is therefore a matter not of *having* competences but of *using* them to good effect.

Competences can be defined at three levels:

1 *core competences* – these apply to the organisation as a whole. They refer to what the organisation has to be good at doing if it is to succeed. This could include such factors as customer orientation, producing high-quality goods or delivering high-quality services, innovation, adding value through the effective use of resources and managing costs (driving unnecessary cost out of the business). Core competences can be linked to the 'balanced scorecard' of measuring organisational success as developed by Kaplan and Norton (1992), discussed in Chapter 15.

2 *generic competences* – these are shared by a group of similar jobs – financial accountants, systems analysts, team leaders etc. They cover the aspects of the work that they have in common, and define the shared capabilities required to deliver the results they are expected to achieve.

3 *role-specific competences* – these are unique to a particular role. They define the special tasks that they have to be able to do, in addition to any generic competences they

may share with other people carrying out broadly similar roles.

Competence is analysed by a process called functional analysis, described later in this chapter.

Competency defined

Competency is sometimes defined as referring to the dimensions of behaviour that lie behind competent performance. These are often called behavioural competencies, because they are intended to describe how people behave when they carry out their role well.

When defined as competencies these behaviours can be classified in such areas as the following, used by Manchester Airport for senior managers:

☐ *understanding what needs to be done* – critical reasoning, strategic capability, business know-how

☐ *getting the job done* – achievement drive, a proactive approach, confidence, control, flexibility, concern for effectiveness, persuasion, influence

☐ *taking people with you* – motivation, interpersonal skills, concern for output, persuasion, influence.

Many organisations have now developed their own lists of 'generic competencies' describing the behaviour they believe to be important.

These are sometimes called competency frameworks or models when they cover all the key jobs in an organisation. They may refer to all the jobs in a 'job family' – ie a related set of jobs with similar skills or competencies but applied at different levels and often in a hierarchy (such as retail assistants, departmental managers and the store managers in a retailing company). The use of 'generic' for competencies is another example of the confusion that permeates the whole concept of competence. It can be used either to denote the competencies shared by those carrying out similar roles, or to the competencies that apply throughout the organisation. Confusion is worse confounded when consultants and personnel managers refer to generic competencies as core competencies.

Because competencies refer to behaviour they can be

regarded as 'soft'. The assumption is made that if you behave as required by the competency definitions of good behaviour, then you will deliver good results. This assumption is based on an analysis of the behaviours of people who do perform well. That being so, it is said, other people who behave in the same way will also perform well.

The analysis of competencies will sometimes produce a list of 'differentiating' competencies that list positive and negative indicators of the level of competence. These are derived from analysis of how good and poor performers behave in this area of competency. For example, the differentiating competencies for a typical competency, judgement, might be defined as follows:

Judgement

Definitions
Reaching appropriate conclusions and making sensible decisions on the basis of analysis and experience.

Positive indicators

☐ Alternative courses of action are carefully explored before reaching a decision.

☐ Decisions are founded on logical inferences and are based on factual information.

☐ Quickly identifies what needs to be achieved in a given situation.

☐ Reaches sound decisions that indicate clearly the most appropriate course of action and the goals to be achieved.

☐ Decisions or recommendations can be and are implemented effectively.

Negative indicators

☐ Fails to take account of some of the key factors in situations.

☐ Fails to think through the implications of the decision.

☐ Frequently comes to an incorrect conclusion because of flawed assumptions, inadequate analysis, or inability to make good use of experience.

Competence analysis

The concept of competence is more meaningful in practical terms than that of competency because it is about what people have to do to achieve results. It is not about *how* they do it, which may or may not result in the required performance and tends to produce lists of generalised personality characteristics such as persuasiveness, assertiveness and achievement motivation. In fact, a number of well-known organisations, such as ICL and the Midland Bank, have rebelled against using the term competence and adopt the term capability instead to denote the things that people are able to do effectively. These are measurable in terms of results in more objective ways than any attempt to measure personality characteristics or traits can be.

Methods of analysis

To analyse competences it is necessary to obtain answers to the following questions:

☐ What are the elements of this job – what does the job-holder have to do (expressed as main tasks or key result areas)?

☐ For each element, what is an acceptable standard of performance?

☐ What levels and types of knowledge and skills are required to ensure that the job-holder is fully capable in each element of the job?

☐ How will role-holders and their managers know that the required levels of competence have been achieved?

The best approach is to get a group of people together in similar jobs and ask them three questions:

1   What do you think are the most important things someone in your sort of job (or one similar to yours) has to be capable of doing?

2   What do people do when they are carrying out each part of their role well?

3   How can you tell that they are doing well?

The answers to these questions from the group should be

written up *in their own language* on flipcharts. Brainstorming rules should apply: any contribution is welcome, and no one will be allowed to rubbish it.

The brainstormed list of answers is then discussed by the group and distilled into a number of statements to the effect that:

> People will be carrying out this part of their job well when they ...

The blank is filled up by statements of what they do, what they have to know to do it, and how they do it. This is in line with the Glaxo Wellcome definition of competence, which states that competence is 'what you do, what you know and how you do it to perform effectively in a role'. The 'how' part of this process in the Glaxo Wellcome definition refers to behaviour, but it is always behaviour anchored to what people do to get results in a specific element or area of a job. It is not about generalised statements of behavioural characteristics or traits.

The most important feature of this approach is that people are involved in writing the competence definitions in their own language. This means that they are much more likely to be acceptable and used as a basis for agreeing performance targets and standards, establishing evidence of the performance achieved, applying performance measures to that evidence and reviewing performance by reference to targets and measures. When it comes to agreeing PDPs (see Chapter 13), participation in the competence-definition process and familiarity with the language used to define competences will help people to identify learning needs and subscribe to a programme for meeting them.

Functional analysis

Functional analysis is the method used to define competence-based standards for National Vocational Qualifications. This starts by describing the key purpose of the occupation and then identifies the key functions undertaken.

A distinction is made between *tasks*, which are the activities undertaken at work, and *functions*, which are the purposes of activities at work. The distinction is important because the analysis must focus on the outcomes of activities in order to establish expectations of workplace performance as the information required to define standards of competence.

When the units and elements of competence have been defined, the next question asked is, 'What are the qualities of the outcomes in terms of the performance criteria that an NVQ assessor can use to judge whether or not an individual's performance meets the required standards?'

Functional analysis is directed towards the definition of NVQ standards by producing definitions of units and elements of competence, performance criteria and range statements. The latter accompany each element and express the range of circumstances in which the competence will be applied. This term is used more loosely in some organisations to express the different levels of competence that will be assessed (see example in Appendix C). Functional analysis will not result directly in the development of definitions of the behavioural dimensions of competence, especially when generic definitions are required for a whole occupational area – for example, managers or team leaders.

Competence analysis at the Southern Focus Trust

A comprehensive competence analysis programme was completed in 1998 by line management at the Southern Focus Trust (then called Portsmouth Housing Trust). The first step was to define the core competences of the Trust, which provides care in the form of accommodation and help for people with learning difficulties, young people, ex-offenders and others in need of assistance.

A working group consisting of managers, team leaders, and support (care) workers and trade-union representatives was set up to define the Trust core competencies, using the techniques discussed above. The essential question was, 'What has the Trust got to be good at doing if it is to achieve its purpose?' The agreed core competence headings were:

□ provide a quality service

□ manage the business and the provision of services effectively

- ensure that accountabilities are defined, accepted and fulfilled
- acquire, develop and use professional expertise to deliver services
- develop and apply interpersonal skills to achieve aims and standards and to comply with the Trust's core values.

The core competences provided the framework for generic role and role-specific competence definitions. The aim was to integrate the generic and specific competences with the organisational core competences. This was to emphasise that they were defined areas of competence at all levels that had to be linked, and that if this did not happen, the organisation was much less likely to thrive – or even survive. Generic competences were developed for the key roles in the Trust, using the same core competence headings as the framework. Workshops were held with groups of team leaders and support workers to produce competence schedules expressed in their words.

The next step was to define role-specific competencies. This was done by team managers with small groups of people with special responsibilities or with individuals. Finally, the generic and role-specific schedules were combined to produce role profiles. These could be generic for some roles (eg team leaders), but might also be a specially tailored mix of generic and specific competencies in certain cases. The role profiles were used as the basis for performance-management processes (called 'competence management' in the Trust).

Using NVQ competence schedules

A number of schedules have been provided by the various NVQ lead bodies defining competence requirements at each of the NVQ levels. These can be used to provide a competence framework, as long as they fit the roles carried out within the organisation. However, this is not always the case, although some organisations have referred to the NVQ schedules for comparable workers and adapted them to suit their requirements.

Competency analysis

Competency analysis is concerned with the behavioural dimensions of roles as distinct from competence analysis, which considers what people have to do to perform well.

Approaches to competency analysis

Some organisations have adapted standardised competency lists developed by occupational psychologists or management consultants. Those produced by reputable people or firms will have been thoroughly researched by reference to actual people carrying out their roles well or not so well. The basic questions are 'How do people in this role behave when they carry it out effectively?' and 'How do people behave in this role when they are carrying it out ineffectively?' The evidence from the answers to these questions is used to derive competency headings and produce definitions of differentiating competencies – positive and negative examples of behaviour.

Management consultants who advise on competency frameworks often produce 'competency dictionaries', which contain examples of differentiating competencies under various headings. They can be applied in an organisation as they stand or, preferably, modified to meet the special requirements of the business. The advantages of adopting this approach is that ready-made competence lists such as those produced for managers by the Management Charter Institute (MCI) save a lot of work and will have been properly researched. But they may not fit the particular circumstances of the business. Generalised definitions, however well based, are not necessarily universally applicable. Rather than painstakingly adapting ready-made lists, some organisations prefer to develop their own tailor-made competence schedules. They do this by conducting workshops, as discussed earlier in relation to competence analysis, but the questions will focus on identifying good and bad behavioural characteristics rather than concentrating on the output factors – those referring to workplace performance.

The preparation of a tailor-made competency schedule is usually carried out by personnel specialists or management consultants, or both. Line managers may be consulted, but eventually the competency frameworks are issued to them to use in accordance with procedures laid down for such processes as performance management.

Although the first draft of a tailor-made competency schedule may be developed in-house, it is frequently the practice to reference home-made schedules to a consultant's dictionary of competence or the standards issued by the MCI.

There are seven approaches to competence analysis. Starting with the simplest, these are:

- expert opinion
- structured interview
- workshops
- functional analysis
- critical-incident technique
- repertory grid analysis
- job competency assessment.

Expert opinion

The basic, crudest and least satisfactory method is for an 'expert' member of the HR department, possibly in discussion with other 'experts' from the same department, to draw up a list from their own understanding of 'what counts', coupled with an analysis of other published lists.

This is unsatisfactory because the likelihood of the competences' being appropriate to the organisation, and realistic and measurable in the absence of detailed analysis, is fairly remote. The list tends to be bland and, because line managers and job-holders have not been involved, unacceptable.

Structured interview

This method begins with a list of competences drawn up by 'experts' and proceeds by subjecting a number of job-holders to a structured interview. This starts by identifying the key result areas or principal accountabilities of the role and goes on to analyse the behavioural characteristics that distinguish performers at different levels of competence.

The basic question is: 'What are the positive or negative indicators of behaviour conducive or non-conducive to achieving high levels of performance?' These may be analysed under such headings as:

☐ personal drive (achievement motivation)
☐ impact on results
☐ analytical power
☐ strategic thinking
☐ creative thinking (ability to innovate)
☐ decisiveness
☐ commercial judgement
☐ team management and leadership
☐ interpersonal skills
☐ ability to communicate
☐ ability to adapt and cope with change and pressure
☐ ability to plan and control projects.

In each area instances will be sought illustrating effective or less effective behaviour.

One of the problems with this approach is that it relies too much on the ability of the expert to draw out information from interviewees. It is also undesirable to use a deductive approach which pre-empts the analysis with a prepared list of competence headings. It is far better to do this by means of an inductive approach that starts from specific types of behaviour and then groups them under competence headings. This can be done in a workshop by analysing positive and negative indicators to gain an understanding of the competence dimensions of an occupation or job, as described below.

Workshops

Workshops bring together a group of people who have 'expert' knowledge or experience of the job – managers and job-holders as appropriate – with a facilitator, usually but not necessarily a member of the personnel department or an outside consultant.

The workshop usually begins by defining the job-related competence areas – the key functions in terms of the outputs required (key-result areas or principal accountabilities). Using the competence areas as a framework, the members of the group develop examples of effective and less effective behaviour, which are recorded on the flipcharts. For example, one of the competence areas for a divisional HR director/manager might be human resource planning, defined thus:

> Prepare forecasts of human resource requirements and plans for the acquisition, retention and effective utilisation of employees that ensure that the company's needs for human resources are met.

The positive indicators for this competence area might include:

☐ seeks involvement in business-strategy formulation
☐ contributes to business-planning by taking a strategic view of longer-term human resource issues likely to affect business strategy
☐ networks with senior management colleagues to understand and respond to the business issues they are facing and their business plans, and define the human resource planning issues they raise
☐ suggests practical ways to improve the use of human resources – for example, the introduction of annual hours.

Negative indicators might include:

☐ takes a narrow view of human resource planning – does not seem to be interested in or understand the wider business context
☐ lacks the determination to overcome problems and deliver forecasts
☐ produces plans that do not face up to the business issues
☐ fails to anticipate skills shortages – for example, unable to meet the multiskilling requirements implicit in the new computer-integrated manufacturing system
☐ does not seem to talk the same language as line management colleagues – fails to understand their requirements
☐ slow in responding to requests for help.

Some of the competence dimensions that could be inferred from these lists are:

□ strategic capability

□ business understanding

□ achievement motivation

□ interpersonal skills

□ communication skills

□ consultancy skills.

These dimensions might also be reflected in the analysis of other areas of competence so that, progressively, a picture of the people-related competences is built up linked to actual behaviour in the workplace.

The facilitator's job is to prompt, help the group to analyse its findings, and assist generally in the production of a set of competency dimensions that can be illustrated by behaviour-based examples. The facilitator may have some ideas about the sort of headings that may emerge from this process, but should not try to influence the group to come to a conclusion that it has not worked out for itself (even if eventually this may require some assistance from the facilitator).

Critical-incident technique

The critical-incident technique is a means of eliciting data about effective or less effective behaviour related to examples of actual events – critical incidents. The technique is used with groups of job-holders, their managers, or other 'experts' (sometimes, less effectively, with individuals) as follows:

□ Explain what the technique is and what it is used for – ie 'to assess what constitutes good or poor performance by analysing events observed to have had a noticeably successful or unsuccessful outcome, thus providing more factual and "real" information than by simply listing tasks and guessing performance requirements'.

□ Agree and list the key areas of responsibility – the principal accountabilities – in the job to be analysed. To save time, the analyst can establish these prior to the meeting, but it is necessary to ensure that they are agreed provisionally by the group, which can be told that the list may well be amended in the light of the forthcoming analysis.

☐ Take each area of the job in turn and ask the group for examples of critical incidents. If, for instance, one of the job responsibilities is dealing with customers, the following request could be made:

'I want you to tell me about a particular occasion at work that involved you – or that you observed – in dealing with a customer. Think about what the circumstances were eg who took part, what the customer asked for, what you or the other member of the staff did, and what the outcome was.'

☐ Collect information about the critical incident under the following headings:
  ▪ what the circumstances were
  ▪ what the individual did
  ▪ the outcome of what the individual did.

This information should be recorded on a flipchart.

☐ Continue this process for each area of responsibility.

☐ Refer to the flipchart and analyse each incident by obtaining ratings of the recorded behaviour on a scale, such as 1 for least effective to 5 for most effective.

☐ Discuss these ratings to get initial definitions of effective and ineffective performance for each of the key aspects of the job.

☐ Refine these definitions as necessary after the meeting: it can be difficult to get a group to produce finished definitions.

☐ Produce the final analysis, which may list the competences required and include performance indicators or standards of performance for each principal accountability or main task.

Repertory grid

Like the critical incident technique, the repertory grid can be used to identify the dimensions that distinguish good from poor standards of performance. The technique is based on Kelly's personal construct theory (Kelly 1955). Personal constructs are the ways in which we view the world. They are personal because they are highly individual and they influence the way we behave or view other people's behaviour. The aspects of the job to which these 'constructs' or judgements apply are called 'elements'.

To elicit judgements, a group of people are asked to concentrate on certain elements, which are the tasks carried out by job-holders, and develop constructs about these elements. This enables them to define the qualities that indicate the essential requirements for successful performance.

The procedure followed by the analyst is known as the 'triadic method of elicitation' (a sort of three-card trick), and involves the following steps:

1   Identify the tasks or elements of the job to be subjected to repertory grid analysis. This is done by one of the other forms of job analysis eg interviewing.

2   List the tasks on cards.

3   Draw three cards at random from the pack and ask the members of the group to nominate which of these tasks is the odd one out from the point of view of the qualities and characteristics needed to perform it.

4   Probe to obtain more specific definitions of these qualities or characteristics in the form of expected behaviour. If, for example, a characteristic has been described as the 'ability to plan and organise', ask such questions as 'What sort of behaviour or actions indicate that someone is planning effectively?', or 'How can we tell if someone is not organising his or her work particularly well?'

5   Draw three more cards from the pack and repeat steps 3 and 4.

6   Repeat this process until all the cards have been analysed and there do not appear to be any more constructs to be identified.

7   List the constructs and ask the group members to rate each task on every quality, using a six- or seven-point scale.

8   Collect and analyse the scores in order to assess their relative importance. This can be done statistically.

Like the critical-incident technique, repertory-grid analysis helps people to articulate their views by reference to specific examples. An additional advantage is that the repertory grid

makes it easier for them to identify the behavioural characteristics or competencies required in a job by limiting the area
of comparison through the triadic technique.

Although a full statistical analysis of the outcome of a
repertory grid exercise is helpful, the most important results
obtained are the descriptions of what constitutes good or poor
performance in each element of the job.

Both the repertory grid and the critical incident techniques
require a skilled analyst who can probe and draw out the
descriptions of job characteristics. They are quite detailed and
time-consuming, but even if the full process is not followed,
much of the methodology is of use in a less elaborate
approach to competence analysis.

Job competency assessment

The job competency assessment method, as described by
Spencer and Spencer (1993) and offered by Hay/McBer (Hay
Management Consultants), is based on David McClelland's
research on what competency variables predict job performance. He established 20 competencies that most often predict
success. These are grouped into six clusters, as follows:

1   achievement cluster
2   helping/service cluster
3   influence cluster
4   managerial cluster
5   cognitive thinking/problem-solving cluster
6   personal effectiveness cluster.

McClelland then developed with his colleagues an expert
system containing a database of competency definitions
under the above headings.

The competency assessment method is used to model the
competencies for a generic role ie a position occupied by a
number of job-holders where the basic accountabilities are
similar, such as research scientists in a laboratory or area
sales managers. The method is based on McClelland's list of
competencies, and may use the expert system developed from
his research.

The starting-point is to assemble a panel of expert

managers to express their vision of the job, its duties and responsibilities, any difficult job components, any likely future changes to the role and the criteria against which the job-holder's performance is measured. The members of the panel nominate job-holders whom they consider to be outstanding and those whom they consider satisfactory.

The next stage is to conduct a 'behavioural event interview' with the nominated job-holders. This interview focuses on the distinction between a person's concepts about what it takes to be successful and what the person actually does to create that success. It employs a structured probe strategy rather than a standard set of questions in order to elicit what the interviewee sees as his or her most critical job experiences. The interview is investigative, not reflective, the object being to gather the most accurate performance data, not to collect a person's ideas about what he or she might have done under similar circumstances. The interviewees are not allowed to draw conclusions about what it takes to do that job; rather, they are pressed for information on their actual behaviour, thoughts and actions by a trained interviewer.

Following this analysis, differentiations can be made between superior and average performers in the form of the:

- competencies that superior performers possess and exhibit that the average performers do not
- activities the average performers undertake that superior performers do not
- competency and performance criteria that both superior and average performers exhibit, but that superior performers exhibit far more frequently.

Which approach?

Techniques such as critical-incident technique and repertory-grid analysis can be used effectively, but they are time-consuming and experience is needed to apply them effectively. Job-competency assessment can be a most effective approach. For those who have not got the time – or the money – to use any of these methodologies, the workshop approach as described above is probably the best. Functional analysis is used when the main objective is to develop NVQ standards.

18   360-DEGREE FEEDBACK

360-degree feedback is the latest and, for some people, the most exciting development in the field of performance management. It hardly existed at all at the time of the 1991 survey, but 11 per cent of the organisations covered by the 1997 survey had some form of 360-degree feedback, and the impression we gained was that many other organisations are contemplating using it.

In this chapter we start by defining 360-degree feedback and describe how it is used and operated. We then discuss its advantages and disadvantages and methods of introduction, and conclude with a summary of the outcome of our special survey.

360-degree feedback defined

360-degree feedback has been defined by Ward (1997) as: 'the systematic collection and feedback of performance data on an individual or group derived from a number of the stakeholders on their performance.' The data is usually fed back in the form of ratings against various performance dimensions. Another way of referring to 360-degree feedback is as multi-source assessment or multirater feedback.

Performance data in a 360-degree feedback process can be generated for individuals (as shown in Figure 20) from the person to whom they report, their direct reports, their peers (who could be team members or colleagues in other parts of the organisation) and their external and internal customers.

The range of feedback could be extended to include other stakeholders – external customers, clients or suppliers (this is sometimes known as 540-degree feedback). A self-assessment process may also be incorporated using for comparison purposes the same criteria as the other generators of feedback.

Figure 20
360-DEGREE FEEDBACK MODEL

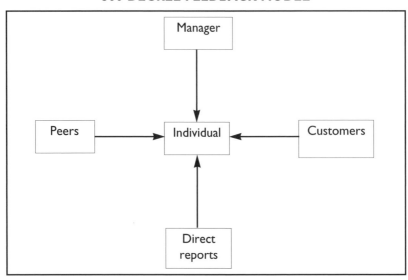

Feedback can be initiated entirely by peers (in a team set-ting) or both by peers and the team leaders. It can also take the form of 180-degree or upward feedback, where this is gen-erated by subordinates to their managers. Feedback may be presented directly to individuals or to their managers, or both. Expert counselling and coaching for individuals as a result of the feedback may be provided by a member of the HR depart-ment or an outside consultant.

Uses of 360-degree feedback

The uses of 360-degree feedback are numerous. Research con-ducted by the Ashridge Management Research Group (Handy *et al* 1996) found that, typically, 360-degree feedback is used as part of a self-development or management development programme. The 45 users covered by the survey fell into the following groups:

☐ 71 per cent used it solely to support learning and develop-ment

☐ 23 per cent used it to support a number of HR processes such as appraisal, resourcing and succession-planning

○ 6 per cent used it to support pay decisions.

A 1997 (unpublished) survey of 22 organisations using 360-degree feedback by the Performance Management Group found that:

○ 77 per cent either disagreed or strongly disagreed with the statement that it is 'a personal development tool and should not be used for wider HR or organisational purposes'

○ 81 per cent disagreed or strongly disagreed that 'the natural use of 360-degree feedback is to provide a basis for reward'.

The survey carried out by the (then) IPD in early 1998 (see pages 327–8) also found that the 51 organisations covered by the research predominantly (92 per cent) used 360-degree feedback to help in assessing development needs, whereas 80 per cent used it to help in overall performance-coaching, only 20 per cent using it to determine a performance grade or pay award.

Use for developmental purposes

As the Ashridge survey noted, where personal development is a priority:

○ performance improvement is important but is viewed as the logical outcome of a successful feedback process

○ the potential for personal change and growth is emphasised rather than current performance

○ strengths and weaknesses are regarded as developmental opportunities

○ a long-term perspective is adopted because the ultimate goal is personal growth

○ the line manager has a nominal role and may be excluded altogether

○ feedback data is 'personal intelligence' and a trigger for change.

The feedback process is used in this case to help managers to formulate personal development plans or as input to a development centre.

Use for appraisal

When 360-degree feedback is used for appraisal, the focus is more on current performance. Feedback goes both to individuals and their managers, and the latter therefore play a greater part. The outcome of the feedback will be included on the agenda for performance review discussions to identify development needs and areas for improvement, and to agree on any actions required.

Use for pay

If 360-degree feedback is used for appraisal it can easily, although controversially, be extended to inform PRP decisions. Ratings are influenced by the feedback and in turn govern, or at least guide, proposals on pay increases. The Ashridge researchers noted that a number of their respondents who rejected a link with reward believed that participants would be so concerned about how their feedback affected decisions about pay that the development opportunities would be lost. As one of their respondents commented, 'Direct links to pay could result in a lack of openness and honesty. This would destroy the value of the feedback.'

The evidence that we collected from organisations and focus groups highlighted the damage to the developmental nature of performance management that can be caused by incorporating ratings and explicit links to pay. If, as we believe should be the case, performance management is primarily a developmental process, then we contend that, when 360-degree feedback is incorporated into performance management, it should not form the basis for performance ratings and should be entirely divorced from pay. Performance management is not simply about judgmental ratings and money.

The case for and against linking 360-degree feedback to pay may be arguable, but it is essential that its purposes, whether regarding development, appraisal or pay decisions, should be defined before embarking on its introduction. And this defined purpose should be communicated to all concerned.

Deciding on the purpose of 360-degree feedback

A number of HR specialists in the organisations we visited where 360-degree feedback was used believed strongly that it should be used only for developmental purposes. The issue is then whether the focus should be on self-development or whether it is believed that development is a joint process between managers and individuals. In the former case, individuals own the feedback, in the latter case it is shared.

The Ashridge researchers found that organisations that directly linked 360-degree feedback to appraisal and pay had a strong performance-management culture, perhaps with PRP. But they came to the conclusion that the best starting-point was to use it for development and then, step by step, extend it to appraisal and pay.

Rationale for 360-degree feedback

The main rationale for 360-degree feedback has been expressed by Turnow (1993) as follows:

> 360-degree activities are usually based on two key assumptions: (1) that awareness of any discrepancy between how we see ourselves and how others see us increases self-awareness, and (2) that enhanced self-awareness is a key to maximum performance as a leader, and thus becomes a foundation block for management and leadership development programmes.

London and Beatty (1993) have suggested that the rationale for 360-degree feedback is that:

□ it can become a powerful organisational intervention to increase awareness of the importance of aligning leader behaviour, work-unit results and customer expectations, as well as increasing employee participation in leadership development and work-unit effectiveness

□ it recognises the complexity of management and the value of input from various sources – it is axiomatic that managers should not be assessing behaviours they cannot observe, and the leadership behaviours of subordinates may not be known to their managers

□ it calls attention to important performance dimensions that may hitherto have been neglected by the organisation.

Trevor Toolan of PILAT said that 360-degree feedback can overcome biased appraisals because the organisation is not relying on one person's view and the inherent prejudices that person may have. Roy Davis of SHL (Saville and Holdsworth (UK) Ltd) said that traditional appraisal schemes were falling down because they were trying to satisfy the interests of too many stakeholders. Organisations are increasingly turning to 360-degree feedback to generate the extra information they need.

Reasons for introducing 360-degree feedback

The following reasons were given by a UK merchant bank for introducing 360-degree feedback:

□ It is seen as best practice.

□ It is suitable for a non-hierarchical, flexible organisation.

□ It assists managers with limited knowledge of performance after restructuring.

□ It reflects value that wider groups should have input into performance management.

The Automobile Association introduced 360-degree feedback as a means of reinforcing the standards of management behaviour and the values they are expected to demonstrate in their everyday dealings with employees. As reported by Handy *et al* (1996), the Forward Trust regarded 360-degree feedback as a tool to embed the new core competency model, which focuses on the desired leadership and managerial behaviours. At W.H. Smith, a pilot scheme was introduced to gain a more comprehensive perspective of performance, including skills, behaviour and outputs and, in particular, to assess how well managers measured up against the organisation's core competencies.

360-degree feedback: methodology

The questionnaire

The processes of 360-degree feedback usually obtain data from questionnaires that measure from different perspectives the behaviours of individuals against a list of competencies. In effect, they ask for an evaluation: 'How well does ... do ...?' The competency model may be one developed within the organisation, or the competency headings may be provided by the supplier of a questionnaire.

The dimensions may broadly refer to leadership, management and approaches to work. The headings used in the Performance Management Group's Orbit 360-degree questionnaire are:

- □ leadership
- □ team player/manage people
- □ self-management
- □ communication
- □ vision
- □ organisational skills
- □ decision-making
- □ expertise
- □ drive
- □ adaptability.

The leadership heading, for example, is defined as:

> Shares a clear vision and focuses on achieving it. Demonstrates commitment to the organisation's mission. Provides a coherent sense of purpose and direction, both internally and externally, harnessing energy and enthusiasm of staff.

The competency model used by SHL as the basis for their questionnaire is shown in Figure 21.

Ratings

Ratings are given by the generators of the feedback on a scale against each heading. This may refer both to importance and performance, as in the PILAT questionnaire asking respondents to rate the importance of each item on a scale of 1 (not important) to 6 (essential), and performance on a scale of 1 (weak in this area) to 6 (outstanding). The scale recommended by Edwards and Ewen (1996) consists of 10 points:

9–10 an exceptional skill
7–8 a strength skill
5–6 appropriate skill level
3–4 not a strength
1–2 least skilled.

Figure 21
COMPETENCY MODEL – SAVILLE & HOLDSWORTH

Area	Competency
Managerial qualities	Leadership Planning and organising Quality orientation Persuasiveness
Professional qualities	Specialist knowledge Problem-solving and analysis Oral communication Written communication
Entrepreneurial qualities	Commercial awareness Creativity and innovation Action orientation Strategic
Personal qualities	Interpersonal sensitivity Flexibility Resilience Personal motivation

The Performance Management Group's approach is to ask assessors to indicate their reaction to a statement such as the example given on leadership above. The scale is: strongly disagree, mostly disagree, neither agree nor disagree, mostly agree, strongly agree. The Local Government Management Board (1995) suggests that scales should be large enough to allow differentiation, small enough to work with, even-numbered to prevent 'sitting on the fence', clearly defined, and anchored with sensible increments between values.

Data-processing

Questionnaires are normally processed with the help of software developed within the organisation or, most commonly, provided by external suppliers. This enables the data collection and analysis to be completed swiftly, with the minimum

Figure 22
360-DEGREE FEEDBACK PROFILE

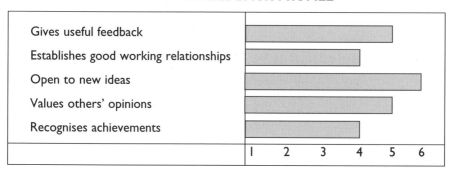

of effort and in a way that facilitates graphical as well as numerical presentation.

Graphical presentation is preferable as a means of easing the process of assimilating the data. The simplest method is to produce a profile as illustrated in Figure 22.

Some of the proprietary software presents feedback data in a much more elaborate form.

Feedback

The feedback is often anonymous and may be presented to the individual (most commonly), to the individual's manager (less common) or to both the individual and the manager. Some organisations do not arrange for feedback to be anonymous, but, as Trevor Toolan of PILAT pointed out, whether or not feedback is anonymous depends on the organisation's culture – the more open the culture, the more likely the source of feedback is to be revealed. Roy Davis of SHL confirmed that there could be cultural barriers to removing anonymity from feedback.

Action

The action generated by the feedback will depend on the purposes of the process ie development, appraisal or pay. If the purpose is primarily developmental, the action may be left to individuals as part of their PDPs, but the planning process may be shared between individuals and their managers if they both have access to the information. Even if the data goes only to the individual, it can be discussed in a performance-review meeting so that joint plans can be made; there is much to be said for adopting this approach.

Development and implementation

To develop and implement 360-degree feedback, the following steps should be taken:

1   *Define objectives* – it is important to define exactly what 360-degree feedback is expected to achieve. It is necessary to spell out the extent to which it is concerned with personal development, appraisal or pay.

2   *Decide on recipients* – ie who is to be at the receiving end of feedback. This may be an indication of who will eventually be covered after a pilot scheme.

3   *Decide who will give the feedback* – the individual's manager, direct reports, team members, other colleagues, or internal and external customers. A decision has also to be made whether HR staff or outside consultants should take part in helping managers to make use of the feedback. A further decision will have to be made whether or not the feedback should be anonymous (it usually is).

4   *Decide the areas of work and behaviour* on which feedback will be given – this may be in line with an existing competency model or may take the form of a list of headings for development. Clearly, the model should fit the culture, values and type of work carried out in the organisation. But it might be decided that a list of headings or questions in a software package would be acceptable, at least to start with.

5   *Decide the method of collecting the data* – the questionnaire could be designed in-house, or a consultant's or software provider's questionnaire could be adopted, with the possible option of amending it later to produce better fit.

6   *Decide data analysis and presentation* – again, the decision is either to develop the software in-house or to use a package. Most organisations installing 360-degree feedback do, in fact, purchase a package from a consultancy or software house. But the aim should be to keep it

as simple as possible.

7   *Plan an initial implementation programme* – it is desirable to pilot the process, preferably at top level or with all the managers in a function or department. The pilot scheme will need to be launched with communications to those involved about the purpose of 360-degree feedback, how it will work and the part they will play. The aim is to spell out the benefits and, as far as possible, allay any fears. Training in giving and receiving feedback will also be necessary.

8   *Analyse the outcome of the pilot scheme* – the reactions of those taking part in a pilot scheme should be analysed and necessary changes made to the process, the communication package and the training.

9   *Plan and implement full programme* – this should include briefing, communicating, training, and support from HR and, possibly, the external consultants.

10   *Monitor and evaluate* – maintain a particularly close watch on the initial implementation of feedback, but monitoring should be ongoing. This process may cause anxiety and stress, or produce little practical gain in terms of development and improved performance for a lot of effort.

Alan Cave of the Performance Management Group told us that the five key areas in which issues seem to arise whenever 360-degree feedback is contemplated are:

1   *fit* – does the intended use of 360-degree feedback square with the organisation's needs and culture?

2   *design* – will the process deliver the goods for its intended use; is it for development purposes alone or will it extend beyond them?

3   *skill* – do the participants have the skills required to make 360-degree feedback work in a positive and constructive way?

4   *communication* – do staff fully understand and support the objectives of 360-degree feedback? Do they trust the process?

5   *administration* – can the growing volume of data and transactions that the processes create be handled efficiently and securely?

Roy Davis of SHL sees the following as the most important things to do when introducing 360-degree feedback: identify the cultural issues that will affect the process, conduct a pilot exercise, get the communication channels right, establish a policy on confidentiality, and train all the individuals concerned.

360-degree feedback: advantages and disadvantages

The survey conducted by the Performance Management Group in 1997 (unpublished) revealed that respondents believed the following benefits resulted from using 360-degree feedback:

- affording individuals a broader perspective than previously possible of how they are perceived by others
- increased awareness, and relevance, of competencies
- increased awareness by senior management that they too have development needs
- more reliable feedback to senior managers about their performance
- gaining acceptance of the principle of multiple stakeholders as a measure of performance
- encouraging more open feedback – new insights
- reinforcing the desired competencies of the business
- provision of a clearer picture to senior management of a given individual's real worth (although there tended to be some 'halo'-effect syndromes)
- clarification for employees of critical performance aspects
- opening up feedback and giving people a more rounded view of performance than they previously had
- identifying key development areas for the individual, a department and the organisation as a whole
- identifying strengths that can be used to the best advantage of the business
- a rounded view of an individual's, team's, or the organis-

ation's performance and what the strengths and weaknesses are

☐ raising the self-awareness of people managers about how they personally affect others – positively and negatively

☐ supporting a climate of continuous improvement

☐ starting to improve the climate or morale, as measured through our employee opinion survey

☐ a focused agenda for development – the process forced line managers to discuss development issues

☐ perception of feedback as more valid and objective, leading to acceptance of results and actions required

But there may be problems. These include:

☐ people not giving frank or honest feedback

☐ people being put under stress in receiving or giving feedback

☐ lack of action following feedback

☐ overreliance on technology

☐ too much bureaucracy.

These can all be minimised, if not avoided completely, by careful design, communication, training and follow-up.

360-degree feedback: criteria for success

The likelihood that 360-degree feedback will be successful is greatest when:

☐ it has the active support of a top management who themselves take part in giving and receiving feedback and encourage everyone else to do the same

☐ there is commitment everywhere else to the process, based on briefing, training and an understanding of the benefits to individuals as well as the organisation

☐ there is real determination by all concerned to use feedback data as the basis for development

☐ questionnaire items fit or reflect typical and significant aspects of behaviour

☐ items covered in the questionnaire can be related to actual events experienced by the individual

- □ comprehensive and well-delivered communication and training programmes are followed
- □ no one feels threatened by the process – this is usually achieved by making feedback anonymous or by getting a third-party facilitator to deliver the feedback
- □ (as SHL points out) recipients are assisted to develop responses to the feedback
- □ feedback questionnaires are relatively easy to complete with clear instructions
- □ bureaucracy is minimised.

SHL survey results

SHL recently conducted research into the use of 360-degree feedback. This was published in 1997 as 'A Survey of the Views of HR Practitioners on 360-Degree Processes'. The main findings, based on responses from over 250 organisations, were as follows:

- □ Users believed that managers should be responsible for their own development, and that feedback is 'the lifeblood of the organisation'.
- □ The most common use of 360-degree instruments was to help individual managers develop.
- □ The least popular reason for using the instruments was for decision-making processes, especially those concerned with determining pay and rewards.
- □ Most users reported that managers were anxious about receiving feedback, and that probably the biggest barrier to acceptance was posed by emotional issues.
- □ The negative feelings initially experienced by participants were reported to have disappeared almost entirely after successful implementation of the methodology.
- □ Virtually all users said that feedback should be given by an HR professional, an independent consultant or a mentor – SHL suggest that best practice is to communicate findings and deliver feedback through channels acceptable to the individuals concerned, who are most likely to be third-party facilitators.

- ○ External consultants are associated with the most successful applications.
- ○ The greatest level of satisfaction was recorded by respondents who used instruments provided by external suppliers.
- ○ A key factor in success was the quality of training given to facilitators, raters and participants.
- ○ Virtually no respondents said that their managers doubted the efficacy of the methodology or that they believed it to be just a passing fad.

IPD survey results

A survey of 360-degree practices was conducted by the (then) IPD in early 1998, covering 51 organisations, 42 in the private and 8 in the public sector (plus one undisclosed). The main findings of the survey are summarised in Table 20.

The salient points emerging from this survey are therefore that feedback:

- ○ largely involves managers
- ○ tends to come from supervisors, subordinates, colleagues and direct reports
- ○ is usually anonymous
- ○ may be fed back by line manager, personnel or directly
- ○ is primarily used for development and coaching
- ○ is felt by only a small proportion of respondents to make people uncomfortable, although a majority feel that, whereas they are generally happy, they have some reservations
- ○ the benefits are mainly concerned with getting good-quality, unbiased data that provides a more rounded view of people
- ○ there are some problems about the creation of anxiety and stress, concern about being honest and lack of expertise in feeding back results.

The overall message emerging from the survey was that 360-degree feedback was felt by the respondents to be worthwhile.

Table 20
IPD SURVEY ON 360-DEGREE FEEDBACK

Finding	Percentage of organisations responding positively
Feedback applied:	
mainly to senior managers	54
to other managers	55
Feedback generated by supervisors,	
subordinates and peers	88
Feedback provided in a special form	90
Feedback anonymous	90
Feedback provided by:	
line manager	27
personnel	25
direct	24
external consultant	8
Feedback is used to:	
assess development needs	92
help in performance-coaching	80
raise quality/level of customer service	49
provide basis for pay award	20
Reactions of people to feedback	
happy and comfortable	35
generally happy with some reservations	55
uncomfortable	10
Benefits	
more rounded view of people	84
less bias	78
better-quality data	73
helps people to perform well in a wider area	47
Problems	
anxiety/stress	35
individuals fear being too honest	35
lack of expertise in feeding back results	33
less than honest answers	27
individuals providing feedback are vengeful	14
bureaucratic	10
time-consuming	8

19 CONDUCTING PERFORMANCE AND DEVELOPMENT REVIEWS

Performance and development reviews provide those involved with the opportunity to reflect on past performance as a basis for making development and improvement plans. Obtaining historical perspective through analysis is a necessary part of the review, but reaching agreement about what should be done in the future is really what it is all about.

Key aspects of performance and development reviews

The purpose of performance and development reviews is to enable those concerned to get together so that they can engage in a dialogue about the individual's performance and development and the support provided by the manager. They are not occasions for top-down appraisals, although some feedback will be provided. Neither are they interviews in which one person asks the questions and the other provides the answers. They should be more like free-flowing, open meetings in which views are exchanged so that agreed conclusions can be reached. Performance and development reviews should be regarded as a conversation with a purpose, the latter being to reach firm and agreed conclusions about the individual's development, and, if applicable, any areas for improvement, including how such improvements are to be achieved.

The basis of the performance and development review

The five key elements of performance review meetings are:

1   *measurement* – assessing results against agreed targets and standards

2   *feedback* – providing information on how a person has been doing

3   *positive reinforcement* – emphasising what has been done well so that it will be done even better in the future and making only constructive criticisms (ie those that point the way to improvement)

4   *exchange of views* – ensuring that the discussion involves a full, free and frank exchange of views about what has been achieved, what needs to be done to achieve more and what reviewees think about their work, the way they are managed, and their aspirations

5   *agreement* – jointly coming to an understanding about what has to be done by both parties to improve performance, knowledge and skills and overcome any work problems raised during the discussion.

There is no one right way to conduct a performance review. The approach will depend on the circumstances and the people involved. But there are certain guidelines to be taken into account, summarised below.

Preparing for the meeting

Both parties should prepare for the meeting in order for consideration to be given to the points for discussion.

The reviewer

The person conducting the review (the reviewer) should consider:

☐ how well the individual (the reviewee) has done in achieving work objectives and meeting performance standards since the last review meeting

☐ to what extent, and with what effect, the personal development plans (PDPs) agreed at the last meeting have been implemented

☐ the feedback to be provided at the meeting and the evidence that will be used to support it

☐ the factors that have affected performance, both those within and outside the reviewee's control

- the points for discussion on the possible actions that can be taken by both the reviewee and the reviewer to further development or improve performance
- possible directions that the reviewee's career could take
- possible objectives for the next review period.

The reviewee

The reviewee should consider:

- achievements in meeting performance objectives and standards
- any examples of where objectives and standards have not been achieved, with explanations
- progress in implementing PDPs
- successes, with examples
- any aspects of work in which improvement is required, and how such improvements may be achieved
- development and training needs
- any requirements for better support or guidance
- aspirations for the future
- possible objectives for the next review period.

Self-assessment

Preparation by the reviewee as described above is, in effect, self-assessment or self-appraisal. This means getting people to analyse and assess their own performance as the basis for discussion and action. The advantages of self-assessment are that it:

- helps to generate less inhibited and more positive discussion
- involves reviewees actively in the review process
- is likely to reduce defensive behaviour
- provides scope to run the review meeting as a constructive and open dialogue by reducing the top-down element of traditional performance appraisals and minimising their unilateral nature.

But self-assessment raises a number of issues. First, individuals must have clear targets and standards against which they can assess their performance. Second, there has to be a climate of mutual trust between the reviewee and the reviewer. Reviewees must believe that reviewers will not take advantage of an honest self-assessment. Third, there is the risk that individuals, especially where there is money at stake, will overestimate their performance, leaving their reviewers in the awkward position of having to correct them. In practice, if there are no ratings for performance-related pay (PRP) purposes, many people *under*estimate themselves. This makes life easier for reviewers, who can take the opportunity to boost the confidence of the reviewee.

Guidelines for the meeting

Reviewing performance is *not* something that managers do to their subordinates. It *is* something that they carry out together. The meeting is essentially about:

☐ what individuals have learned or need to learn
☐ where they have got to
☐ where they are going
☐ how they are going to get there
☐ what they believe they know and can do
☐ what help or guidance can be provided for them by the organisation or their manager.

Agenda-setting

It can be said that whoever sets the agenda directs the meeting. But the whole point of the review is that it should be a joint affair. Neither party should dominate. The agenda is therefore set by both the reviewer and the reviewee, ideally through their pre-meeting analyses. It may consist of the following items:

☐ a review of each key element in the job (accountabilities or main activities), with discussion of what has gone well or less well, and why
☐ a point-by-point examination of the results of the objectives, actions and PDPs agreed at the last meeting

□ a discussion and agreement on the performance objectives for the next period, in the shape of targets and standards of performance

□ a discussion and agreement on the reviewee's developmental objectives

□ a discussion and agreement on the actions to be taken to ensure that the performance and developmental objectives are achieved, which should include the formulation of a PDP

□ a general discussion of any other matters or concerns, including the reviewee's aspirations

□ a check that there is mutual understanding of the objectives and action plans

□ an agreement on action plans to conclude the meeting.

An alternative approach is to structure the discussion around forms to be completed in advance by the reviewer and the reviewee covering the preparation points listed earlier.

Conducting a constructive review meeting

A constructive review meeting is most likely to take place if reviewers:

□ encourage reviewees to do most of the talking

□ listen actively to what they say

□ allow scope for reflection and analysis

□ analyse performance, not personality – ie concentrate on what reviewees have done, not on the sort of people they are

□ keep the whole period under review, not concentrating on isolated or recent events

□ adopt a 'no-surprises' approach – performance problems should have been identified and dealt with at the time they occurred

□ recognise achievements and reinforce strengths

□ end the meeting positively with agreed action plans and an understanding of how progress in implementing them will be reviewed.

Performance review skills

The main skills applied to performance reviews are asking the right questions, listening actively and providing feedback as discussed below. Performance review meetings also provide opportunities for coaching and counselling but, as these activities can take place at other times, they are considered in Chapter 20.

Asking the right questions

The aim of a performance and development review meeting is to obtain effective interaction. This can be promoted by asking the right questions, allowing thinking time for response, listening carefully (see below) and maintaining a friendly atmosphere. Only one question at a time should be asked and, if necessary, unclear responses should be played back to check understanding.

The two main approaches to use are open and probe questions.

Open questions

These are general, not specific. They provide room for people to decide how they should be answered and encouragement for them to talk freely. They set the scene for the more detailed analysis of performance that will follow later, and may be introduced at any point to open up a discussion on a new topic. Open questions help to create an atmosphere of calm and friendly enquiry, and can be expressed quite informally. For example:

- □ How do you think things have been going?
- □ What do you feel about that?
- □ How can we build on that in the future?
- □ What can we learn from that?

Open questions can be put in a 'tell me' form, such as:

- □ Tell me, why do you think that happened?
- □ Tell me, how did you handle that situation?
- □ Tell me, how is this project going?
- □ Tell me, what do you think your key objectives are going to be next year?

Probe questions

These seek specific information on what has happened, and why. They can:

- show interest and encouragement by making supportive statements followed by questions: 'I see, and then what?'
- seek further information by asking 'Why?', 'Why not?' or 'What do you mean?'
- explore attitudes: 'To what extent do you believe that …?'
- reflect views: 'Have I got the right impression? do you feel that …?'

Listening

Reviewers need to develop and practise the art of listening carefully. Good listeners:

- concentrate on the speaker, alert at all times to the nuances of what is being said
- respond quickly when appropriate, but do not interrupt unnecessarily
- ask questions to clarify meaning
- comment as necessary on the points made to demonstrate understanding, but not at length.

Giving feedback

Giving feedback based on fact, not subjective judgement, is an important part of a performance and development discussion. In this respect at least, performance meetings have some of the characteristics of a system, in that they provide for information to be presented (feedback) to people on their performance, which helps them to understand how well they have been doing and how effective that behaviour has been. The aim is for feedback to promote this understanding so that appropriate action can be taken. This may be corrective action, where the feedback has indicated that something has gone wrong, or, more positively, action may be taken to make the best use of the opportunities the feedback has revealed. In the latter case, feedback acts as a reinforcement, and positive feedback can be a powerful motivator, because it is a recognition of achievement. The following are some guidelines on giving feedback:

□ *Build feedback into the job.* To be effective, feedback should be built into the job. Individuals or teams should be able to find out easily how they have done from the control information readily available to them. If it cannot be built into the job, it should be provided as quickly as possible after the activity has taken place – ideally within a day or two.

□ *Provide feedback on actual events.* Feedback should be provided on actual results or observed behaviour.

□ *Describe, don't judge.* The feedback should be presented as a description of what has happened. It should not be accompanied by a judgement.

□ *Refer to specific behaviours.* The feedback should be related to specific items of behaviour; it should not transmit general feelings or impressions.

□ *Ask questions.* Ask questions rather than make statements eg 'Why do you think this happened?', 'On reflection, is there any other way in which you think you could have handled the situation?', 'What are the factors that influenced you to make that decision?'

□ *Get people to work things out for themselves.* Encourage people to come to their own conclusions about what they should do or how they should behave. Ask such questions as 'How do you think you should tackle this sort of problem in the future?', 'How do you feel you could avoid getting into this situation again?'

□ *Select key issues.* Select key issues and restrict the feedback to them. There is a limit to how much criticism anyone can take. If it is overdone, the shutters will come down and the discussion will get nowhere.

□ *Focus.* Focus on aspects of performance that the individual can improve. It is a waste of time to concentrate on areas about which the individual can do little or nothing.

□ *Show understanding.* If something has gone wrong, find out whether this has happened because of circumstances beyond the individual's control, and, if so, indicate that this is understood.

More consideration is given to dealing with performance problems in Chapter 21.

20 COACHING AND COUNSELLING

An important, although sometimes neglected, aspect of performance management is the provision of support to employees. As Marchington and Wilkinson (1996) point out, support can take the form of mentoring, coaching and the removal of any barriers that may prevent excellent performance. Support can and should be provided on an everyday basis, as the need arises. But it can be given more specifically through coaching and counselling, which take place during formal performance review meetings, but should be carried out at any time of the year as required. And coaching may well play an important part in a personal development plan.

Coaching

Coaching is a person-to-person technique designed to develop individual knowledge, skills and attitudes. It is most effective if it takes place informally as part of the normal process of management or team leadership.

Aims

The aims of coaching are to:

- help people become aware of how well they are doing, where they need to improve and what they need to learn
- put controlled delegation into practice; in other words, managers can delegate new tasks or enlarged areas of work, provide guidance as necessary on how the tasks or work should be carried out, and monitor performance in doing the work
- get managers and individuals to use whatever situations arise as learning opportunities
- enable guidance to be provided on how to carry out specific

tasks as necessary, but always on the basis of helping people to learn, rather than spoon-feeding them with instructions on what to do and how to do it.

The coaching sequence

Coaching can be carried out in the following stages:

□ Identify the areas of knowledge, skills or capabilities where learning needs to take place to qualify people to carry out the task, provide for continuous development, enhance transferable skills or improve performance.

□ Ensure that people understand and accept the need to learn.

□ Discuss with people what needs to be learned and the best way to undertake the learning.

□ Get people to work out how they can manage their own learning while identifying where they will need help from you or someone else.

□ Provide encouragement and advice to people in pursuing the self-learning programme.

□ Provide specific guidance as required where people need your help.

□ Agree how progress should be monitored and reviewed.

Counselling

Workplace counselling can be defined as:

> any activity in the workplace where one individual uses a set of skills and techniques to help another individual to take responsibility for and to manage their own decision-making, whether it is work related or personal.
>
> Institute of Personnel and Development (1994)

Counselling is central to the management and development of people. Managers frequently engage in some activity during their normal working life that could be termed as counselling. It is therefore a natural component of managing people – an everyday activity that can arise from immediate feedback, or play an important part during a performance and development review.

Aims of counselling

The most important aim is to encourage people to accept much of the responsibility for their own performance and development. What people feel and find out for themselves, with some guidance as necessary, is likely to make much more impact on their behaviour than anything handed down to them by their manager.

Counselling stages

The counselling process as described by the IPD (now the CIPD) consists of three stages:

o   *recognition and understanding* – recognising the existence of problems and issues

o   *empowering* – enabling employees to recognise their own problem or situation and encouraging them to express it, work out a solution and take action to implement it

o   *resourcing* – managing the problem, which will include deciding on any further help individuals may need from their managers, a specialist or an outside resource.

It should be remembered, however, that the counselling role is intended to help people resolve problems concerning their work behaviour. Managers cannot be expected to play the part of amateur psychotherapists in addressing personality disorders or any other deep-seated behavioural problem. They should be briefed that, if they meet a situation which they believe themselves not qualified to handle, then they should enlist the support of the HR department, which may employ a professional counsellor.

Approach to counselling

A non-directive approach is best, which means not telling people what their problem is or what they should do about it. Instead, it is preferable to do the following:

o   *Listen with intelligence and understanding.* People in difficulty cannot fail to benefit if they are encouraged to discuss their problems with a sympathetic listener. Attentive silence is often the counsellor's best contribution. When listening, they are trying to understand the perspective of the other person (ie empathy, putting themselves in the other's shoes). They should attempt to communicate their understanding so that both parties can agree on what the situation or problem is. This may mean asking 'reflecting' questions, which ensure that the problem is expressed as the individual sees it. 'From what you have been telling me, am I right in believing that your situation/problem is ...?'

☐ *Avoid being judgemental.* A counselling session aims to help people, not to criticise them (ie by making unwelcome moral judgements). If an individual engaged in counselling is judgemental, the other party is likely to clam up or go on the defensive, and the rapport established by attentive listening will be destroyed.

☐ *Define the problem.* Encourage individuals to define the problem for themselves with the aid of sympathetic listening and careful questions. A considerable amount of listening and questioning may be necessary before the point becomes clear, because clarity of expression and strong emotions seldom go together. It is desirable to summarise, reflect and probe gently, asking such questions as 'Is this what you are telling me?', 'Is that the situation?', 'Is there anything else you think you want to tell me?', 'Are there any other factors that preceded this situation?', 'Is there anything more you can tell me about the circumstances in which this problem arose?', 'What part did you play?', 'Who else was involved, and what did they do?'

☐ *Change the perspective.* Talking through the problem may change a person's perspective and lead towards the development of a solution. But this does not always happen. It may be necessary to ask more challenging questions to encourage the person to see the situation or problem in a new light – such questions as 'On reflection, do you think there is any other way in which you could look at this problem?', 'Have you considered ...?', 'What would happen if you ...?' If an open atmosphere of trust and acceptance has been created in the initial listening stage, it will be possible to use these 'challenging' questions to help the person to understand more about what can be done about the problem.

☐ *Stay alert and flexible* – the meeting ought to be planned to decide broadly how it should be tackled, but the counsellor should be prepared to change direction in the light of new information.

☐ *Observe behaviour* – how the person talks, reacts and responds.

☐ *Conclude the meeting* – help people to work out a solution to the problem that they can put into effect, possibly with some help from the manager or another person. They can be prompted by asking such questions as 'Well, what do you think you should do now?', 'What do you think is the best way to deal with this situation?', 'Where do we go from here?', 'How could I help?', 'Is there any other help you feel you need?'

21 PERFORMANCE PROBLEM-SOLVING

Performance management is a positive process. It helps people to build on success, but it also provides the impetus for people to improve their performance – to solve their work problems. In this chapter, we examine the overall approach to managing underperformers, the basic steps that are required to address work problems, how performance weaknesses can be dealt with at review meetings, and the part that discipline and capability procedures play in managing performance.

The overall approach

The approach to solving performance problems should be based on re-inforcement theory. As Handy (1989) has put it, this is about 'applauding success and forgiving failure'. He suggests that mistakes should be used as an opportunity for learning – 'something only possible if the mistake is truly forgiven because otherwise the lesson is heard as a reprimand and not as an offer of help'.

What organisations can do to solve performance problems

Poor performance may be a result of inadequate leadership, bad management or defective systems of work. All are probably the result of a failure of whoever is at the top of the organisation to establish well-defined and unequivocal expectations for superior performance. As Robert Schaffer (1991) has said, 'The capacity for demand-making may be the most universally underdeveloped managerial skill.'

Organisations can provide the climate and the processes for solving performance problems by:

☐ creating a culture in which success is applauded but in which the approach is to minimise the likelihood of failure; if it does occur, steps should be taken to ensure that lessons are learned to prevent repetition in the future

☐ developing performance-management processes that set standards against which performance can be reviewed and deficiencies rectified by individuals, the individuals' managers or by both acting jointly

☐ training managers in how to handle performance and disciplinary problems

☐ continually monitoring performance and analysing the reasons for failure in order to develop organisational solutions (improvement in processes and systems, better resourcing and organisational development programmes)

☐ ensuring that organisational learning is encouraged, so that if performance problems occur, people will generally know what to do to avoid repetition

☐ foster a 'double-loop' learning approach, in which the root causes of problems are analysed and dealt with, rather than simply taking short-term corrective action.

What individuals can do to solve performance problems

The responsibility for solving performance problems rests with individuals and their managers. A joint problem-solving approach should be adopted, as described in this chapter. Coaching and counselling should be provided or organised by managers whenever appropriate during the year. Performance review meetings should provide 'quality time' in which the parties can reflect on general performance issues (no *post mortems* on isolated events) and agree on what is to be done by either or both in the future. Personal development plans (PDPs) should specify the areas of performance or behaviour in which learning needs to take place and the means by which this learning is to be achieved.

Addressing performance problems

As Stewart and Stewart (1982) suggest, 'Managing poor performance falls into three parts: spotting that there is a problem, understanding the causes of the problem and attempting a remedy'. Managers, as Schaffer (1991) suggests, sometimes use a variety of psychological mechanisms for avoiding the unpleasant truth that performance gaps exist. These mechanisms include:

□ *evasion through rationalisation*. Managers may escape having to demand better performance by convincing themselves that they have done all they can to establish expectations. They overlook the possibility of obtaining greater yields from available resources.

□ *reliance on procedures*. Management may rely on a variety of procedures, programmes and systems to produce better results. Top managers say, in effect, 'Let there be performance-related pay, or performance management or whatever' and sit back to wait for these panaceas to do the trick, which, of course, they will not unless they are part of a sustained and coherent effort led from the top, and are based on a vision of what needs to be done to improve performance.

□ *attacks that skirt the target*. Managers may set tough goals and insist that they are achieved, but still fail to produce a sense of accountability in subordinates.

Robert Schaffer suggested the following steps for dealing with these problems:

□ Select the goal.
□ Specify the minimum expectations of results.
□ Communicate expectations clearly.
□ Allocate responsibility.

Managing underperformers

Managing underperformers is a positive process which is based on feedback throughout the year that looks forward to what can be done by individuals to overcome performance problems and, importantly, how managers can help. The five basic steps required to manage them are these:

1 *Identify and agree the problem*. Analyse the feedback and, as far as possible, obtain agreement from the individual on what the shortfall has been. Feedback may be provided by managers, but it can in a sense be built into the job. This takes place when individuals are aware of

their targets and standards, know what performance measures will be used, and either receive feedback/control information automatically or have easy access to it. They will then be in a position to measure and assess their own performance and, if they are well motivated and well trained, take their own corrective actions. In other words, a self-regulating feedback mechanism exists. This is a situation that managers should endeavour to create, on the grounds that prevention is better than cure.

2 *Establish the reason(s) for the shortfall.* When seeking the reasons for any shortfall, the manager should not crudely be trying to attach blame. The aim should be for the manager and the individual jointly to identify the facts that have contributed to the problem. It is on the basis of this factual analysis that decisions can be made on what to do about it by the individual, the manager or the two of them working together.

It is necessary first to identify any causes outside the control of the individual. These include external pressures, changes in requirements, systems faults, inadequate resources (time, finance, equipment), jobs or tasks allocated to people without the necessary experience or attributes, inadequate induction and continuation training, and poor leadership, guidance or support from the manager, team leader or colleagues. Any factors within the control of the individual or the manager can then be considered. What has to be determined is the extent to which the reason for the problem is that individuals:

  □ did not receive adequate support or guidance from their manager
  □ did not fully understand what they were expected to do
  □ could not do it (ability)
  □ did not know how to do it (skill)
  □ would not do it (attitude).

3 *Decide and agree the action required.* Action may be taken by the individual, the manager, or both parties as follows:

  □ Jointly take steps to improve skills.

□ Change behaviour. This is up to individuals, as long as they accept that their behaviour needs to be changed. The challenge for managers is that people will not change their behaviour simply because they are told to do so. They can only be helped to understand that certain changes to their behaviour could be beneficial not only to the organisation but also to themselves. Approaches to behavioural modification are described below.

□ Change attitudes. Changing behaviour is easier than changing attitudes, which may be deep-rooted. The sequence is therefore to change behaviour first, so far as this is possible, and allow attitude changes to follow.

□ The manager provides more support or guidance.

□ Jointly clarify expectations.

□ Jointly develop abilities and skills. These are joint in the sense that individuals may be expected to take steps to develop themselves, but managers may provide help in the form of coaching, additional experience or training.

□ Jointly redesign the job. Whatever action is agreed, both parties must understand how they will know that it has succeeded. Feedback arrangements can be made but individuals should be encouraged to monitor their own performance and take further action as required.

4   *Resource the action.* Provide the coaching, training, guidance, experience or facilities required to enable agreed actions to happen.

5   *Monitor and provide feedback.* Both managers and individuals monitor performance, ensure that feedback is provided or obtained and analysed, and agree on any further actions that may be necessary.

Behavioural modification

Behavioural modification uses the behavioural principle *operant conditioning* (ie influencing behaviour by its consequences). Five steps for behavioural modification have been defined by Luthans and Kreitner (1975):

1   *Identify the critical behaviour* –what people do or do not do that has to be changed.

2   *Measure the frequency* – obtain hard evidence that a real problem exists.

3   *Carry out a functional analysis* – identify the stimuli that precede the behaviour and the consequences in the shape of reward or punishment that influence the behaviour.

4   *Develop and implement an intervention strategy* – this may involve the use of positive or negative reinforcement to influence behaviour (ie providing or withholding financial or non-financial rewards).

5   *Evaluate the effects of the intervention* – what improvements, if any, happened and, if the interventions were unsuccessful, what should be done next?

Handling problems at performance review meetings

Although the management of performance is a continuous process, formal performance reviews provide a good opportunity to analyse and to reflect on performance problems and to agree solutions. These discussions will be based on feedback that involves providing constructive criticism or self-assessment as described in Chapter 18.

Criticising constructively is not something all managers either like doing or do well. Fletcher (1993a) believes that:

> when tackling performance weaknesses you should remember that there may be aspects of a person's performance that are only weak in comparison with that individual's overall performance and not weak in comparison with other people. If this is the case, you should point it out to the appraisee saying, in effect, that your aim is to help the good to become better.

He has suggested the following methods of handling criticism:

☐ Let reviewees know that their frankness in identifying any shortcomings is appreciated.

☐ Get reviewees to produce their own ideas on remedial action.

☐ Provide reviewees with reassurance if they mention an

aspect of their performance that falls below their own standards but that you think is satisfactory.

☐ If reviewees do not agree that there is a problem, be firm but specific, giving examples.

☐ Confine comments to weaknesses that can be put right; don't try to alter the reviewee's personality.

☐ Don't tackle more than two weaknesses in one meeting – there is a limit to how much criticism individuals can take without becoming defensive.

Performance management and discipline

The positive approaches to solving performance are joint analysis and problem-solving, and counselling. If these and the other ways of managing performance mentioned earlier in this chapter do not produce the desired improvements, there may be no alternative but to leave the performance-management process and enter the disciplinary procedure. This should start with an informal warning, followed by a formal written warning if the informal warning is not heeded and, as a last resort, dismissal or some other disciplinary action.

Disciplinary procedures should be handled in accordance with the principles of natural justice, which are these:

☐ Individuals should know the standards of performance they are expected to achieve and the rules to which they are expected to conform.

☐ They should be given a clear indication of where they are at fault or what rules they have broken.

☐ They should be given a chance to explain or defend themselves.

☐ Except in cases of gross misconduct, they should be given an opportunity to improve before disciplinary action is taken.

Warnings should always spell out the problem and indicate as specifically as possible what employees have to do, or how they are expected to behave, to avoid the invocation of the next stage of the disciplinary procedure. Employees should be given every chance to respond to the warning and be allowed to appeal against it if, in spite of their objections, the warning is confirmed. Help in the form of further counselling, coaching or training should be offered wherever possible: the aims are to ensure that the informal warning will overcome the problem and that no further disciplinary action has to be taken.

Although disciplinary action can be used as a means of overcoming performance problems, it should be treated as a separate procedure that is not regarded as part of the normal processes of performance management. These processes may help to identify performance problems that should be dealt with on the spot, if at all possible. Only if this fails should these problems be transferred to the disciplinary system for resolution.

This separation of performance-management processes from disciplinary procedures is important because of the serious harm that would be done to the positive performance improvement and developmental aspects of performance management if employees felt that the process were simply being used to collect evidence for use against them. Performance reviews can become threatening affairs if they are perceived as placing in the hands of management sticks with which they can beat employees.

If the problem has to be transferred to the disciplinary procedure for resolution, it is highly desirable to state what it is in full, with any available supporting evidence. Reference can be made to the fact that the problem was identified earlier as part of the continuing process of performance management, but the content of any performance-review form produced following a review meeting should not be used as evidence. The disciplinary warning must be complete in itself.

Handling disciplinary interviews

As described by Fowler (1995), the following steps to conducting a disciplinary interview should be adopted:

☐ Make sure that you have got all the facts in advance and decide how you are going to tackle the interview.

☐ Give employees notice that the interview is going to take

place so that they can be prepared and can get a representative to accompany them.

□ Arrange for a colleague to be present to help conduct the interview and to take notes.

□ State the complaint to the employee, giving chapter and verse, and also giving supporting statements from other people involved, where appropriate.

□ Allow employees to give their side of the story and call any supporting witnesses.

□ Question employees and their witnesses and allow them to do the same.

□ Allow time for a general discussion of the issues raised and any other relevant issues.

□ Give employees an opportunity to have a final say, and mention any mitigating circumstances.

□ Sum up the points emerging from the meeting as you see them, but allow employees to comment on them, and be prepared to amend your summary.

□ Adjourn the meeting so that you can consider your decision on the basis of what has come out in the interview. It is best not to announce the decision during the initial meeting. The adjournment may be only half an hour or so in a straightforward case. It could be longer in a more complex one.

□ Reconvene the meeting and announce your decision.

□ Confirm your decision in writing.

Substandard work – the main points to watch

As stated in the Industrial Relations Legal Information Bulletin No. 452 (July 1992), the main points to watch in dealing with substandard work are:

□ careful recruitment – fitting the right person into the right job

□ a probationary period, where appropriate

□ giving employees adequate guidance on the standards required and proper training

□ if poor performance is suspected, establishing the position by an appropriate method of assessment – in some circumstances a single or extreme act of negligence or incompetence may make such assessment unnecessary

□ establishing the cause of substandard work, which may be incapability or misconduct, or a combination of the two

□ fair procedures for dealing with poor-performance problems

□ dismissal, if an employee's performance persistently falls short of the required standard, although alternatives should be considered, such as transfer to more suitable work

□ redundancy, if substandard work has arisen because the job has changed and the employee lacks the necessary skills (and cannot acquire them), and there is no suitable alternative work

□ compensation, if the dismissal for substandard work is found to be unfair, although the sum may be reduced if the employee contributed to the dismissal.

Capability procedure

There is much to be said for having a capability procedure to deal specifically with performance problems, leaving other disciplinary matters such as absenteeism to be dealt with through a disciplinary procedure. The following is an example of a capability procedure as set out in the *Croner Employment Digest*, 17 May 1993, page 2.

Policy
The company will at all times endeavour to ensure that employees achieve and maintain a high standard of performance in their work. To this end it will ensure that standards are established, performance is monitored and employees are given appropriate training and support to meet these standards.

Procedure
1 Where the manager/supervisor first establishes that an employee's performance is unacceptable, an informal discussion will be held with the employee to try to establish the reason. Should this discussion result in a decision that the

established standards are not reasonably attainable, the standards will be reviewed.

2 Should the interview establish that the performance problems are related to the employee's personal life, the necessary counselling/support will be provided. However, if it becomes apparent that the poor performance constitutes misconduct, the disciplinary procedure will be invoked.

3 If it is decided that the poor performance emanates from a change in the organisation's standards, those standards will be explained to the employee and help will be offered to obtain conformity with the standards.

4 Should the employee show no (or insufficient) improvement over the next ... weeks/months, a formal interview will be arranged between the employee (together with a representative if so desired) and ... The aims of this interview will be to:

(a) identify the cause(s) of the performance and to determine what – if any – remedial treatment (eg training, retraining, support, etc) can be given

(b) explain clearly the shortfall between the employee's performance and the required standard

(c) obtain the employee's commitment to reaching that standard

(d) set a reasonable period for the employee to reach the standard and agree on a monitoring system during that period and

(e) tell the employee what will happen if that standard is not met.

The outcome of this interview will be recorded in writing and a copy will be given to the employee.

At the end of the review period a further formal interview will be held, at which time:

(a) if the required improvement has been made, the employee will be told of this and encouraged to maintain the improvement

(b) if some improvement has been made but the standard has not yet been met, the review period will be extended

(c) if there has been no discernible improvement ... will explain to the employee that he or she has failed to improve. Consideration will be given to whether there are alternative vacancies which the employee would be competent to fill. If there are, the employee will be given the option of accepting such a vacancy or being dismissed.

(d) if such vacancies are available, the employee will be given full details of such vacancies, in writing, before being required to make a decision

(e) in the absence of suitable alternative work, the employee will be told that the employee will be invited to give his or her views on this before the final decision is taken.

Employees may appeal against their dismissal by writing to ... at the company's address, stating the reasons for their appeal. The appeal must be made within ... working days.

PART V

DEVELOPING AND MAINTAINING PERFORMANCE MANAGEMENT

22 INTRODUCING PERFORMANCE MANAGEMENT

It is not too difficult to conceive how performance management should function. It is much harder to ensure that it works in practice. It takes time, energy and determination to launch performance management successfully. It is necessary to start by understanding the development framework and the contextual factors affecting performance management. Against this background, the next steps are to:

□ conduct a diagnostic review

Figure 21
THE DEVELOPMENT FRAMEWORK

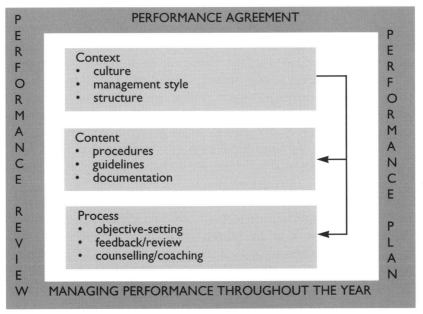

□ set objectives for performance management
□ prepare and carry out the development and implementation
   programme.

The development framework

Performance management can be regarded as a framework, as
illustrated in Figure 21 (adapted from Armstrong 1994),
within which a number of factors operate affecting how it
should be developed, introduced and evaluated.

The framework for performance management is provided
by the arrangements for agreeing performance requirements
or expectations, preparing performance plans, managing performance throughout the year and reviewing performance.

Environmental (cultural and structural) factors

Inside this framework lie the contextual factors of culture,
management style and structure, which will strongly influence
the content of performance-management procedures, guidelines and documentation, and the all-important processes that
make it work (objective-setting, attribute and competence
analysis, providing feedback, counselling and coaching).

Cultural considerations affect performance management
because the latter works best when it fits the existing values
of the organisation. Ideally, these should support high performance, quality, involvement, openness, freedom of communication and mutual trust. These may not have been put
into practice in full, however vigorously they have been
espoused. But top management must genuinely want to move
in these directions, and have to make it clear that they, like
everyone else, should go along with them, using performance
management as a lever for change.

Structural considerations also affect the way in which performance management is introduced. In a highly decentralised
organisation, or one in which considerable authority and
power are devolved to some functions or divisions, it may be
appropriate to encourage or permit each unit or function to
develop its own approach to performance management, as long
as they conform to central guidelines on its basic principles.

The cultural and structural factors to be taken into account vary considerably between organisations, which is why there is no single best way to develop and introduce performance management.

Performance-management development programme

The starting-point for the development programme should be a diagnostic review, as described below. On the basis of this review, agreement can be reached on the drivers for performance management. The procedural and design points can then be dealt with, and the final arrangements for pilot schemes and implementation made.

Diagnostic review

The diagnostic review should cover the following points:

Context – data on:

- the organisation's culture, values and management style
- structure – the degree of centralisation and devolution, and the extent to which the organisation is hierarchical, or team- or process-based
- systems and processes
- strategic plans
- organisational core competences/critical success factors
- stakeholders – an analysis of who they are, what part they play, what their expectations are, what influence they exert.

Strengths and weaknesses of present arrangements for:

- managing, measuring and reviewing performance
- paying for performance
- developing performance, skill and competence
- integrating business, team and individual objectives.

A *diagnosis* of:

- what needs to be done
- why it needs to be done
- how it should be done.

An *assessment* of:

☐ costs
☐ benefits.

Drivers for introducing performance management

The drivers for performance management should be determined and agreed by top management. The aims could include some or all of the following:

☐ To reinforce a performance-oriented culture, or to help change an existing culture to becoming more performance-oriented.

☐ To weld together different parts of the organisation with different cultures.

☐ To improve the performance of individuals and teams – performance-driven performance management.

☐ To develop the skills, competences and potential of employees – development-driven performance management.

☐ To provide the information on performance required for performance-related pay (PRP) – reward-driven performance management.

☐ To provide for increased and sustained motivation – motivation-driven performance management.

☐ To empower people – giving them more scope to exercise control over and take responsibility for their work.

☐ To help in the integration of organisational, functional, departmental, team and individual objectives.

☐ To provide for an extra channel of communication about matters concerning work.

☐ To provide a framework within which managers can improve their performance in the processes of clarifying responsibilities, delegation, monitoring and reviewing performance, and developing their staff.

☐ To attract and retain skilled staff.

☐ To support total quality management (TQM).

Procedural points

Where and how should performance management be introduced? Performance management is usually introduced on an organisation-wide basis, starting at the top. In most cases the philosophy, principles and key procedures and processes are developed centrally.

In a highly decentralised organisation, separate business units may be allowed to decide for themselves whether they want performance management, and, if they do, to develop it on their own.

An intermediate approach adopted by some decentralised organisations is for the centre (top management) to require all divisions and business units to introduce performance management in accordance with certain general principles, which the centre lays down. The business units proceed to develop their own processes, but the centre provides help as required, and may monitor the introduction of performance management in each division to ensure that it is happening according to plan and in line with corporate principles and values.

The most common, and the best, method of introduction is to set up a project team or working group for this purpose, with management and staff representatives. This provides for different opinions and experiences to be considered, serves as a base for wider consultation and communications to take place, and generally helps to achieve ownership.

There may be a central project team to draw up the basic principles of performance management, but some organisations have also provided for the full involvement of line management and employees by introducing it progressively in each major division or function. The management team of the department acts as its own working group, and decides in full consultation with members of the department how it will operate. A series of workshops may be held within the division or department to brief and train managers and staff. Assistance will be given to this development programme by members of the central project team or the HR department, or an external consultant. This approach is also designed to enhance ownership: the aim is to get each division or department to believe that this is their scheme, which fits into their normal pattern of working (objective-setting, planning and reviewing). Members of the project team and other champions of performance management can perform the important role of advising and guiding their colleagues on performance-management processes.

Who should be covered?

Another important decision to be made at the outset is who should be covered by performance management. At one time most schemes were restricted to managers, but performance management is now more generally being extended to all professional, administrative, technical and support staff. Some organisations also include shop-floor workers, especially high-tech firms, those that rely on production by high-performance work teams, companies with integrated pay structures and terms and conditions of employment (often high-tech or international firms) and companies with PRP for manual workers.

Different approaches according to level?

If performance management does cover managers and professional or technical staff, administrative, clerical and support staff and (possibly) manual workers, a decision has to be made on whether the same approach should be used for everybody.

Many organisations believe that it would be invidious to distinguish between levels so far as the essence of the approach is concerned, although different performance measures may be used. Some organisations do distinguish between roles where, on the one hand, quantified and regularly updated short-term objectives will be set and, on the other, those where continuing performance standards are more usual. In the former case they may refer to the key-result areas of the job as 'principal accountabilities'; in the latter they may use such terms as 'main tasks' or 'key activities'.

It may also be recognised that the objective-setting and review process in more routine jobs may not need to be as exhaustive as for those in managerial or professional roles.

Design points

The following points should be considered when designing performance-management processes:

- the process model – performance agreements
- use of objectives and competencies
- how objectives will be cascaded down, and how individuals and teams will contribute to their formulation
- link to PRP, if any
- ratings, if any
- what performance measures will be used
- how competencies will be defined and measured
- what documentation will be required, and who keeps it
- the extent to which flexibility will be allowed in carrying out performance-management processes.

Development and implementation points

The following points should be clarified for the development and implementation programme:

- the people who will be involved in the programme and their responsibilities
- the timetable for development and implementation
- arrangements for communicating details of the plan and the scheme to employees (it is vital that this should be done thoroughly and in good time)
- arrangements for training (also vital)
- pilot-scheme arrangements (it is generally desirable to pilot-test the scheme)
- success criteria
- arrangements for monitoring and evaluating implementation.

Pilot tests

There is much to be said for pilot-testing at least some aspects of performance management – bearing in mind that the usual cycle lasts 12 months, and it may therefore be difficult to pilot-test the whole process.

The aspects of performance management that can be tested are drawing up performance agreements, objective-setting and document completion.

Prepare briefing papers

Overall brief

It is desirable to issue an overall description of performance management to all employees that sets out its objectives and method of operation, along with the benefits it is expected to provide for the organisation and its managers and employees. Some organisations have prepared elaborate and lengthy briefing documents but fairly succinct documents often suffice, as long as they are written in simple language and are well produced.

Oral briefings

It is desirable to supplement written with oral briefings through a briefing group system, if there is one, or a special briefing programme. In a large or dispersed organisation, this briefing will have to be carried out by line managers, and they should be issued with special briefing packs and, possibly, a list of typical questions and their answers. An example of a question-and-answer document for use by managers when briefing is given in Appendix I.

Plan implementation programme

The implementation programme should cover the:

☐ date of introducing performance management in the whole, or different parts of, the organisation (phased as necessary)
☐ briefing plan
☐ training programme
☐ procedure for evaluating the process (see Chapter 24).

Case-studies on developing and implementing performance management

The following examples refer to the experiences of organisations in introducing performance management.

HR consultancy

When a large HR consultancy set about developing a performance management system for partners, they reviewed opinion about what was needed and found massively different opinions in different parts of the business. They decided to identify a number of key principles (relating to objective-setting in the strategic domains, and giving and receiving feedback), and not to design a process.

Individual discussions were held with the partners responsible for each office in order to encourage them to take ownership and responsibility for the partner-review process in accordance with agreed principles. Each partner was free to work out how the processes of collecting feedback, objective-setting, and conducting performance reviews etc were going to work in their office.

Edinburgh City Council
Background

This information refers to the former Lothian Regional Council, which was abolished at the time of local government re-organisation in Scotland in April 1986, when Edinburgh City Council was formed. There were about 18,000 employees in 15 departments in Lothian Regional Council, which has been promoted as a best-practice approach within Edinburgh City Council.

The evolution of the Lothian Regional Council process

The initial step in developing a performance-management process to replace an existing performance appraisal scheme was taken in 1990. In that year, the administration produced a strategic four-year plan for its years in office. Departmental heads were required to develop work plans to help achieve the strategic objectives contained in the four-year plan. Simultaneously the Accounts Commission for Scotland produced performance indicators for councils that had to produce information on performance for each indicator. Thus the concept of measuring performance was reinforced.

Within Lothian Regional Council, attitude surveys were carried out in the larger departments that indicated a significant proportion of staff would welcome a performance management approach.

The Department of Management and Information Services, Personnel Division drew up the basic principles of the desired approach to performance management (see below). Departmental working groups were set up with a brief to develop a process that suited them within the overall framework. Personnel facilitated the groups. The unions were consulted (NALGO, then UNISON), and were broadly in favour of performance management, but were absolutely opposed to PRP. Ten out of the 15 departmental groups developed and introduced performance management. The differences between approaches were often insignificant.

The performance-management process in Lothian Regional Council covered only chief officials, professional, technical, administrative and clerical staff. Manual workers were excluded (this would have been too difficult at that time).

The basic principles are:

- the process should be based on agreeing objectives (cascaded from council strategic objectives)
- performance should be monitored against objectives
- management information should be made available to measure performance
- an annual appraisal meeting should take place, with an emphasis on employee development
- communications and involvement are important – passing on information, team briefing etc
- emphasis on teamwork – teams setting their own objectives, monitoring their performance and making improvements.

The process starts with a joint meeting to agree objectives. The review meeting is regarded as a stocktaking exercise. There should be no surprises, and performance problems should be dealt with during the year as and when they arise. The disciplinary procedure is entirely separate and evidence emerging from formal performance reviews is not allowed in disciplinary hearings.

Evaluation

Sheena Robertson, senior employee development adviser, carried out evaluation formally and by means of a focus group with working-group leaders. One important result is that training is much more focused on individual needs.

A few managers were hostile ('a waste of time'), indifferent or cynical (they'd seen it all before). Professional staff generally felt that they were there to be professional, not to achieve objectives. However, a number of young administrative staff liked the scheme because they saw it as 'a way of proving that I am competent and want to get on'. Favourable comments by working-group leaders included the following:

- ☐ 'Difficult to establish if improvements in service delivery flow directly from performance management. It is considered, however, that the clearer objectives and timescales have contributed to improved performance.'

- ☐ 'As a result of performance management, we have developed better communications with our target groups through regular information newsletters, and have become more responsive through clearer consultations.'

- ☐ 'Generally, setting and reviewing objectives has, along with the introduction of the resource management system, produced a better understanding of monitoring management. Need to go back to customers to see if service delivery has improved.' (This department had carried out a customer survey prior to developing a system for introducing performance management and therefore should be able to assess any improvements.)

- ☐ 'The setting of objectives has allowed work to be more focused, eg preparation of annual reports. Reduced complaints. Improved staff morale.'

- ☐ 'Performance review procedure is being adopted within ISO 9902.'

- ☐ 'Helped to identify issues and tackle them.'

- ☐ 'By properly identifying and targeting needs of staff, service should improve.'

Lessons learned

The main lessons learned from the evaluation were first the importance of visible commitment by senior management, especially because the process relies on cascading objectives from departmental to individual level, and second that the annual review process needs strong drivers to take the process forward and make sure timetables are adhered to. Where these were lacking, the process soon ground to a halt. By having one-to-one appraisal interviews with their immediate line manager, employees had a better understanding of what was expected of them, and felt their needs and problems were being addressed – especially during the period prior to local government reorganisation. Training budgets were increased in some areas to meet the demand for individual training identified through the appraisal process.

Introducing performance-management systems developed by working groups (which comprised representatives from every level of the department or division, including a trade-union representative) can be time-consuming. However, the evaluation showed that consultation and involvement did lead to more commitment to the principles of managing for performance from both managers and employees.

Cummins Engine Company

Jose Pottinger, director–personnel, believes that performance management should be introduced by an educative process – 'encouraging, supporting and setting a sense of direction'.

Car manufacturer

The importance of context was emphasised by the HR manager, who explained that 'I had to design something that could be easily understood by everyone that related to this office and to the work in this office.'

Food manufacturer

The implementation of performance management was mainly about pulling together a number of component parts. It was concerned more with making explicit links between the business plan, people plans and individual objectives than it was about making a fundamental change. HR people from all the regions were brought in for training, and given resources and presentation packs to take back to their business units.

Kent County Council

Formal evaluations through attitude surveys were conducted in 1992 and 1993. Further detailed management feedback was obtained from two large departments in the 'making connections' programme.

The main findings of this initial evaluation were that:

☐ the quality of appraisal was patchy

☐ the pay factor was not so motivating as had been hoped – people felt that PRP was unfair, that it was spread too thinly and that it went only to staff who had the opportunity to demonstrate effectiveness

☐ the process was a 'ritual bureaucracy'

☐ people questioned the reason for doing it because 80 per cent got an increment

☐ the review was crammed into a busy time of the year

☐ rewards were made inconsistently.

It was then decided, in 1995, that the system should be changed to reflect these concerns and new thinking about the process within Kent County Council. Chief officers were given freedom to develop departmental schemes that best meet service and development needs, as long as these are aligned to the principles of 'the Kent scheme'.

Financial services organisation

Prior to the introduction of a new appraisal system, focus groups were conducted with staff all around the country, facilitated by external consultants. Draft copies of assessment forms and guidance notes were prepared and 'played back' to more focus groups in an iterative process that resulted in 81 versions. Ahead of the launch, workshops were run for regional HR people, which included helping them to tailor the implementation locally. This was very different from the old culture, in which everything was done from the centre.

Utilities-sector organisation

'Best practice' was identified by benchmarking externally and by consulting the old personal development process used in the corporate centre. It was entirely driven by HR people, with no external consultants. Unions were invited to comment at the end of the process rather than participate in the development.

A pilot scheme, including introduction, training and follow-up, was run. This identified two major issues:

☐ Initially, the training was delivered by external providers. It was criticised for being too focused on theory and not relevant. In the full implementation, all training was delivered by the appraisals manager.

☐ The complexity of the paperwork was also criticised; this too was addressed.

The implementation has proceeded far less painfully than was expected. In the opinion of the personnel manager, the strengths of their approach were:

☐ openness – the implementation was accompanied by a large-scale communication exercise

☐ the fact that there was a pilot scheme enabling issues to be resolved prior to full implementation

☐ the fact that the pilot covered all functions – front and back office – meant that the final product was designed to suit everyone.

23 LEARNING ABOUT PERFORMANCE MANAGEMENT

There was no doubt that the research evidence we collected, including the focus group discussion, indicated that one of the keys to success in introducing and sustaining performance management was the range and quality of training provided to managers, team leaders and individuals.

The approach to performance-management training

As Armstrong and Murlis (1994) point out, recent developments in performance-management training have treated it as a developmental process that enables managers to get to the heart of how they can manage and coach people more effectively, and that helps other staff to get the most out of their involvement. Typical approaches to performance-management training are likely to focus on:

□ delivering training on a 'just-in-time' basis to ensure that learning is re-inforced as soon as possible after it has been received

□ concentrating initially on learning styles (eg Kolb's) because people have to understand how they themselves learn and how they can help others to learn

□ working on organisation climate and management style, so that those responsible for performance management gain a well-articulated idea of the ways in which their own management styles affect the organisational climate

□ conducting coaching workshops so that the principles of coaching to improve performance are properly understood and related to the current operating environment

□ working on performance-planning in relation to both the 'what' and 'how' of performance, so that a fully rounded understanding of performance against business objectives is built in, together with means of tracking performance and personal development through the year

□ conducting performance-review workshops to re-inforce the coaching and feedback messages of earlier training, and to ensure that reviewers have the chance to get some coaching and support when they need help, notably with any intractable performance problems

□ working on the consistency of review, reward and recognition processes to ensure that common values apply and to reduce the risk of patchy implementation; the relationship of performance management with both the pay system (if applicable) and development processes should be clearly distinguished so that people understand the purpose and nature of each of them.

Objectives

Performance management training has three main objectives:

1 To let people know about the whys and wherefores of the processes with which they will be involved – these will include the business drivers that have led the organisation to introduce performance management as well as a description of the processes involved.

2 To spell out their contribution – why it is important, how they make it and the benefits that will accrue to them and the organisation.

3 To train people in the skills they have to use.

The whys and wherefores

It was suggested to us by Allen Cave of the Performance Management Group that training in performance-management processes and skills should concentrate on answering the following questions:

□ *Why performance management?* – defining the business case for it

□ *What does performance management consist of?* – getting people to understand the processes involved.

□ *How should performance processes be carried out?* – the skills involved.

All these areas are important, but it is vital to make the business case for performance management: 'This is what it will contribute to improving organisational effectiveness and overall performance.'

Performance management may be regarded with suspicion ('a waste of time', 'another method of coercion') or cynicism ('we've seen it all before', 'it won't work'). The reasons for introducing it should be spelled out in a briefing document or performance-management guide and presented orally to employees (see Chapter 22). This should clarify why the organisation believes performance management is important – how it is thought it will help to drive improved performance to the benefit of all the stakeholders.

But this information should be re-inforced with face-to-face briefings. These can be conducted through briefing groups or, in a dispersed organisation, a travelling roadshow. Without being too slick, the presentations should make good use of visual aids.

Seminars or workshops can be used to provide more in-depth understanding. Opportunities can then be created not only to discuss reasons and benefits, but also for people who have voiced any doubts and fears to have them answered. A detailed description of each stage in the performance-management process and who does what and why can also be carried out.

The focus is ideally on formulating performance agreements, preparing and implementing personal development plans (PDPs), including the learning opportunities available, and monitoring and reviewing performance and development.

Contribution

It is important to re-inforce the broad briefing on the processes with more precise information on the parts played by managers, team leaders, teams and individuals. The emphasis should be on the need for partnership and dialogue, the open and honest exchange of information (feedback), and sharing the process to the mutual benefit of both parties.

When spelling out the contribution of managers and team leaders, the message should be that they are there to help and to coach, not to judge. For individuals, the message will be how they can benefit from self-assessment and the part they can play in developing themselves.

Skills

Performance management is not easy. It requires high levels of skill by everyone involved, but the skills are likely to be ones that have not yet been developed or put into practice. Providing feedback, for example, that will motivate and help to develop people does not come easy to those who have not done it before. Receiving, responding to and acting on feedback are similarly unfamiliar skills for many people.

The agreement of objectives and competence requirements, the application of performance measures and methods of analysing and using the outcomes of reviews may be strange. The concepts of personal development planning and self-managed learning will also be new to many people.

The main performance-management skills that people need to learn are:

☐ defining accountabilities and key-result areas
☐ defining objectives
☐ identifying and using performance measures
☐ defining and assessing competencies and behavioural requirements
☐ giving and receiving feedback
☐ questioning and listening
☐ identifying development needs and preparing and implementing PDPs
☐ diagnosing and solving performance problems
☐ coaching
☐ counselling.

These skills can be covered in a performance-management learning programme, which may take the form of modules dealing with the overall processes and skills – for example, a programme on reviewing performance such as the example given below.

Workshop aims

On completing this workshop, participants will:

☐ understand the purpose of performance reviews
☐ know how to prepare for a constructive review
☐ know how to conduct an effective performance review
☐ be able to provide good feedback
☐ have gained some initial understanding of the processes of coaching and counselling.

Programme

09.00	Objectives of the workshop
09.30	The purpose of the performance reviews
10.00	Preparing for the review
10.30	Coffee
10.45	Giving feedback
11.15	Conducting the review
12.30	Lunch
13.15	Practice in conducting reviews (1)
15.00	Tea
15.15	Practice in conducting reviews (2)
16.15	Introduction to coaching and counselling
17.00	Putting the review to good use
17.30	Close.

Examples of training programmes operated by Zeneca Pharmaceuticals are given in Appendix E.

Methods

Learning, especially skills development, should be achieved by participative methods: guided discussions, role plays and other exercises.

Guided discussion

The aim of guided discussions is to get participants to think through for themselves the learning-points. When covering review meetings, the trainer asks such questions as:

☐ What do you think makes for a good review meeting? Can you provide any example from your previous experience?

☐ What do you think can go wrong with a meeting? Have you any examples?

☐ Why is it important to create the right environment?

☐ How do you set about doing so?

☐ What sort of things should be discussed in a review meeting?

☐ Why is it important for managers to let the individual do most of the talking?

☐ Why could self-assessment be useful?

Role plays

Role plays are usually based on a written brief that defines the same situation from each participant's point of view so that they can understand what it feels like to be in either position.

Course members are then asked to play out the roles, after which fellow members assess their performance (this in itself provides some practice in performance assessment). Each person playing the role also describes his or her feelings about the review and assesses the other person's performance or behaviour.

Exercises

A more realistic approach is to get participants to perform a task on which they are appraised by fellow course members. This could be a group exercise. If there is sufficient time, each member can take it in turn to lead the group and be appraised on their performance by the rest. Such exercises may also be used to practise formulating team objectives and reviewing team performance.

A further variation, suggested by Clive Fletcher (1993a), is to get one course member to give a short presentation on a topic, have a second one assess the presenter and get a third person to assess the quality of the assessment. As Fletcher suggests:

The point about exercises of this kind is that, whilst they only allow the appraisal of performance in one isolated event, they do offer an opportunity to practise appraisal skills on genuine behavioural examples. The course members are ego-involved to the extent that they find it a demanding task with the minimum of artificiality.

Use of videos

The use of videos (there are a number available on the market) can be a valuable supplement to the other training methods, although they cannot replace them. They are particularly helpful if relatively inexperienced trainers have to be used (and, with the best will in the world, some organisations cannot afford to engage a highly skilled trainer in this subject).

Interactive video

Interactive video combines two powerful training technologies: computer-based training and video. It is both individualised and interactive, and the learner's needs and pace of learning can be accommodated with the software. Because it is interactive, it is an ideal method of learning performance-management skills.

Multimedia

Multimedia training uses (as the name suggests) a variety of media including audio, video, text, graphics, photography and animation combined to create an interactive programme delivered on a PC. It is well suited to learning about the interpersonal relations aspects of performance management, where scenarios and role plays can be used to practise and develop the skills required.

24 EVALUATING PERFORMANCE MANAGEMENT

One of the more interesting findings of our research was that only 44 per cent of organisations with performance management evaluated its effectiveness. But, as we have noted a number of times, performance management is easy to conceive but hard to deliver. To ensure that it is delivering what it was expected to deliver, it is essential to evaluate performance management, and it is quite remarkable that fewer than half the survey respondents attempted to do so.

This chapter considers how organisations can properly evaluate performance management. It contains a list of the areas to examine, a diagnostic check-list of what should be looked for when carrying out evaluations, and a review of the main methods of evaluation.

Areas for examination

Engelmann and Roesch (1995) have suggested that the following areas should be examined when evaluating a 'performance system':

- [ ] how well it supports the organisation's objectives
- [ ] how it is linked to the organisation's critical success factors
- [ ] how well it defines and establishes individual objectives
- [ ] how well it relates to job responsibilities and performance expectations
- [ ] how effectively it encourages personal development
- [ ] how easy (or difficult) it is to use
- [ ] how objective or subjective, clear or ambiguous evaluation criteria are

☐ whether it addresses company policies and procedures
☐ whether it is fairly and consistently administered
☐ how well supervisors and employees are trained to use and live under the system
☐ how it is linked to pay.

Diagnostic check-list: evaluation

To evaluate performance management, you must look for the following:

1 Performance-management processes fit the culture of the organisation, the context in which it operates and the characteristics of its people and work practices.

2 There is commitment and support from top management.

3 There is shared ownership with line managers and employees generally.

4 Processes are aligned to the real work of the organisation and the way in which, generally, performance is managed.

5 Performance-management processes help to integrate organisational, team and individual objectives.

6 It can be demonstrated that performance management adds value in terms of both short-term results and longer-term development.

7 Performance-management processes are integrated with strategic and business-planning processes.

8 Performance-management processes are integrated with other HR processes.

9 Performance-management processes can operate flexibly to meet local or special circumstances.

10 Performance-management processes are readily accepted by all concerned as natural components of good management and work practices.

11 All stakeholders within the organisation are involved in the design, development and introduction of performance management. These compose top management, line managers, team leaders, teams, individual employees and trade-union or employee representatives.

12 Performance-management processes are transparent and operate fairly and equitably.

13 Managers and team leaders take action to ensure that there is a shared understanding generally of the vision, strategy, goals and values of the organisation.

14 Performance-management processes recognise that there is a community of interests in the organisation and respect individual needs.

15 Performance-management processes are used by managers and team leaders to help people feel that they are valued by the organisation.

16 Performance-management processes help to align organisational and individual goals, but this is not a matter of a top-down 'cascade' of objectives. Individuals and teams are given the opportunity to put forward their views on what they can achieve, and their views are listened to.

17 The focus of performance management is demonstrably on the development of people. Financial rewards are a secondary consideration if, indeed, they are associated with performance management at all.

18 There are competence frameworks in place developed specially for the organisation with the full involvement of all concerned.

19 The aims and operation of performance management and how it can benefit all concerned are communicated thoroughly and effectively.

20 Training in performance-management skills is given to managers, team leaders *and* employees generally.

Evaluation methods

Questionnaires following review meetings

Evaluation can take place by asking individuals to complete a questionnaire immediately following a review meeting. The questionnaire could ask people to rate the effectiveness of the review meetings on a points scale. They would, for example, be asked to indicate their reactions – fully agree, partly agree, partly disagree, fully disagree – to the following statements (the questions might also establish how many people actually received a formal review):

1 I was given plenty of opportunity to contribute to formulating my objectives.
2 I am quite satisfied that the objectives I agreed to were fair.
3 I felt that the meeting to agree objectives helped me to focus on what I should be aiming to achieve.
4 I received good feedback from my manager during the year on how well I was doing.
5 My manager was always prepared to provide guidance when I ran into any problems with my work.
6 The performance review was conducted by my manager in a friendly and helpful way.
7 My manager fully recognised my achievements during the year.
8 If any criticisms were made during the review, they were based on fact, not on opinion.
9 I was given plenty of opportunity by my manager to discuss the reasons for any problems with my work.
10 I felt that generally the comments made by my manager at the review meeting were fair.
11 The review meeting ended with a clear plan of action for the future with which I agreed.
12 I felt well motivated after the meeting.

Attitude surveys

Attitude surveys can be conducted periodically using broadly the same questions as those referred to above. These could be an alternative to an immediate expression of opinion after a meeting.

Focus groups

Focus groups could be used to provide more in-depth feedback on how well performance management is working. The questions for discussion could be along the lines of those set out above, but there would be an opportunity to hear extended views supported by the reasons for expressing them. Interaction between members of the group may also create useful additional insights into the effectiveness, understanding and acceptance of performance management.

PART VI

CONCLUSIONS

25   THE REALITY OF PERFORMANCE MANAGEMENT

Overall findings of the research

The overall findings of the research were that, since the last survey by the (former) IPM (now the CIPD) of performance management in 1991, considerable changes in the approach to performance management have taken place, as shown in Figure 23.

These developments can be summarised as follows:

○ *From system to process.* In 1991, performance management was regarded as a 'system', a sort of mechanistic set of techniques that could be applied rigidly to any organisation, with the guarantee that it would deliver results in the form of improved performance. It is now more gener-

Figure 23
**DEVELOPMENTS IN PERFORMANCE MANAGEMENT
SINCE 1991**

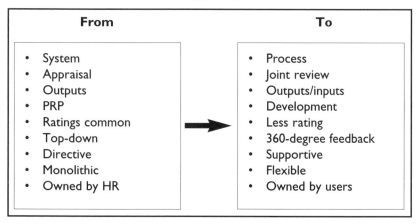

From	To
• System	• Process
• Appraisal	• Joint review
• Outputs	• Outputs/inputs
• PRP	• Development
• Ratings common	• Less rating
• Top-down	• 360-degree feedback
• Directive	• Supportive
• Monolithic	• Flexible
• Owned by HR	• Owned by users

ally seen as an integrated set of processes concerned with ways in which managing performance can be carried out. The emphasis is much more on *how* the management of performance is carried out – what the people involved do, and how they do it – than on a set of prescribed procedures and practices to be followed rigidly by all concerned.

☐ *From appraisal to joint review.* Performance management in the early 1990s still carried the baggage of the traditional performance appraisal scheme, in which the appraisal meeting was an annual event involving top-down and unilateral judgements by 'superiors' of their 'subordinates'. Since then, it has increasingly been perceived as a continuous process, involving reviews that focus on the future rather than the past, and for which the key words are 'dialogue', 'shared understanding', 'agreement' and 'mutual commitment'.

☐ *From outputs to inputs.* In 1991, the emphasis was still on objective-setting and the appraisal of results against goals ie outputs. This was more baggage – a hangover from the discredited management-by-objectives system. The difference now is that there is a realisation that a fully rounded view of performance must embrace *how* people get things done as well as *what* gets done ie inputs as well as outputs. This means using the so-called mixed model, considering skills and competence as well as results, inputs as well as outputs.

☐ *From PRP to development.* In the early days, performance management was associated closely with PRP, which to many people epitomised the 'system'. Lip-service may have been paid to the use of performance appraisal as a means of identifying training needs (to be met by sending people on courses), but the developmental aspects of the process were, strangely, neglected. It did not seem to be appreciated that the greatest added value to be derived from performance management was the role it could play in continuous development and self-development. Personal development plans (PDPs) had not been heard of in 1991. Yet in 1997–98 they became a major feature of per-formance-management processes. This does not mean that they always work as well as they are expected to, but the philosophy of planning personal development as part of the overall process has now become firmly embedded in the policies and practices of a large proportion of the organisations covered by our research.

☐ *Less prominence given to ratings.* At one time, performance appraisal was synonymous with performance-rating – another hangover from the old days (in this case, merit-rating). The need for rating is often justified by the need to have a basis for PRP decisions. Yet about a quarter of the organisations with PRP that responded to the IPD survey did *not* have ratings. The focus group research revealed considerable hostility to ratings shared by people at all levels in the organisations concerned. Increasingly, people are realising that ratings, as one HR director put it to us, 'denigrate the performance-management process'.

☐ *From top-down appraisal to 360-degree feedback.* The use of 360-degree feedback is still fairly small (11 per cent of the respondents to the IPD questionnaire). But interest is growing as the value of obtaining feedback from a number of different sources is becoming recognised.

☐ *From a directive to a supportive approach.* 'Best-practice' organisations recognise that performance management is not just another means of obtaining compliance to the achievement of objectives that have been cascaded down from some remote height. They treat it as a joint process that requires managers and team leaders to identify in discussion with individual team members (or their teams as a whole) what support they need to do their work well. This support may be provided in a number of ways, including exercising more effective leadership skills, coaching, counselling, guidance, training, redesigning roles or redefining team responsibilities, providing better resources (in the shape of equipment and facilities), and generally demonstrating that people are valued for what they contribute. A supportive approach is in line with the belief that individuals and teams are, in effect, the internal customers of their managers.

☐ *From monolithic to flexible.* Traditionally, performance

appraisal has been a monolithic and bureaucratic system imposed on line managers by the personnel department. Everyone had to conform to the same procedure, and the most important output has been a set of ticks on an elaborate form which, once made, were soon forgotten. Today there is much less bureaucracy in many organisations: forms are no longer the be-all and end-all of performance management. It has also been recognised by many people that performance management is a tool for managers to use in association with the members of their teams, and that they will use it most effectively if they apply it in their own particular way in accordance with their own particular circumstances. It is still desirable to define and communicate certain principles of the approach to performance management that are likely to produce the best results. And it is often desirable to provide structure and guidance that can be built around some fairly simple forms and procedures. Helping everyone to learn about how they can gain the most benefit from performance management is also important. But this is no longer regarded by many of the organisations we contacted as a set of prescriptions that everyone must follow to the letter.

☐ *From ownership by HR to ownership by the line.* The best-practice organisations we visited all stressed that they were concerned with the management of performance as the responsibility of line managers in conjunction with their teams. The idea that the personnel function was the sole guardian of performance standards through the performance appraisal-schemes it administered has been rejected for the nonsense that it is.

Best practice

We regard the concept of 'best practice' with some suspicion, because it seems to imply that, in the words of F. W. Taylor, there is 'one best way'. Best fit is more important than best practice, but it is still interesting to note what could be regarded as 'good practice' among the organisations we contacted. These can be

summarised as follows (the words in italics identify the organisation or sector providing the judgement):
A clear understanding of aims:

- [ ] enhance performance – *manufacturing*
- [ ] develop individuals to increase the added value they provide – *manufacturing*
- [ ] integration of objectives – 'We were deeply concerned that they should integrate,' – *HR director, services*
- [ ] achieving enhanced performance in the round – *agency*
- [ ] provide space for individuals to perform and grow – *oil company*
- [ ] provide support for individuals – *oil company*
- [ ] integral part of culture-change programme – *local authority*
- [ ] clarify expectations, link organisational and individual objectives, focus on improvement – *manufacturing*
- [ ] improve customer service – *financial services*
- [ ] define expectations, provide feedback – *charity*
- [ ] change culture, focus on performance – *manufacturing*
- [ ] improve business performance by raising each individual's effectiveness – *pharmaceuticals*
- [ ] foster better management – *NHS Trust*.

Principles:

- [ ] a management tool that will help managers to manage better – *charity*
- [ ] driven by corporate purpose and values – *manufacturing*
- [ ] inherent – 'We don't have to fight the ideological argument for performance management – it's there in the corporate thinking,' – *food industry*
- [ ] to obtain 'solutions that work' – *food industry*
- [ ] only interested in things you can do something about and get a visible improvement – *manufacturing*
- [ ] focus on changing behaviour rather than paperwork – *financial services*
- [ ] 'It's about how we manage people, it's not a system,' – *manufacturing*

- 'the company will not grow unless its people grow,' – *oil company*.

Development of process:

- agree principles and then devolve application to line managers – 'Right, over to you. These are the principles, you put them in place. We are here to give you support and advice on how to do this, if you want it,' – *head of management and career development, financial services.*
- maximum involvement of staff and trade unions at all stages – *charity*
- incremental – pick off departments one by one, leaving them to adapt principles to meet own requirements – *local authority*
- use line managers to sponsor or facilitate implementation – *pharmaceuticals*
- set framework to be filled by each directorate in line with principles – *local authority*
- recognise diversity – *museum*
- don't over-engineer – *financial services.*

Evaluation:

- comprehensive use of attitude surveys and focus groups – *retail*
- emphasis on mentoring and evaluation – *charity*
- use of balanced scorecard – *charity.*

Objectives:

- explicit cascading of objectives – 'As near to management by objectives as you can get without being in a state of rigor mortis,' – *HR director, services*
- clear distinction between objectives and standards – *museum*
- recognition that a different approach has to be taken in more routine jobs – *local authority.*

Competences/competencies:

- reaction against the competence concept – *clearing bank, museum*

□ use everyday language – *charity, NHS Trust*

□ develop organisational core competences (not competencies) and integrate role generic and specific competences with them – *charity*.

Views about performance management

The field research conducted by means of focus groups and attitude surveys revealed much more positive attitudes to performance management than the stereotyped views of many academic and other commentators might have led one to expect. Both managers and individuals on the whole *liked* the performance review process – the phrase 'quality time' recurred frequently. They liked the opportunity it gives for structured discussion, and they liked the opportunity it gives for managers and individuals to get away together from the hurly-burly of their everyday working lives. To a very large extent, the focus groups indicated that both parties felt they gained from the process. Remarkably few comments were made to the effect that it was a waste of time. Certainly, the outcome of the research was a very positive endorsement of this aspect of performance management. Nonetheless, there was much hostility to rating, which confirmed the belief that introducing a performance-appraisal or -rating element into performance management can seriously detract from what we, along with the majority of those who participated in the research, believed to be the main purpose of performance management: its focus on personal development.

Problems/issues identified by field visits

The following problems and issues were identified in the field visits:

□ culture of 'cram it all into one meeting,' – *financial services*

□ 'One number was your life; every other HR process locked on behind the appraisal,' – *financial services*

□ ability of managers to deliver the reward package – *financial services*

☐ excellent design, patchy implementation – *food industry*

☐ need to deliver on promises – *services*

☐ link between performance management and reward – *IT company, charity*

☐ excessive use of competence approach – *financial services*

☐ inadequate or no evaluation in many cases – *services.*

Conclusion: key issues

The key issues revealed by the research were:

☐ *managerial focus* – what do individual members of staff get out of it? Is performance management, as the academics claim, simply a manipulative device adopted by managements to obtain compliance? Is it all about 'cascading' objectives? Are the views of those at the receiving end of the cascade taken into account? Is it all about direction – developing a command-and-control culture? Are the principles of procedural justice applied? Is management aware that it is there to provide support as well as to exercise control? To what extent is management in the business of developing transferable skills and employability, beyond as well as within the firm? These questions must be answered by anyone contemplating the introduction of performance management or thinking about revising existing arrangements.

☐ *overengineering* – some schemes still contain a lot of elaborate documentation. There are two extreme schools of thought. One is that you must provide lots of boxes into which managers can enter ticks, because if you don't do that, *they* won't know what to do. The other extreme advocates the use of a blank sheet of paper, which gives managers freedom to do their own thing. An approach somewhere between these extremes is usually desirable. Managers generally like some sort of framework, but it should be helpful and easy to use.

☐ *a need to define what is meant by performance and how performance-management processes will enhance performance.* Performance management should address both aspects of performance: what people achieve, and how they achieve it. This enables performance expectations to be defined and managed, and provides the basis for taking steps to improve performance by changing behaviour or developing skills and competences. It should be focused on the things that matter in organisations – the critical success factors and core competences.

☐ *performance management for teams*. It was noticeable how few of the organisations we contacted made any special arrangements to operate performance management for teams. In view of the emphasis they all placed on teamwork, this is surprising, to say the least. Performance-management processes should address ways of developing more effective teams. They should not concentrate on individuals.

☐ *need for involvement and communication*. Managers, team leaders, individuals and their representatives should be involved in the design of performance-management processes to ensure that they meet their needs and to resolve any doubts about how useful and fair the processes will be. The use of a range of communication channels is desirable to ensure that everyone understands what performance management means, how it will affect them, and the part they will be expected to play.

☐ *need for thorough and all-round training*. Performance management requires skills that need to be developed. These skills are exercised by managers *and* individuals. Both need to be trained. There is no doubt that the favourable reactions to performance management in most of the focus groups we conducted arose because of the care with which all-round training had taken place.

☐ *easy to design, tough to implement*. It is easy to design forms and produce handbooks. It is much more difficult to get people to carry out performance-management processes effectively and with conviction. Time spent on implementation is always time well spent. The problems that may arise in achieving 'buy-in' by all concerned should never be underestimated: hence the importance of involvement, communication and training.

☐ *ownership by those who experience the process*. People

have got to feel that this is *their* process, which will help them as well as the organisation.

Keys to success

We conclude by quoting again what Gillian Henchley, head of personnel at the Victoria and Albert Museum, told us were what she believed to be the keys to the successful introduction and application of performance management:

- being clear about what is meant by performance
- understanding what the organisation is and needs to be in its performance culture
- being very focused on how individual employees will benefit and play their part in the process.

APPENDIX A

THE PERFORMANCE MANAGE-MENT SURVEY QUESTIONNAIRE

Section A – What is performance management?

1   Please indicate the extent to which you agree/disagree with the following statements.

	Strongly agree	Slightly agree	Slightly disagree	Strongly disagree
The most important aspect of performance management is the setting of challenging and stretching goals				
Performance management will inevitably become a bureaucratic chore				
Performance management will only succeed if it is part of an integrated approach to the management of people				
Performance management will only succeed if it integrates the goals of individuals with those of the organisation				
Performance-related pay is an essential part of performance management				
It is essential that line managers own the performance management system				
The focus of performance management should be developmental				
Performance management should be a continuous and integrated part of the employee – line manager relationship				
The main objective of performance management should be to motivate individuals				
Performance management is an essential tool in the management of organisational culture				
The effectiveness of performance management is easier to measure in qualitative rather than quantitative terms				
Everyone must be trained in performance management techniques for a PM system to be successful				
Performance management distracts people from more important core activities				
It is essential that performance management is accompanied by extensive communication to ensure its aims are fully understood				
Performance management should be distanced as far as possible from payment systems				
Quantifiable measures of performance are essential to successful performance management				

Section B – Organisational background

1   Which of the following economic sectors best describes your organisation?

Public sector $\square_1$ Private-sector manufacturing $\square_2$

Private-sector service/voluntary $\square_3$ Other (*please specify*) .... $\square_4$

2   Approximately how many people does your organisation employ?

50–99 $\square_1$ 100–499 $\square_2$ 500–999 $\square_3$ 1000 plus $\square_4$

How has this changed in the last two years (ie since January 1995)?

Up $\square_1$ Down $\square_2$ No change $\square_3$

3   What are the major elements of your business strategy at present? (Please rank those which you think are relevant in order of importance, with 1 being most important.)

Reduce costs $\square_1$ Increase productivity $\square_2$

Expand/develop markets $\square_3$ Develop skills/competence of workforce $\square_4$

Increase efficiency $\square_5$ Reduce headcount $\square_6$

Reduce production time $\square_7$ Develop new products or services $\square_8$

Improve quality $\square_9$ Other (*please specify*) .... $\square_{10}$

Section C – Nature of current performance arrangements

1   Does your organisation operate formal performance-management processes?

Yes $\square_1$ No $\square_2$

If yes, which of the following groups of employees do these processes apply to?

Senior managers $\square_1$ Other managers/team leaders $\square_2$

Technical/clerical $\square_3$ Professionals $\square_4$

Manual/blue-collar $\square_5$ Other (*please specify*) .... $\square_6$

Do the performance management processes you operate differ between the above groups?

Yes $\square_1$ No $\square_2$

If yes, please complete the rest of this questionnaire only for those performance-management arrangements which apply to the *largest group* within your workforce, and please specify by ticking the relevant boxes below which employees are included within this largest group.

Senior managers $\square_1$ Other managers/team leaders $\square_2$

Technical/clerical $\square_3$ Professionals $\square_4$

Manual/blue-collar $\square_5$ Other (*please specify*) .... $\square_6$

If you do not operate formal performance-management processes, have you any plans to do so within the next two years?

Yes ❑₁   No ❑₂   Don't know ❑₃

and have you had a performance-management system at any time in the last 10 years?

Yes ❑₁   No ❑₂   Don't know ❑₃

If yes, why did you abandon it?

Too costly   ❑₁ Too time-consuming   ❑₂
Lack of commitment from line managers ❑₃ Did not achieve objectives ❑₄
Other (*please specify*)................................. ❑₅

Please only proceed if you *do* operate formal performance management processes. If you do not, please return the form now in the pre-paid envelope provided.

2   Please indicate which of the following features of performance-management processes are included in your arrangements, and how effective you believe these to be.

	Are a feature	Very effective	Mostly effective	Partly effective	Not effective
Annual appraisal					
Twice-yearly (bi-annual) appraisal					
Rolling appraisal					
360-degree appraisal					
Peer appraisal					
Self-appraisal					
Subordinate feedback					
Continuous assessment					
Competence assessment					
Objective-setting and review					
Performance-related pay					
Coaching and/or mentoring					
Career management and/or succession-planning					
Personal development plans					
Other (*please specify*)					

3 Are individual, team, and organisational objectives linked? Yes ❏₁ No ❏₂

If yes, how are they linked? ....

4 Who sets the performance requirements for individuals? (Please tick as many boxes as appropriate.)

Senior managers   ❏₁   Line managers/team leaders   ❏₂
Personnel staff   ❏₃   Other (*please specify*) .... ❏₄

5 Is your organisation unionised?

Yes   ❏₁   No ❏₂   Partly ❏₃

If yes or partly, were current performance-management arrangements agreed with the union(s)?

Yes   ❏₁   No ❏₂

What was the attitudes of the union(s)?

Positive ❏₁   Neutral ❏₂   Negative ❏₃

6 Are the current performance-management arrangements:

A new system (ie developed within the last two years) ❏₁
A development of an older system   ❏₂
An old-established system   ❏₃
Other (*please specify*) .... ❏₄

7 How long did it take to develop the system?

Less than one year   ❏₁   More than one year but less than two years   ❏₂
More than two years   ❏₃

8 How long did it take to implement the system?

Less than one year   ❏₁   More than one year but less than two years   ❏₂
More than two years   ❏₃

9 Who was involved in the development and design of the system? (Please tick as many boxes as appropriate.)

All staff   ❏₁ Senior managers   ❏₂ Other managers/team leaders ❏₃
TU officials   ❏₄ Staff representatives ❏₅ Personnel staff   ❏₆

10 Who (if anybody) receives training in performance-management techniques? (Please tick as many boxes as appropriate.)

All staff   ❏₁   Appraisers ❏₂   Heads of department ❏₃
Personnel staff ❏₄   No one   ❏₅

Section D – Process of performance management

1 To what extent do you agree that the following statements describe per-formance-management processes in your organisation?

	Strongly agree	Slightly agree	Slightly disagree	Strongly disagree
Performance-related pay is an essential part of performance management				
Line managers own and operate the performance-management process				
Performance management is an integrated part of the employee–line manager relationship				
Performance management is integrated into other people-management processes				
The focus of performance management is developmental				
Performance management integrates the goals of individuals with those of the organisation				
Performance management motivates individuals				
Performance management is used to manage organisational culture				
The effectiveness of performance management is measured in qualitative rather than quantitative terms				
Performance management sets stretching and challenging goals				
Performance management is bureaucratic and time-consuming				
The aims and objectives of performance management are well communicated and fully understood				

2 Do you give an overall rating for performance?

Yes ❑1   No ❑2

If yes, what sort of categories do you use?

Numerical/alphabetical	❑1	Verbal (all positive)	❑2
Verbal (positive and negative)	❑3	Other (*please specify*)	❑4

3   Do you use any of the following to achieve consistency in ratings across different parts of the organisation?

Forced distribution ☐₁   Management group review ☐₂
Points rating system ☐₃   Grandparenting system ☐₄
Prior estimates by management group ☐₅   Peer review of outcomes ☐₆
Standard setting workshops or seminars ☐₇   Others (*please specify*) ....☐₈

4   Who keeps the documentation?

Personnel department ☐₁   Line manager ☐₂   Individual ☐₃
Other (*please specify*)... ☐₄

Section E – Performance management outcomes

1   Is there a formal system for the evaluation of performance management?

Yes ☐₁   No ☐₂

If yes, please specify the process you use to evaluate.

Opinion/attitude surveys ☐₁   Focus groups ☐₂
Informal feedback (verbal) ☐₃   Formal feedback (written) ☐₄
Other (*please specify*) .... ☐₅

2   How important are the following criteria in the measurement of individual performance in your organisation?

	Very important	Important	Not very important	Not used as a measure
Customer care				
Quality				
Flexibility				
Competence				
Skills/learning targets				
Business awareness				
Working relationships				
Contribution to team				
Financial awareness				
Productivity				
Aligning personal objectives with organisational goals				
Achievement of objectives				

3   How is the performance management system regarded by

	Very effective	Moderately effective	Effective	Not very effective
Senior managers				
Other managers/team leaders				
Other staff				
Personnel				

4   Are you proposing to make any changes to your performance-management arrangements over the next 12 months?

Yes   ❑₁   No   ❑₂   Don't know   ❑₃

5   What are the key factors which you use to determine whether performance management is effective? (Please rank the relevant factors only in order of importance, with 1 being most important.)

Achievement of financial targets   ❑₁   Productivity   ❑₂
Development of skills   ❑₃   Development of competence   ❑₄
Improved customer care   ❑₅   Improved quality   ❑₆
Changes in behaviour   ❑₇   Changes in attitude   ❑₈
Motivation   ❑₉   Labour turnover   ❑₁₀
Other (*please specify*) .... ❑₁₁

6   In general, how effective have your organisation's performance-management processes proved in improving overall performance?

Very effective   ❑₁   Moderately effective   ❑₂
Effective   ❑₃   Ineffective   ❑₄
Don't know   ❑₅

7   How do you rate the overall performance of your organisation against the rest of UK organisations operating in your industrial sector in each of the following categories?

	Top 25%	Middle 50%	Bottom 25%	Don't know
Quality of goods or service				
Innovative capacity				
Cost				
Market share				
Return on investment				
Profitability				
Quality of workforce				
Efficiency				

Are there any other comments you would like to make about your performance-management arrangements not covered in the questions above?

....

....

....

....

As part of this research we are planning to visit a number of companies to discuss their performance-management arrangements in more depth. Would you be prepared to take part in these follow-up discussions?

Yes ❑   No ❑

If yes, please give contact details:

Name ....

Company ....

Address ....

Tel. No. ....

APPENDIX B
THE EMPLOYEE ATTITUDE SURVEY

1   What do you understand by the term performance management?
(Please indicate by ticking the box which of the following features you think should form a part of performance management.)

Performance appraisal or review ☐
Regular meetings with boss/supervisor to review progress ☐
Setting objectives ☐
Assessment of training and development needs ☐
Personal development plans ☐
Pay based on performance ratings ☐

Other *(please specify)* ....

2   Have you carried out all the requirements of your own organisation's per-formance-management arrangements in the last year (ie set objectives, had a performance review)?   Yes ☐   No ☐

If no, why not?

Too busy ☐
Not necessary ☐
Irrelevant to current job ☐

Other *(please specify)* ....
....

If yes, what actions were carried out as a result?

Attended a training course ☐
Implemented a programme of self-development ☐
Received a pay rise ☐
Identified career development ☐
Agreed improvements to way work done ☐

Other *(please specify)* ....
....

3   Please indicate the extent to which you agree or disagree with the following statements.

	Strongly agree	Slightly agree	Slightly disagree	Strongly disagree
I have authority to determine my work objectives				
I receive a lot of feedback on my performance				
The people in my work group are committed to the organisation				
The most important thing about my job is the pay				
Hard work is not necessarily recognised or rewarded				
My organisation values my contribution				
I fully understand my organisation's business goals and objectives				
My organisation is a good employer				
The people who get the best pay rises are those who ask for them				
I know what is expected of me by my organisation				
My work objectives are unrealistic and difficult to achieve				
I have autonomy over the way I perform my work				
I find it difficult to discuss work problems with my line manager				
My organisation is committed to my training and development				
My organisation communicates well				
My work colleagues and I have respect for each other				
I feel I am constantly being compared with my work colleagues				
My work colleagues and I work as a team				

4   Please indicate the extent to which you agree or disagree with the following statements as descriptions of performance management generally.

	Strongly agree	Slightly agree	Slightly disagree	Strongly disagree
Performance management is about individuals and their long-term development				
Performance management helps people to do a better job				
Performance management is about managers controlling people				
Performance management does not help to develop careers, only improve work performance				
Performance management is only of use to personnel people				
Performance management is about deciding how much to pay people				
Performance management provides a way for people to discuss their progress openly and honestly				
Performance management is a two-way process, with both manager and employee expressing their views				
Performance management is a way of keeping a record of an individual's progress and performance				
Performance management is about getting people to work harder				
Performance management has no value for individuals, only for organisations				
Performance management values the contribution of the team				
Performance management motivates people and makes them feel part of the organisation				

5   Please indicate the extent to which you agree or disagree with the following statements regarding performance management as it applies to you personally in your current role.

	Strongly agree	Slightly agree	Slightly disagree	Strongly disagree
Performance management helps me to do my job better				
Performance management helps me to develop my skill and potential				
The objectives/performance standards agreed with my manager are realistic				
I get useful feedback from my performance management review				
I am not satisfied with the way my manager/team leader conducts my performance review				
Assessments of my performance are consistent, fair and unbiased				
I feel motivated after a review meeting				
I do not understand how my manager/team leader decides my rating/assessment				
Managers/team leaders give the best ratings/assessments to people they like				
I fully understand how my objectives/performance standards relate to the business needs of the organisation				
I have received adequate training in performance management				
The system of performance management used here works well and does not need to change				
Time spent on performance management is worthwhile				
The information disclosed in performance reviews is used sensitively and productively by the organisation				

For managers/team leaders who conduct performance reviews only

Please indicate the extent to which you agree or disagree with the following statements regarding performance management as it applies to you as a line manager in your organisation.

	Strongly agree	Slightly agree	Slightly disagree	Strongly disagree
Performance management helps me to motivate my team				
Performance management helps me decide what to pay members of my team				
Performance management helps me to develop the skills and capabilities of my team				
Performance management helps my team to perform better				
Performance management helps me to communicate to my team what is expected of them				
I am not comfortable with conducting performance reviews				
Performance management is generally only of use to the personnel department, not individual line managers				
I have not been adequately trained to get the best out of the performance-management process				
The information generated from performance reviews is unproductive and of no value				
I have no difficulty in agreeing objectives or performance standards with individual members of my team				
The time I spend on performance reviews could be used more productively elsewhere				
The documentation associated with performance management is unclear and unhelpful				
The current performance-management system works well and does not need to change				
I am satisfied that I give consistent and fair ratings to members of my team				

APPENDIX C
EXAMPLES OF PERFORMANCE-MANAGEMENT DOCUMENTATION

The following examples of performance-management documentation are reproduced with the kind permission of the organisations concerned. Each illustrates a slightly different approach and, taken together, they should provide pointers that will help most organisations generate their own material. **AA Insurance** uses a review form incorporating a personal development plan. **The Corporation of London** has adopted an even more pared-down performance and development review, which nonetheless includes team and individual objectives as well as a training plan. Finally, **New Forest District Council** shows how the analysis of *competency* can form the heart of a performance and development review form.

These forms have necessarily been edited in places to facilitate reproduction.

AA Insurance

Personal Performance Review

For: Staff

Mid-Year

Name .... Staff No. ....

Job title .... Grade ....

Department/location ....

Review period from .... to ....

Review carried out by ....

Reviewer's job title ....

Date ....

Year End

Job title .... Grade ....

Department/location ....

Review period from .... to ....

Review carried out by ....

Reviewer's job title ....

Date ....

Mid-Year		**Year End**	
Summary Rating		Summary Rating	

PERSONAL OBJECTIVES

YOUR OBJECTIVES SHEET FOR EACH REVIEW SHOULD BE INCLUDED WITH THIS PERFORMANCE REVIEW DOCUMENT AND INSERTED IN YOUR PERSONAL PORTFOLIO

Objectives are determined at the beginning of the review period. Summarise in the appropriate columns on a separate sheet the main objectives (usually not more than 8) and the standards/targets that will be used in assessing achievement. Ensure that the most important aspects of your role are covered.

Objectives should be relevant and appropriate. Assessment should not be made against an objective you do not have the opportunity to undertake.

To be completed at the end of the review period as a result of joint discussion between reviewer and job holder. When rating an individual objective please use this scale:

1 = Excellent performance in exceeding objective
2 = Objective met at a level of performance above required standard
3 = Objective met at the standard required
4 = Performance has not met some of the requirements of the objective. May have some development needs
5 = Performance has met few of the requirements of the objective and performance must improve significantly
6 = Unable to assess

MID-YEAR	YEAR END
REVIEWER'S COMMENTS Signature .... Date	**REVIEWER'S COMMENTS** Signature .... Date ....
JOB HOLDER'S COMMENTS Signature .... Date	**JOB HOLDER'S COMMENTS** Signature .... Date ....
OVERVIEWER'S COMMENTS Signature .... Date	**OVERVIEWER'S COMMENTS** Signature .... Date ....

PERSONAL COMPETENCE

Different roles will make varying demands on the person, and an individual's competence rating is only relevant against the context of a role. The competency is measured against the expectation of the relevant grade.

Ratings:

A Well above the requirements of the role   D Below the requirements of the role
B Above the requirements of the role   E Well below the requirements of the role
C Matches the requirements of the role   U Unable to assess

		Mid-Year Rating	Year End Rating
CAPABILITY – Readiness and capacity to perform			
Relevant knowledge and technical expertise	Has an appropriate level of business awareness, experience, knowledge and skill for the professional and technical requirements of the role.	_____	_____
Analytical and reasoning skills	Able to handle and interpret data, identify key issues, resolve problems and derive solutions when in contact with customers.	_____	_____
Amount of direct supervision or guidance required	Sufficiently confident and able to operate competently without an ongoing need for detailed rules or close supervision.	_____	_____

Comments, including examples of where competence has been demonstrated.

		Rating	Rating
MOTIVATION – Drive, commitment and willingness			
Wants to learn and grow	Seeks and uses all learning opportunities to gain self-awareness, improve own performance and realise full potential.	_____	_____
Energy and application	Conscientious and hard-working to achieve required results.	_____	_____
Customer- and service-focused	Aware of the importance of meeting customer needs and delivering a quality service.	_____	_____
Flexible and adaptable	Responds positively and co-operatively to change, challenges and conflicting demands.	_____	_____

Comments, including examples of where competence has been demonstrated.

EFFICIENCY – Management of self and other resources

		Mid-Year Rating	Year End Rating
Well planned and organised	Plans ahead and demonstrates good personal organisation.	_____	_____
Prioritises	Takes action to meet customer requirements in order of importance where appropriate.	_____	_____
Delivers to time, quality and costs	Consistently meets due dates and deadlines; works to high standards and service levels; cost-conscious.	_____	_____
Shows resilience and stamina	Resilient and able to handle disappointments, rejection and set-backs positively. Copes effectively with ambiguity and change.	_____	_____

Comments, including examples of where competence has been demonstrated.

EFFECTIVENESS – Approach to achieving results

		Rating	Rating
Decisive, exercising sound judgement	Considers options and makes timely decisions; considers the implications and usually selects the best possible option or right course of action.	_____	_____
Proactive	Identifies areas where action and improvement is required, implementing change and better ways of doing things.	_____	_____
Innovative	Generates and tries out new ideas and approaches successfully.	_____	_____

Comments, including examples of where competence has been demonstrated.

PRESENCE – Management of self and other resources

Mid-Year Year End
Rating   Rating

		Mid-Year Rating	Year End Rating
Effective team player	As a team member, able to work effectively with peers. Contributes fully to the team.	_____	_____
Communicates and influences effectively	Communicates clearly and persuasively when speaking and writing. Listens effectively and shows empathy. Open and honest.	_____	_____
Builds strong working relationships	Gains the necessary trust, support and co-operation from others.	_____	_____

Comments, including examples of where competence has been demonstrated.

PERSONAL DEVELOPMENT REVIEW

Recent development
List training and development activities undertaken during the review period, **and attach training and development evaluation forms.**

Mid-Year

Year End

Disability
Discuss the possible existence of a disability and identify any training, development or equipment which would help the job-holder to work with a disability.

Where would you like to be? Career aspirations

Long Term:

Short Term:

PERSONAL DEVELOPMENT PLAN

Please identify below any training and development training needs which have been identified during the course of your performance review.

Your Personal Development Plan should:

(a) Enable you to undertake your present job to a satisfactory standard.

(b) Enable you to develop skills and competencies to reach a standard of excellence in your job and to develop your abilities for the future.

(c) All training and development **must be** clearly linked to business and personal objectives.

IF FURTHER EDUCATION IS IDENTIFIED AS A NEED, PLEASE COMPLETE A FURTHER ED. APPLICATION FORM.

What development/ training, further ed. need is identified?	Method/How is it to be delivered?	Identify link to business objective	To be achieved by – when?	Who is going to organise it?	What will be the improvement to your performance/competence?

Please continue on separate sheet if necessary.

The Corporation of London
Performance and development review

NAME: **JOB TITLE:**   **DEPARTMENT:**

The purpose of this form is to review the way in which you carry out your work and how you can be even more effective in the coming year. You may want to talk about your work output; your job knowledge; your effectiveness; the quality of your work; your work relationships and how satisfied you are with your job.

WHAT WENT WELL AND WHY?

WHAT DID NOT GO SO WELL, AND WHY?

WHAT NEEDS TO HAPPEN TO BE EVEN MORE EFFECTIVE?

SUMMARY OF DISCUSSION

Objective-setting and performance review

TEAM: _____   DEPARTMENT: _____   DATE SET: _____

NAME: _____   JOB TITLE: _____

The purpose of this form is to set new objectives and performance standards against which performance will be reviewed over the following year. Number and provide a title for each task/objective, and identify the performance standard that you need to be met over the coming year. At the review, assess the level of your achievement in meeting these objectives over the past year, and summarise, using the third column.

TASKS/OBJECTIVES	PERFORMANCE STANDARDS	LEVEL OF ACHIEVEMENT IN MEETING OBJECTIVES

Team-based objective-setting and performance review

TEAM: _____ DEPARTMENT: _____ DATE SET: _____

NAME: _____ JOB TITLE: _____

The purpose of this form is to set team-based objectives and performance standards against which performance will be reviewed over the following year. Number and provide a title for each task/objective, and identify the performance standard that needs to be met by the team over the coming year. At the review, assess the level of your personal achievement/individual contribution to the team objectives over the past year, and summarise, using the third column.

TASKS/OBJECTIVES	PERFORMANCE STANDARDS	LEVEL OF ACHIEVEMENT/ INDIVIDUAL CONTRIBUTION TO TEAM OBJECTIVES

Development review: training plan

NAME: _____ JOB TITLE: _____

DEPARTMENT: _____ DATE OF REVIEW: _____

The purpose of this form is to review what training and development is needed to help you achieve performance and fulfil your longer-term potential. This plan is then the joint responsibility of you and your manager. Please consider training courses, projects, planned work experience, coaching etc when determining the 'action required'. It could also include consideration of team development needs.

TRAINING & DEVELOPMENT NEED	ACTION REQUIRED	BY WHOM	TARGET COMPLETION DATE	COMMENTS

Performance and development review

ACTION POINTS			
APPRAISER	**by date**	**APPRAISEE**	**by date**

APPRAISEE COMMENTS

(continue on separate sheet if necessary)

APPRAISEE _____ (sign) _____ (date)

APPRAISER _____ (sign) _____ (date)

APPRAISER'S MANAGER _____ (sign) _____ (date)

New Forest District Council
Performance and development interview
SKILLS ASSESSMENT

(To be completed by Manager or Supervisor for all employees)

COMPETENCE LEVEL ➡ SKILL ⬇	1 Performance is above job expectations. Plays a key role in helping to achieve business-unit objectives. Exceeds job requirements.	2 Performance meets job expectations but further improvement would play a key role in helping to achieve business-unit objectives.	3 Performance is below the expectations reasonably required by the business unit and needs to be improved with training and development.	4 Performance which training and development may not resolve.	COMMENTS
RELATIONSHIPS – COLLEAGUES The extent to which the employee communicates and maintains effective relationships with colleagues.	☐ Maintains very good relationships with colleagues and promotes business unit effectively.	☐ Good relationships with colleagues. Meets job expectations.	☐ There are currently some difficulties being experienced with colleague relationships. This is an area for improvement during next period.	☐	
RELATIONSHIPS – CUSTOMER CARE The extent to which the employee effectively communicates and maintains relationships with customers.	☐ Maintains very good relationships with customers and promotes New Forest District Council effectively.	☐ Good relationships with customers. Meets job expectations.	☐ There are currently some difficulties being experienced with customer relationships. This is an area for improvement during the next period.	☐	
RELATIONSHIPS – MANAGER The extent to which the employee effectively communicates and maintains relationships with their manager/ supervisor.	☐ Maintains very good relationships with manager and effectively helps promote business unit and achieve business objectives.	☐ Good relationships with manager. Meets job expectations.	☐ There are currently some difficulties being experienced with relationships in this area. This is an area for positive development during the next period.	☐	
RELATIONSHIPS – MEMBERS The extent to which the employee effectively communicates and maintains relationships with Members. NOT APPLICABLE ☐	☐ Maintains very good relationships with Members and effectively helps promote business unit and New Forest District Council.	☐ Good relationships with Members. Meets job expectations.	☐ There are currently some difficulties being experienced with Member relationships. This is an area for positive development during the next period.	☐	

COMPETENCE LEVEL ⟶ ↓ SKILL	1 Performance is above job expectations. Plays a key role in helping to achieve business-unit objectives. Exceeds job requirements.	2 Performance meets job expectations but further improvement would play a key role in helping to achieve business-unit objectives.	3 Performance is below the expectations reasonably required by the business unit and needs to be improved with training and development.	4 Performance which training and development may not resolve.	COMMENTS
COMPETENCE The extent to which employee demonstrates competence (skills and knowledge) relating to the business-unit activity.	☐ Very competent. Consistently demonstrates sound understanding of business-unit objectives and activities detailed in business/service plan. Performance exceeds job expectations.	☐ Full competence is developing and this will improve as role within the team develops further. There is a good understanding of business/service plan. Meets expectations of the job.	☐ Competence level is an area needing attention and an action programme is being developed to improve to acceptable standards. This is an area for positive development during next period.	☐	
KNOWLEDGE The extent to which the employee has an effective knowledge of their own role, the work of the business unit and the Council.	☐ Very good knowledge of own role, the business unit and work of the Council. Knowledge exceeds that required by job expectations.	☐ Knowledge is good and meets expectations of the job.	☐ Knowledge is below the levels reasonably expected. It is an area requiring improvement during next period.	☐	
JUDGEMENT The extent to which judgement is effective and consistent in achieving business-unit objectives.	☐ Judgement consistently very good and leads to achievement of business-unit objectives. Exceeds job expectations.	☐ Judgement is good. Meets expectations of job.	☐ Judgement is below the levels reasonably expected. This is an area requiring improvement during next period.	☐	
COMMUNICATION SKILLS How effective is the employee with verbal and written communication?	☐ Very good in all written and verbal communication. Above job expectations.	☐ Verbal and written communication skills are good and meet the expectations of the job.	☐ Has some difficulty with verbal or written communication. An issue for training and improvement during next period.	☐	
TEAMWORK How well does the employee work with others to accomplish goals of the business unit?	☐ Works very well with others and responds enthusiastically to new business challenges. Exceeds job expectations.	☐ Good team worker. Plays an active role in helping to achieve business objectives.	☐ Has some difficulty in accepting change and can become disruptive team member. Issue for discussion and improvement during next period.	☐	

COMPETENCE LEVEL ⟶ SKILL ↓	1 Performance is above job expectations. Plays a key role in helping to achieve business-unit objectives. Exceeds job requirements.	2 Performance meets job expectations but further improvement would play a key role in helping to achieve business-unit objectives.	3 Performance is below the expectations reasonably required by the business unit and needs to be improved with training and development	4 Performance which training and development may not resolve	COMMENTS
ATTITUDE What is the employee's attitude to job aspects such as commitment, enthusiasm, motivation, dependability and loyalty to business unit?	☐ Very good attitude to job and achieving business-unit objectives. Attitude exceeds job expectations.	☐ Attitude towards job and achieving business-unit objectives is good and meets job expectations.	☐ Attitude towards job and or achieving business-unit objectives is an issue for training and improvement during next period.	☐	
EFFECTIVENESS How effective and productive is the employee in achieving business-unit objectives? Both individual and team objectives.	☐ Very effective and productive. Always meets agreed targets and deadlines. Meets both individual and team objectives. Exceeds job expectations.	☐ Effectiveness and productivity are good and meet job expectations.	☐ Effectiveness and or productivity are areas which need to be improved and are an issue for improvement during the next period.	☐	
INITIATIVE The extent to which the employee uses their own initiative and resolves issues within their power to help achieve work objectives.	☐ Continuously uses initiative to achieve business objectives. Initiative is used appropriately and boundaries known and adhered to.	☐ Use of initiative is good and in line with job expectations.	☐ Inappropriate or ineffective use of initiative. This is an area for training improvement during next period.	☐	
PRIORITISING AND DECISION-MAKING Extent to which prioritising and decision-making positively contribute to the achievement of business objectives.	☐ Prioritising and decision-making are consistently good and play a key role in achieving business-unit objectives. Job expectations are exceeded.	☐ Prioritising and decision-making skills are good and meet the expectations of the job. Further development would play a key role in achievement of business-unit objectives.	☐ Prioritising and decision-making skills are below the competence levels reasonably expected. This is an issue requiring improvement during the next period.	☐	
ACCURACY How accurate/ systematic and careful is the employee in achieving their work objectives to timescale?	☐ Very accurate and systematic in achieving work objectives. Exceeds job expectations.	☐ Good accuracy and systematic approach. Meets job expectations.	☐ Accuracy and systematic approach could be improved and are issues for improvement and training during the next period.	☐	

COMPETENCE LEVEL → SKILL ↓	1 Performance is above job expectations. Plays a key role in helping to achieve business-unit objectives. Exceeds job requirements.	2 Performance meets job expectations but further improvement would play a key role in helping to achieve business-unit objectives.	3 Performance is below the expectations reasonably required by the business unit and needs to be improved with training and development.	4 Performance which training and development may not resolve.	COMMENTS
HEALTH & SAFETY AWARENESS Is the employee aware of personal and business Health and Safety requirements?	☐ Highly motivated towards Health and Safety. Encourages others likewise.	☐ A good attitude to Health and Safety.	☐ Health and Safety is an area for programmed training during the next period.		
TIME-KEEPING What is the employee's pattern of time-keeping?		☐ Time-keeping is acceptable.	☐ Time-keeping is an issue for discussion and improvement. (See Comments)		
OVERALL An overall assessment of the employee's performance contribution to the achievement of business objectives based on above criteria.	☐ Very good performance which exceeds job expectations. Above job expectations. Plays a key role in helping to achieve business-unit objectives.	☐ Performance has been good and meets job expectations. Further improvement will play a key role in helping to achieve business-unit objectives.	☐ Performance is below the competence levels reasonably expected by the business unit. There is a need for positive improvement in a range of areas.		

Progress over last period with personal and team objectives
LINKED TO ACHIEVING BUSINESS PLAN

Topic or Objective	No.	Target Date Agreed	Progress with Topic/ Objective Include development/ training undertaken	Agreed actions (to be completed at interview)

APPENDIX D

AN ANALYSIS OF THE RESULTS OF THE IPD* SURVEY

by
David E. Guest
and
Neil Conway

* The IPD became the Chartered Institute of Personnel and Development (CIPD) in July 2000.

Introduction

Performance management (PM) has been a popular and widely applied concept in industry for a number of years. It has also been the subject of considerable criticism. There are two main bases for this criticism. The first is that the concept is diffuse: it is all things to all people, and increasingly provides little more than an umbrella under which to describe a number of well-tried and often rather dated ideas. The second criticism is that any rigorous evaluation has failed to show that PM has any impact on performance, calling into question the whole rationale behind the approach.

The (then) Institute of Personnel Management (IPM) undertook a major study of PM in the early 1990s (IPM 1992), which confirmed much of the scepticism. It reported a wide variety of practices, a generally piecemeal approach and no evidence that PM increased performance. It might be hoped that the wide publicity given to the findings encouraged a more strategic approach to PM. The IPD took another careful look at performance management, and this report is part of that exercise. Using multivariate statistical analysis, the report explored two main issues: the first was whether those using PM report any underlying coherence in their beliefs about and approach to it, the second was whether PM had any impact on performance and, if so, what it was about PM systems that seemed to have the impact.

The analysis is based on a questionnaire returned by 562 personnel practitioners of whom 388 reported that their organisation was using formal PM processes.

The aim of this first section of the report is to determine whether PM represents a coherent approach as perceived by personnel specialists and as used in their organisations. The first section therefore explores beliefs about PM. The second compares the views of personnel practitioners who are using formal PM processes and those who are not. The third looks at the practices adopted by those organisations engaged in PM. We then try to link beliefs to practices, and business strategy to practices, and all of these to performance. Ideally, we might hope to see a clear link between business strategy and PM in practice.

Beliefs about PM

PM can mean many different things. The aim of this analysis is to determine whether personnel managers' perceptions of it display any coherence and consistency. Indeed, in the extensive literature on PM it is possible to detect the following perspectives:

□ PM as an integration of organisational and individual goals – the old management-by-objectives
□ PM as essentially performance-related pay (PRP)
□ PM as a goal-setting-based form of motivation
□ PM as primarily a developmental activity
□ PM as primarily a traditional appraisal process
□ PM as an innovative approach to appraisal
□ PM as a bureaucratic chore.

We were interested in whether personnel managers emphasised one or more of these. As a first step, we asked them to indicate to what extent they agreed or disagreed with 16 statements about PM that were designed to cover the perspectives listed above.

It was possible to compare the responses of those who currently do and do not use PM. We might expect, for example, that more non-users would perceive it as a bureaucratic chore. A factor analysis should identify any coherence in the responses. Since we might expect greater coherence among users of PM than among non-users, who might be less familiar with it, we analysed them separately. The results of the actor analysis for the 388 users of PM are shown in Table 1. Figures in brackets show the percentage of respondents in the full sample who positively endorsed the statement. The five factors accounted for 49.8 per cent of the variance.

The five factors imply some coherence, in that they are readily interpretable. Factor 1 views PM as an on-going, developmental, integrated process; it reflects a kind of soft, qualitative approach. Factor 2 is concerned with PRP. Factor 3 contains the three items that concern the bureaucracy of PM. Factor 4 is mainly concerned with PM as goal-based motivation. However, it also contains an item about PM as management of culture, which fits less well, as does the item on

Table 1

FACTOR ANALYSIS OF BELIEFS ABOUT PM AMONG PERSONNEL MANAGERS IN ORGANISATIONS USING PM

Figures in brackets = % respondents endorsing the statement	1	2	3	4	5
PM as an on-going, developmental integrative process					
The focus should be developmental (91)	.683				
Training in PM techniques is essential for its success (79)	.656				
Effectiveness of PM is more easily measured qualitatively (62)	.460				
PM should be an integrated part of employee–manager relations (99)	.449				
PM succeeds only by integrating individual and organisational goals (97)	.444				
PM as performance-related pay					
Performance-related pay is an essential part of PM (39)		.824			
PM should be distanced as far as possible from payment systems (57)		−.816			
PM as bureaucracy					
PM distracts people from more important core activities (14)			.753		
PM will inevitably become a bureaucratic chore (31)			.670		
It is essential that line managers own the PM system (97)			−.460		
PM as goal-based motivation					
Most important aspect of PM is setting challenging goals (96)				.716	
Main objective of PM should be to motivate individuals (97)				.705	
PM is an essential tool in management of organisational culture (91)				.507	
It is essential that there is extensive communication of aims of PM (98)				.365	
Criteria for success of PM					
Quantifiable measures are essential to the success of PM (87)					.711
PM will only succeed as integrated approach to people management (99)					.578

communication. Factor 5 is less easily interpretable, but both items are concerned with what is required for PM to succeed, and therefore the factor appears to reflect an underlying concern about the success of PM.

As expected, the factor analysis of the non-users produced a rather different set of factors, which did not cluster in the same way. For brevity, we shall not reproduce them here.

Even with the combined population, most of these statements are strongly endorsed and can be viewed as 'motherhood' statements about PM. Exceptions concern PRP, on which responses are fairly evenly split, though a majority want it separated from PM. Also, and predictably in the light of the other responses, few saw PM as a bureaucratic chore. In short, we have a population of personnel managers who are very enthusiastic about a broad, integrative approach to PM.

The results of this initial analysis appear to be quite encouraging, in the sense that beliefs about PM carry an underlying coherence. The next step in any conventional analysis would be to turn each of the factors into a scale that can be used as a single item in the subsequent analysis. Unfortunately, the standard test to determine whether the items could be scaled, the alpha test, showed that all the factors fell some way below the acceptable level. (The alpha score ranged between .314 and .451, where we should be looking for above .60 and preferably above .70.) This suggests that the initial clusters emerging from the factor analysis are less coherent than we might have hoped.

Comparison of beliefs about PM among users and non-users

If PM has any importance, we would expect that representatives of those organisations using it would have different beliefs about it from those who did not use it. Ideally, we would have explored this by comparing scores on the scales that emerged from the factor analysis. However, because users and non-users provided different factors, and because in neither case could we turn the factors into acceptable scales, we are forced to make an item-by-item comparison. This was achieved using T-tests on each of the 16 items used in the factor analysis, which appear in Table 1. Only a small number of differences emerged.

Users of PM were more likely to agree with the following statements:

☐ The most important aspect of PM is the setting of challenging and stretching goals.
☐ PM will succeed only if it integrates the goals of individuals with those of the organisation.
☐ It is essential that line managers own the PM system.
☐ PM should be a continuous and integrated part of the employee–line manager relationship.
☐ PM is an essential tool in the management of organisational culture.

In contrast, users were less likely to agree that:

☐ It is essential that PM is accompanied by extensive communication to ensure its aims are fully understood.

The items that appear to be given greater emphasis by users of PM are those concerned with aspects of integration into mainstream management activity, in particular incorporating line management. It is impossible to tell whether this is the wisdom of hindsight or a long-standing view.

The practice of PM

If PM is to have an impact, we would expect the practices in use to cluster together in a coherent way to meet the relevant objectives. A long list of possible practices was provided. Those using PM were asked to indicate which processes were included in their arrangements. The factor analysis revealed six factors that accounted for 60.4 per cent of the variance.

Table 2
FACTOR ANALYSIS OF PERFORMANCE-MANAGEMENT PRACTICES

Figures in brackets = % respondents endorsing the statement	I	2	3	4	5	6
Innovative approaches						
Subordinate feedback (20)	.728					
Peer appraisal (9)	.715					
360-degree appraisal (12)	.658					
Career-related development practices						
Personal development plans (69)		.783				
Career management and/or succession-planning (32)		.633				
Objective-setting and review (85)		.546				
Timing of appraisal						
Annual appraisal (84)			−.823			
Bi-annual appraisal (24)			.770			
Continuous assessment						
Continuous assessment (17)				.654		
Rolling appraisal (12)				.651		
Performance-related pay (44)				.531		
Competence assessment (31)					.743	
Self vs support systems						
Coaching and/or mentoring (39)						.840
Self-appraisal (45)						−.471

The percentage who report use of each of the practices are shown in brackets. They are shown in Table 2.

Most of these factors may be interpreted as suggesting that organisations do consider PM practices in a coherent way. Factor 1 is concerned with what might be described as innovative approaches to appraisal, but essentially concerns alternatives to appraisal by the immediate superior. Factor 2 covers career-related development issues. Factor 3 is concerned with the traditional timing of appraisal. Factor 4 is concerned with continuous assessment, although it is not clear why PRP fits in here. Factor 5 includes only competence assessment, suggesting that it does not fit easily into PM systems. Finally, Factor 6 is concerned with the role of self *versus* others in performance development, and implies provision of support. The range of factors, some of which are probably mutually exclusive, highlights the variety of practices that constitute PM.

Although the main factors listed above appear to indicate some coherence, we again found that they did not translate into scales with an acceptable alpha score. The implication, as with the beliefs, is that the superficial appearance of coherence is not sustained in more rigorous analysis. This lack of underlying coherence may have consequences when we explore the impact of PM. Despite the problems of scaling, we can combine the scores within each factor through a simple count of practices, and this is the process adopted in the later analysis.

Relationship between beliefs about PM and practices adopted

Ideally, we might expect to see some link between the beliefs concerning the nature of PM and the kind of systems in place. The link might not be straightforward, because the responses on beliefs about PM are likely to reflect personal views, whereas the practices might well have been introduced by others in the organisation. Unfortunately, the failure to obtain acceptable scales from the factor analyses means that this analysis cannot be conducted.

Links between use of PM and business strategy

Some of the responses discussed have already identified concern to integrate PM into mainstream activities in organisations. This might also be expected to relate to the decisions to use PM. One way of exploring this is to compare those organisations that are, or are not, using PM. Do they have a different set of business priorities, or do they differ in any other respects?

The way in which this was achieved was through the use of discriminant function analysis. This seeks to identify any background characteristics that successfully discriminate between those organisations that do and those that do not use PM. In this case, only a limited number of background variables was available. These were sector, numbers of employees employed, change in numbers of employees employed and business strategy. Nine aspects of business strategy were offered (eg reduce costs, improve quality, improve productivity), and respondents were asked to rank those that were relevant in order of importance. Chance would predict whether or not an organisation used PM on 50 per cent of occasions. Using these four variables, it was possible to estimate use accurately on 59.2 per cent of occasions. This is only a modest improvement, and only one of the background variables contributed significantly to this improved prediction. It was business strategy and, in particular, giving priority to reducing production time.

The coherence of PM: a summary

We have now explored the coherence of PM from several perspectives. Although the factor analyses promised some evidence of coherence, it proved impossible to develop acceptable scales for further statistical analysis. This raises questions about the coherence of beliefs and about the practices associated with PM. It was also impossible to identify any very coherent differences between those using PM and those who where not. There were some differences in beliefs, but no helpful differences in organisational characteristics. The single discriminating item – a strategic emphasis on reducing production time – does not really point to any useful insights.

PM and performance

In the previous section we were unable to find coherent clusters of PM practices. This will make any evaluation of the impact of PM both more difficult to undertake and, arguably, less likely to lead to the identification of any clear explanation of performance differences. Before we can attempt to examine explanations for the impact of PM, we first need to determine whether organisations make any serious attempt to evaluate its impact and, if so, what criteria are used. These can then be related to subjective evaluations of PM effectiveness.

Is PM evaluated?

Before we can report any convincing data on the impact of PM, we need more information about how any judgements about it are arrived at. One question asked whether there was a formal system for the evaluation of PM. The result was that 165 (or 44.8 per cent) of those who answered the question said that there was. This was explored further by asking about the evaluation process. Disappointingly, the most popular method of formal evaluation cited was 'informal evaluation (verbal)', reported by 103 (or 62.4 per cent) of those who undertake formal evaluation. This was followed by opinion/attitude surveys reported by 84 (or 50.9 per cent) of those with formal evaluation. Third was use of 'formal feedback (written)', cited by 62 (or 37.6 per cent). The final main form of formal evaluation was use of focus groups reported by 36 (or 21.8 per cent). A further 20 cited other random means of formal evaluation.

These data show that only a minority of respondents claim to have any system of formal evaluation in place, and even among these, only a small proportion conduct what can be described as serious evaluation. This suggests that we should view the subjective reports of the success of PM with considerable caution.

Factors used to determine the effectiveness of PM

A list of possible criteria was provided, and respondents were asked to identity the most important. They could rank as many as they wished from the list of nine criteria provided,

Table 3

KEY CRITERIA USED TO DETERMINE THE EFFECTIVENESS OF PERFORMANCE MANAGEMENT

Criterion	Top priority %	Top three priority %	Some ranking %
Achievement of financial targets	28.4	40.2	68.3
Development of skills	8.2	27.0	69.8
Development of competence	7.7	25.8	60.6
Improved customer care	7.5	31.2	61.1
Improved quality	6.4	26.3	66.2
Changes in behaviour	5.9	21.1	57.5
Productivity	5.4	21.9	52.3
Other (unspecified)	5.2	9.3	9.3
Changes in attitude	1.8	10.0	50.5
Motivation	1.5	15.4	53.6
Labour turnover	0.8	2.9	32.0

and add others of their own. The results are shown in Table 3.

The key criteria combine concern to develop skill and competence with improved customer care and quality, and achievement of financial targets. Some sort of logical link among these could be detected. It is reasonable to assume that, in arriving at judgements about the effectiveness of PM, some of these criteria are used.

Ratings of the effectiveness of PM

The effectiveness of PM was measured through a series of subjective ratings. Because these are used later in the report as the key dependent measures, the descriptive results are presented in Table 4. The aim was to identify judgements of effectiveness from the perspective of senior managers, other managers, staff in general and the personnel function. Since the responses generally come from personnel managers, they have either to guess how others will respond or base their assessment on what they know from the formal evaluation process. One issue, therefore, is whether those who claim to have a system of formal evaluation report different outcomes from those without it.

Table 4
RATINGS OF EFFECTIVENESS OF PM

%	Very effective	Moderately effective	Effective	Not very effective/ ineffective
Senior managers	17.8	64.4	11.1	1.5
Other managers/team leaders	12.6	59.3	16.2	4.1
Other staff	4.1	41.0	34.8	9.8
Personnel	12.9	49.0	22.4	6.2
Contribution to improving overall performance	7.0	41.0	29.9	8.2

The second general measure was a single item asking about the effectiveness of PM contributing to improvements in overall performance. In both cases a similar four-point scale was used.

It should be noted that not all the figures in Table 4 add up to 100 per cent, because some either failed to answer or claimed not to know the answer.

The results in Table 4 are interesting in that they reflect a belief that senior managers are more positive about the impact of PM than those in the personnel department; and that other staff, who are often on the receiving end, are the least positive. Despite these variations, the results are generally positive, well under 10 per cent providing ratings of either 'less than effective' or 'ineffective'.

The final element in the evaluation asked about the performance of the firm in comparison with others in its sector in the UK. This covered a number of outcomes, some of which, as we have just seen, are judged to be relevant in evaluating PM. Factor analysis revealed that these fell neatly into two clusters, one concerned with internal performance and the other with external performance. These had encouragingly high alpha scores and could therefore be turned into scales. The assumption is that if PM is successful, there will be a positive correlation between ratings of PM and these broader ratings of overall performance. In a survey of this sort, we should be a little cautious in assuming the direction of causality. It is possible that strong financial performance leads to positive ratings on the PM system rather than vice versa.

It should be noted that personnel managers generally rated the performance of their organisation very positively. The benchmark question asked them about performance against major competitors, and whether they felt their organisation was in the top 25 per cent, the bottom 25 per cent or the middle 50 per cent. On internal performance, about which they might be expected to be more confident, the proportion claiming their organisation was in the top 25 per cent ranged from 57 per cent in the case of 'quality of goods and services' to 28 per cent for 'efficiency'. Those rating their organisation in the bottom 25 per cent ranged from 0.5 per cent on 'quality of goods and services' to 9 per cent for 'innovation'. About 15 per cent declined to answer the question. For external performance, this rose to about 40 per cent who were either unwilling or unable (public sector) to answer. For external performance, 35 per cent claimed to be in the top 25 per cent on market share and 27 per cent on profits and ROI. About 9 per cent fell into the bottom 25 per cent on each item. It seems likely that many of these estimates are overoptimistic.

The factor analysis of the measure of overall organisational performance is reported in Table 5.

The two factors accounted for 54.5 per cent of the variance. Factor 1 is concerned with internal performance, and Factor 2 is a measure of external performance. An attempt to turn the

Table 5
FACTOR ANALYSIS OF OVERALL RATINGS OF ORGANISATIONAL PERFORMANCE

	Factor 1	Factor 2
Internal performance		
Quality of workforce	.779	
Quality of goods and services	.698	
Efficiency	.673	
Innovative capacity	.613	
Cost	.496	
External performance		
Return on investment		.914
Profitability		.872
Market share		.563

Table 6

INTERCORRELATIONS BETWEEN EFFECTIVENESS RATINGS

		2	3	4	5
1	Contribution to overall performance	.48	.58	.56	.55
2	Senior management view		.63	.52	.64
3	Other managers/team leaders view			.67	.66
4	Other staff view				.63
5	Personnel view				

factors into scales revealed acceptable alphas of .699 and .739 respectively.

Intercorrelations between measures of PM effectiveness

Because all the measures of the overall effectiveness of PM are provided by the same respondent, it is possible that they are highly intercorrelated and can indeed be seen as representing a single factor. We therefore examined the correlations and subjected the effectiveness measures to a further factor analysis. The results of the intercorrelations are shown in Table 6.

All the correlations in Table 6 are highly significant. We factor-analysed the four sets of views about the effectiveness of PM. (We kept the item on contribution to overall performance separate, because it was asking about something rather different and presupposes the purpose of the scheme.) The factor analysis revealed a single factor accounting for 72.1 per cent of the variance. This was converted into a scale with an alpha score of .869, which is well above the level of acceptability. We shall therefore use this scale score in our subsequent analysis to indicate the effectiveness with which the PM scheme is viewed inside the organisation.

We can take the exploration of outcome measures a step further by exploring the correlations between the ratings of the overall contribution of PM to performance and ratings of current organisational effectiveness on the scales of internal and external performance market and financial criteria. The correlation with external performance is .280, which is statistically significant, but the correlation with internal performance is only .077, which is not statistically significant. The intercorrelation between internal and external performance is .428. This is a somewhat unexpected finding, because the internal performance factor contains items concerned with efficiency and cost that fit well with the strategy of 'reduced production time', and are also the criteria that, intuitively, we would expect PM to have an impact on before it could have any impact on external performance. However, we know from the earlier analysis of evaluation criteria that any evidence about some internal criteria is going to be very sketchy at best.

In summary, this analysis indicates that we have a range of possible measures of the effectiveness of PM. They should all be viewed with extreme caution, because they are often based on either a very limited form of formal evaluation or an absence of any formal evaluation. Having said this, the evaluations are overwhelmingly positive. Any sensible model of the impact of PM would predict that its impact diminishes as we move from ratings of its general effectiveness through its impact on internal organisational performance to external criteria judged in comparison with major competitors in the market-place. The next stage is therefore an attempt to identify which aspects of PM are associated with variations in these three levels of evaluation of PM.

What determines the form and effectiveness of PM?

To enable us to undertake this part of the analysis, a model of the PM process was developed. It is outlined in Figure 1.

Figure 1
A MODEL OF PM

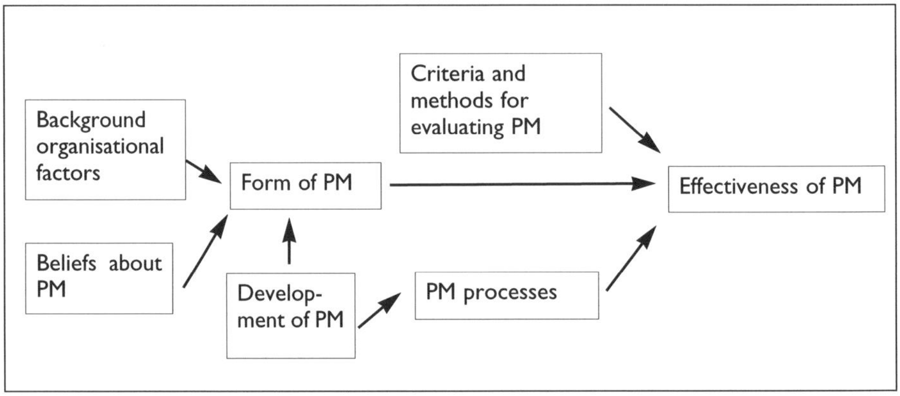

This model has a number of steps:

1   It is assumed that organisational background factors such as sector, size and strategy will have an influence on the focus and goals of PM. So too will beliefs about the nature of PM, although these are the beliefs of the personnel manager.

2   The actual form and operation of PM will also be influenced by the way in which it is introduced, including union involvement, development time and training provision.

3   The effectiveness of PM will be determined by the form it takes in the organisation, by the processes in place to ensure its application (such as the role of line management, the coverage of the system and its age), the way it was introduced, and the monitoring of and concern with effectiveness.

The aim was to test this model with the survey data. However, we were severely constrained by the inability to turn sets of data into single scales. As a result, we had to conduct complex regression analyses using large numbers of individual items. This is a consequence of the failure to find coherence in the way in which PM was approached in organisations. Not surprisingly, this lack of coherence is also reflected in the results.

The attempt to determine the influences on the various criteria of effectiveness is inconclusive. Firstly, a wide range of influences appear. Secondly, the range of influences is inconsistent across the various criteria of effectiveness. Thirdly, and as a result of the previous points, it is difficult to detect any coherent pattern of responses. In the light of the lack of coherence of practices and limited systematic evaluation, we should not be too surprised at this apparently negative outcome.

Despite the failure to find coherent results, the regression analysis shows that the various factors included do have an influence on effectiveness. They explain 29 per cent of the variation in ratings of PM effectiveness, 27 per cent of the variation in ratings of the contribution of PM in improving overall performance, 19 per cent of the variance in judgements of internal performance, and 17 per cent of the variation in judgements of external performance. The declining amount of influence as we move from the evaluation of PM to the more 'distant' evaluation of financial and market performance is very much in line with expectations.

Looking across the four figures that summarise the results, we can struggle to detect signs of coherence. An arbitrary emphasis on any items that appear more than once suggests that general effectiveness is enhanced when the business strategy emphasises increased productivity; when career-development practices are emphasised within PM; when there is a system of formal evaluation that places some emphasis on general employee contribution (an average of the items 'flexibility', 'competence', 'working relationships' and 'contribution to team'); when PM is applied to manual workers; when the system in use is an old one; when line managers keep the documentation but do not set performance targets; and when individual–team–organisation objectives are linked.

We took the analysis one step further. So far, we have explored which aspects of the PM system appear to determine PM effectiveness, which aid the contribution of PM to organisational performance, and which influence the internal and external performance measures. We can also examine how far the effectiveness of PM determines its contribution to organisational performance and, more importantly, how far it contributes to ratings of organisational performance. Using the process of step-wise regression, the analysis confirms that ratings of the effectiveness of PM have a major impact on ratings of the contribution that it makes to organisational effectiveness. However, this is what we might expect, because the two measures may be covering much the same underlying issue; as Table 6 reveals, they are quite highly intercorrelated. However, PM effectiveness has no impact on either internal or external performance. This is the more rigorous analysis, and is further confirmation of the weakness of the case that PM has an impact on organisational performance. Because the measures of internal and external performance include some of the variables identified as most important in assessing the effectiveness of PM, this is an even more challenging result, and raises serious questions about the basis for the generally positive assessment of PM effectiveness.

Some conclusions

This multivariate analysis has been conducted to explore determinants of PM effectiveness. Although the performance or outcome measures show some coherence when subjected to statistical analysis, the same has not proved to be the case for the 'input' measures. One possible reason for this is the nature of the practice items in the questionnaire (yes/no responses rather than ratings). However, a more likely explanation is the inconsistent application of PM.

Despite the absence of systematic evaluation, personnel managers were generally very positive in their judgements about the effectiveness of PM, and considered senior managers to be even more positive. It should be borne in mind that they cited as key criteria in arriving at this judgement the achievement of financial targets, achievement of quality and customer service goals, and employee-development goals. Yet our analysis failed to demonstrate consistent evidence of any link between the practice of PM and these outcomes. An optimistic conclusion might be that PM really does work, and it makes little difference what form of it is used or how it is introduced or monitored.

However, the alternative interpretation that there is as yet no identifiable evidence that PM has an impact on performance is more plausible. It is worth emphasising that this result has been obtained even though the ratings of effectiveness and of performance are entirely subjective. This allows for some internal consistency of responses, which might be expected to lead to more positive results. From this exercise, and indeed from the previous work undertaken by the IPD, we must therefore raise questions about how far the positive evaluation reported by personnel managers is soundly based.

On the basis of the evidence provided by this survey we are unable to *prove* that PM has a positive impact on organisational effectiveness. However, the strength of opinion among managers and the examples of best practice collected by other means do indicate that it *is* felt to play a positive role in the majority of organisations that engage in it. Our failure to prove the case for it can be attributed, at least in part, to the lack of systematic evaluation and the incredible diversity of actions that take place under the banner of PM.

APPENDIX E

PERFORMANCE-MANAGEMENT TRAINING AT ZENECA PHARMACEUTICALS

Performance-management workshop

Objectives

A two-day workshop providing the knowledge and skills necessary to operate the whole performance-management process effectively. The workshop also offers an opportunity for refresher training where required. By the end of the workshop participants will be able to:

- describe the four-stage performance-management process and the key skills required
- apply a structured approach to help them establish team objectives, personal targets and development plans, and conduct effective performance reviews
- explain the difference between performance review and career review
- show they have practised the key skills required to operate each stage of the performance-management process
- to operate, supported by coaching from their manager, the performance-management process back in the workplace.

Format

A two-day, non-residential workshop.

Designed for

Those requiring an understanding of and a chance to practise the concepts and skills of performance management.

Coaching skills
Objectives

Coaching is the ability to take the opportunities presented by the job itself and use them in a conscious manner to improve the knowledge, skills, competencies, and therefore performance, of the learner. It is fundamental to performance management and generally to good management practice.

By the end of the workshop participants will:

☐ be able to describe and apply factors that help others to learn

☐ be able to apply a systematic approach towards achieving learning through the conscious use of on-the-job opportunities

☐ have practised skills/behaviours associated with effective coaching.

Format

A one-day workshop.

Designed for

People who have some existing experience of operating the performance-management system.

Individual development workshop

The aim of this workshop is to enable participants to gain a clear understanding of what development planning is, and how they can implement it effectively.

Objectives

By the end of the workshop participants will be able to:

☐ derive an agreed individual development plan

☐ implement the skills associated with improving performance.

Format

A one-day workshop. In order to make the most practical use of the one-day event, participants will be invited to work on real issues and situations, and tutors will demonstrate real examples. Case-studies and role plays will not be used.

Designed for

Those who have some experience of performance management and who want to improve their understanding and skill in individual development planning.

Performance-review workshop

Performance management is a continuous process aiming to increase business effectiveness by improving the performance of individuals. The planning, development and evaluation of performance throughout the year require frequent review between the people involved to monitor targets, discuss achievements, and progress development plans. This workshop will enable people to conduct effective discussions throughout the year and at the annual performance summary review session. It explores how reward in its widest sense can be used to reinforce performance.

Objectives

By the end of the workshop, participants will be able to:

☐ describe good practice for reviewing performance
☐ apply a structured approach to preparing for and conducting review meetings
☐ create conditions that encourage good performance
☐ apply a variety of methods to reward performance.

Format

A one-day workshop.

Designed for

People at all levels who have a good understanding of performance management and who want to enhance their ability to conduct effective performance review discussions and reinforce good performance.

REFERENCES

ACAS *see* ADVISORY, CONCILIATION AND ARBITRATION SERVICE

ADVISORY, CONCILIATION AND ARBITRATION SERVICE (1988) *Employee Appraisal.* London, Advisory, Conciliation and Arbitration Service.

AMERICAN COMPENSATION ASSOCIATION *see* Engelmann and Roesch 1996.

ANTONIONI D. (1994) 'Improve the performance management process before discontinuing performance appraisals'. *Compensation & Benefits Review.* May–June. pp29–37.

ARGYRIS C. (1992) *On Organisational Learning.* Cambridge, Mass., Blackwell.

ARGYRIS C. (1993) *Knowledge for Action: A guide to overcoming barriers to organisational change.* San Francisco, Calif., Jossey Bass.

ARMSTRONG M. (1976) *A Handbook of Personnel Management Practice.* 1st edn. London, Kogan Page.

ARMSTRONG M. (1992) Address to Royal Institute of Public Administration Conference, Edinburgh. May.

ARMSTRONG M. (1996a) *A Handbook of Personnel Management Practice.* 6th edn. London, Kogan Page.

ARMSTRONG M. (1996b) *Employee Reward.* London, Institute of Personnel and Development.

ARMSTRONG M. *and* BARON A. (1995) *The Job Evaluation Handbook.* London, Institute of Personnel and Development.

ARMSTRONG M. *and* MURLIS H. (1994) *Reward Management: A handbook of remuneration strategy and practice.* 3rd edn. London, Kogan Page.

ARMSTRONG M. *and* RYDEN O. (1996) *The IPD Guide on Broadbanding.* London, Institute of Personnel and Development.

AUDIT COMMISSION (1987) *Performance Review in Local Government.* London, Audit Commission.

BAGULEY P. (1994) *Improving Organisational Performance.* Maidenhead, McGraw-Hill.

BAILEY R. T. (1983) *Measurement of Performance*. Aldershot, Gower.

BANDURA A. (1977) *Social Learning Theory*. Englewood Cliffs, N.J., Prentice-Hall.

BANDURA A. (1982) 'Self-efficacy mechanism in human agency'. *American Psychologist*. Vol. 37. pp132–147.

BANDURA A. (1986) *Social Boundaries of Thought and Action*. Englewood Cliffs, N.J., Prentice-Hall.

BARLOW G. (1989) 'Deficiencies and the perpetuation of power: latent functions in performance appraisal'. *Journal of Management Studies*. September. pp499–517.

BATES R. A. *and* HOLTON E. F. (1995) 'Computerised performance monitoring: a review of human resource issues'. *Human Resource Management Review*. Winter. pp267–288.

BEAVER G. *and* HARRIS L. (1995) 'Performance management and the small firm: dilemmas, tensions and paradoxes'. *Journal of Strategic Change*. Vol. 4. pp109–119.

BECKHARD R. (1969) *Organization Development: Strategy and models*. Reading, Mass., Addison-Wesley.

BEER M. *and* RUH R. A. (1976) 'Employee growth through performance management'. *Harvard Business Review*. July–August. pp59–66.

BENNIS W. (1960) *Organisational Development*. Reading, Mass., Addison-Wesley.

BERNADIN H. K., KANE J. S., ROSS S., SPINA J. D. *and* JOHNSON D. L. (1995) 'Performance appraisal design, development and implementation', in G. R. Ferris, S. D. Rosen and D. J. Barnum (eds), *Handbook of Human Resource Management*. Cambridge, Mass., Blackwell.

BEVAN S. *and* THOMPSON M. (1991) 'Performance management at the crossroads'. *Personnel Management*. November. pp36–39.

BIRCHALL D. *and* LYONS L. (1995) *Creating Tomorrow's Organisation Today: Unlock the benefits of future working*. London, Pitman.

BITICI U. S., CARRIE A. S. *and* MCDEVITT L. (1997) 'Integrate performance management systems: audit and development goals'. *The TQM Magazine*. Vol. 9, No. 1. pp46–53.

BONES C. (1996) 'Performance management: the HR contribution'. Address at the Annual Conference of the Institute of Personnel and Development, Harrogate. October.

BOWLES M. L. *and* COATES G. (1993) 'Image and substance: the management of performance as rhetoric or reality?' *Personnel Review*. Vol. 22, No. 2. pp3–21.

BOYATZIS R. (1982) *The Competent Manager*. New York, Wiley.

BOYETT J. H. *and* CONN H. P. (1995) *Maximum Performance Management*. Oxford, Glenbridge Publishing.

BROWN D. (1998) Address to the Compensation Forum Meeting. February.

BROWN D. *and* ARMSTRONG M. (1997) 'Terms of endearment'. *People Management*. 11 September. pp36–38.

BRUMBACH G. B. (1988) 'Some ideas, issues and predictions about performance management'. *Public Personnel Management*. Winter. pp387–402.

BURDETT J. O. (1991) 'What is empowerment anyway?' *Journal of European Industrial Training*. Vol. 15, No. 6. pp23–30.

BURGOYNE J. (1994) As reported in *Personnel Management Plus*. May. p7.

CAMPBELL J. P. (1990) 'Modelling the performance prediction problem in industrial and organizational psychology', in M. P. Dunnette and L. M. Hugh (eds), *Handbook of Industrial and Organizational Psychology*, Cambridge, Mass., Blackwell.

CARDY R. L. *and* DOBBINS G. H. (1994) *Performance Appraisal: Alternative perspectives*. Cincinnati, Ohio, South-Western Publishing.

CARLTON I. *and* SLOMAN M. (1992) 'Performance appraisal in practice'. *Human Resource Management Journal*. Vol. 2, No. 3. Spring. pp80–94.

CAVE A. (1994) *Organisational Change in the Workplace*. London, Kogan Page.

CAVE, A. *and* THOMAS C. (1998) 'The reward portfolio'. *The Training Directory*. p34.

CHELL E. (1992) *The Psychology of Behaviour in Organisations*. 2nd edn. Basingstoke, Macmillan.

CHILD J. (1972) *Organisation: A guide to problems and practice*. London, Harper & Row.

COOPER D. (1965) 'The anti-hospital: an experiment in psychiatry'. *New Society*. March. pp4–6.

DANIELS A. C. (1987) 'What is PM?' *Performance Management*. July. pp8–12.

DEMING W. E. (1986) *Out of the Crisis*. Cambridge, Mass., Massachusetts Institute of Technology, Centre for Advanced Engineering Studies.

DRUCKER P. (1955) *The Practice of Management*. London, Heinemann.

EARLEY D. C. (1986) 'Computer-generated performance feedback in the magazine industry'. *Organisation Behaviour and Human Decision Processes.* 41. pp50–64

EDWARDS M. R. *and* EWEN A. T. (1996) *360-Degree Feedback.* New York, American Management Association.

EDWARDS M. R., EWEN A. T. *and* O'NEAL S. (1994) 'Using multi-source assessment to pay people not jobs'. *ACA Journal.* Summer. pp6–17.

EGAN G. (1995) 'A clear path to peak performance'. *People Management.* 18 May. pp34–37.

ENGELMANN C. H. *and* ROESCH C. H. (1996) *Managing Individual Performance.* Scottsdale, Ariz., American Compensation Association.

EPSTEIN S. *and* O'BRIEN E. J. (1985) 'The person-situation debate in historical perspective'. *Psychological Bulletin.* 83. pp956–974.

FAYOL H. (1916) *Administration Industrielle et Générale.* Translated by S. Storrs as *Industrial and General Management,* London, Pitman, 1949.

FISHER C. M. (1994) 'The difference between appraisal schemes: variation and acceptability – part 1'. *Personnel Review.* Vol. 23, No. 8. pp33–48.

FLANAGAN J. C. (1954) 'The critical incident technique'. *Psychological Bulletin.* Vol. 51. pp327–358.

FLETCHER C. (1993a) *Appraisal: Routes to improved performance.* London, Institute of Personnel and Development.

FLETCHER C. (1993b) 'Appraisal: an idea whose time has gone?' *Personnel Management.* September. pp34-37.

FLETCHER C. *and* WILLIAMS R. (1992) 'Organisational experience'. *Performance Management in the UK: An analysis of the issues.* London, Institute of Personnel Management.

FOUCAULT M. (1981) *Power/Knowledge: Selected interviews and other writings.* Brighton, the Harvester Press.

FOWLER A. (1990) 'Performance management: the MBO of the '90s?' *Personnel Management.* July. pp47–54.

FOWLER A. (1995) *The Disciplinary Interview.* London, Institute of Personnel and Development.

FREEMAN E. (1984) *Strategic Management: A stakeholder approach.* London, Pitman.

FRENCH J. R. *and* RAVEN B. (1959) 'The basis of social power', in D. Cartwright (ed.), *Studies in Social Power.* Ann Arbor, Mich., Institute for Social Research.

FRIEDMAN A. (1977) *Industry and Labour: Class structure and monopoly capitalism.* London, Macmillan.

FURNHAM A. (1996) 'Starved of feedback'. *The Independent*. 5 December.

GANNON M. (1995) 'Personal development planning', in M. Walters (ed.), *The Performance Management Handbook*. London, Institute of Personnel and Development.

GARTH M. *and* MILLS C. W. (eds) (1946) *From Max Weber*. Oxford, Oxford University Press.

GARVIN D. A. (1993) 'Building a learning organisation'. *Harvard Business Review*. July–August. pp78–91.

GENNARD J. *and* JUDGE G. (1997) *Employee Relations*. London, Institute of Personnel and Development.

GEORGE J. (1986) 'Appraisal in the public sector: dispensing with the big stick'. *Personnel Management*. May. pp32–35.

GOMEZ-MEJIA L. R. *and* BALKIN D. B. (1992) *Compensation, Organisational Strategy, and Firm Performance*. Cincinnati, Ohio, South-Western Publishing.

GRINT K. (1993) 'What's wrong with performance appraisal? A critique and a suggestion'. *Human Resource Management Journal*. Spring. pp61–77.

GROSS S. E. (1995) *Compensation for Teams*. New York, Hay.

GUEST D. (1996) 'The management of performance'. Address at the Annual Conference of the Institute of Personnel and Development, Harrogate. October.

GUILE E D. *and* FONDA N. (1998) *Performance Management through Capability*. Issues in People Management No. 25. London, Institute of Personnel and Development.

GUIN K. A. (1992) *Successfully Integrating Total Quality and Performance Appraisal*. New York, Spring, Faulkner and Gray.

HAMPSON S. E. (1982) *The Construction of Personality*. London, Routledge and Kegan Paul.

HANDY C. (1989) *The Age of Unreason*. London, Business Books.

HANDY L., DEVINE M. *and* HEATH L. (1996) *360-Degree Feedback: Unguided missile or powerful weapon?* Berkhamstead, Ashridge Management Group.

HARRINGTON-MACKIN D. (1994) *The Team Building Tool Kit*. New York, Amacom.

HARRISON R. (1992) *Employee Development*. London, Institute of Personnel Management.

HARRISON R. (1997) *Employee Development*. London, Institute of Personnel and Development.

HARTLE F. (1995) *Transforming the Performance Management Process*. London, Kogan Page.

HEGARTY S. (1995) 'Self service'. *Personnel Today*. 6 June. pp25–26.

HENDRY C., BRADLEY P. *and* PERKINS S. (1997) 'Missed'. *People Management*. 15 May. pp20–25.

HERZBERG F. (1968) 'One more time: how do you motivate your employees?' *Harvard Business Review*. January–February. pp109–120.

HILLAGE J. (1994) *The Role of Job Evaluation*. Falmer, Institute of Manpower Studies.

HONEY P. *and* MUMFORD A. (1986) *The Manual of Learning Styles*. Maidenhead, Peter Honey.

HOPE T. (1998) Address to the Compensation Forum, London.

HULL C. (1951) *Essentials of Behaviour*. New Haven CT, Yale University Press.

HUMBLE J. (1972) *Management by Objectives*. London, Management Publications.

IDS *see* Incomes Data Services

INCOMES DATA SERVICES (1997) 'Performance management'. *Study No. 626*. London, Incomes Data Services. May.

INSTITUTE OF PERSONNEL AND DEVELOPMENT (1994) *People Make the Difference*. London, Institute of Personnel and Development.

INSTITUTE OF PERSONNEL AND DEVELOPMENT (1998) *Getting Fit, Staying Fit: Developing lean and responsive organisations*. IPD Research. London, Institute of Personnel and Development.

INSTITUTE OF PERSONNEL MANAGEMENT (1992) *Performance Management in the UK: An analysis of the issues*. London, Institute of Personnel Management.

IPD *see* Institute of Personnel and Development

IPM *see* Institute of Personnel Management

IRS MANAGEMENT REVIEW 'Using human resources to achieve strategic objectives'. Vol. 1:2. July.

JAY A. (1967) *Management and Machiavelli*. London, Hodder and Stoughton.

JONES P., PALMER J., WHITEHEAD D. *and* NEEDHAM P. (1995) 'Prisms of performance'. *The Ashridge Journal*. April. pp10–14.

JONES T. W. (1995) 'Performance management in a changing context'. *Human Resource Management*. Fall. pp425–442.

KANE J. S. (1996) 'The conceptualisation and representation

of total performance effectiveness'. *Human Resource Management Review*. Summer. pp123–145.

KANTER R. M. (1984) *The Change Masters*. London, Allen & Unwin.

KANTER R. M. (1989) *When Giants Learn to Dance*. London, Simon & Schuster.

KAPLAN R. S. *and* NORTON D. P. (1992) 'The balanced score-card – measures that drive performance'. *Harvard Business Review*. January–February. pp71–79.

KAPLAN R. S. *and* NORTON D. P. (1996a) 'Using the balanced scorecard as a strategic management system'. *Harvard Business Review*. January–February. pp75-85.

KAPLAN R. S. *and* NORTON D. P. (1996b) 'Strategic learning and the balanced scorecard'. *Strategy and Leadership*. June. pp20-34.

KATZ D. *and* KAHN R. (1964) *The Social Psychology of Organizations*. New York, Wiley.

KATZENBACH J.R. *and* SMITH D.K. (1993) *The Wisdom of Teams*. Boston, Mass., Harvard Business School Press.

KELLY G. (1955) *The Psychology of Personal Constructs*. New York, Norton.

KERMALLY S. (1997) *Managing Performance*. Oxford, Butterworth-Heinemann.

KESSLER I. *and* PURCELL J. (1992) 'Performance-related pay: objectives and application'. *Human Resource Management*. Spring. pp16–33.

KNOWLES M. S. (1989) 'Everything you wanted to know from Malcolm Knowles'. *Training*. August. pp8–10.

KOLB D. A., RUBIN I. M. *and* McINTYRE J. M. (1974) *Organisational Learning: An experiential approach*. Englewood Cliffs, N.J., Prentice Hall.

KOONTZ H. (1971) *Appraising Managers as Managers*. New York, McGraw-Hill

LATHAM G. P. *and* LOCKE E. A. (1979) 'Goal setting – a motivational technique that works'. *Organisational Dynamics*. Autumn. pp442–447.

LAWLER E. E. (1986) 'What's wrong with point-factor job evaluation'. *Compensation & Benefits Review*. March–April. pp20–28.

LAWSON P. (1995) 'Performance management: an overview', in M. Walters (ed.), *The Performance Management Handbook*. London, Institute of Personnel and Development.

LAZER R. I. *and* WIKSTRÖM W. S. (1977) *Appraising Managerial*

Performance: Current practices and new directions. New York, the Conference Board.

LEVENTHAL G. S. (1980) 'What should be done with equity theory? New approaches to the study of fairness in social relationships', in K. Gerken, M. Greenberg and R. Willis (eds), *Social Exchange: Advances in theory and research.* New York, Plenum Press.

LEVINSON H. (1970) 'Management by whose objectives?' *Harvard Business Review.* July–August. pp125–134.

LEVINSON H. (1976) 'Appraisal of what performance?' *Harvard Business Review.* July–August. pp30–46.

LITTLER C. *and* SALAMAN S. (1982) 'Bravermania and beyond: recent theories of the labour process'. *Sociology.* Vol. 16, No. 2. pp215–269.

LOCAL GOVERNMENT MANAGEMENT BOARD (1995) *Guide to 360-Degree Feedback.*

LOCKETT J. (1992) *Effective Performance Management: A strategic guide to getting the best from people.* London, Kogan Page.

LONDON M. *and* BEATTY R. W. (1993) '360-degree feedback as competitive advantage'. *Human Resource Management.* Summer/Fall. pp353–372.

LONG P. (1986) *Performance Appraisal Revisited.* London, Institute of Personnel Management.

LUTHANS F. *and* KREITNER R. (1975) *Organisational Behaviour Modification.* Glenview, Ill., Scott-Foresman.

MACKAY I. (1992) *A Manager's Guide to the Appraisal Discussion.* London, BACIE.

MARCHINGTON M. *and* WILKINSON A. (1996) *Core Personnel and Development.* London, Institute of Personnel and Development.

MARSICK V. J. (1994) 'Trends in managerial reinvention: creating a learning map'. *Management Learning.* Vol. 25, No. 1. pp11–33.

MCDONALD D. *and* SMITH A. (1991) 'A proven connection: performance management and business results'. *Compensation & Benefits Review.* January–February. pp59–64.

MCGREGOR D. (1957) 'An uneasy look at performance appraisal'. *Harvard Business Review.* May–June. pp89–94.

MCGREGOR D. (1960) *The Human Side of Enterprise.* New York, McGraw–Hill.

MILKOVICH G. *and* WIGDOR A. C. (1991) *Pay for Performance: Evaluating performance appraisal and merit pay.* Washington DC, National Academy Press.

MILLER E. *and* RICE A. (1967) *Systems of Organisation.* London, Tavistock.

MOHRMAN A. M. *and* MOHRMAN S. A. (1995) 'Performance management is "running the business"'. *Compensation & Benefits Review.* July–August. pp69–75.

MUMFORD A. (1989) *Management Development: Strategies for action.* 1st edn. London, Institute of Personnel Management.

MUMFORD A. (1994) *Management Development: Strategies for action.* 2nd edn. London, Institute of Personnel and Development.

NADLER D. A. *and* TUSHMAN M. (1980) 'A congruence model for diagnosing organisational behaviour', in R. H. Miles (ed.), *Resource Book in Macro-Organisational Behaviour.* Santa Monica, Calif., Goodyear Publishing.

NEWTON T. *and* FINDLAY P. (1996) 'Playing god?: The performance of appraisal'. *Human Resource Management Journal.* Vol. 6, No. 3. pp42–56.

OAKLAND J. S. (1993) *Total Quality Management: The route to improved performance.* 2nd edn. Oxford, Butterworth-Heinemann.

PASCALE R. (1990) *Managing on the Edge.* London, Viking.

PEARCE J. A. *and* ROBINSON R. B. (1988) *Strategic Management: Strategy formulation and implementation.* Georgetown, Ontario, Irwin.

PEDLER M., BURGOYNE J. *and* Boydell T. (1986) *Manager's Guide to Self Development.* 2nd edn. Maidenhead, McGraw-Hill.

PETERS T. (1988) *Thriving on Chaos.* London, Macmillan.

PHILPOTT L. *and* SHEPPARD L. (1992) 'Managing for improved performance', in M. Armstrong (ed.), *Strategies for Human Resource Management.* London, Kogan Page.

PICKARD J. (1997) 'A yearning for learning'. *People Management.* Vol. 3, No. 5. pp34–35.

PLACHY R. J. (1987) 'The point-factor job evaluation system: a step by step guide'. *Compensation & Benefits Review.* September–October. pp12–27.

PLACHY R. J. *and* PLACHY S. J. (1988) *Getting Results From Your Performance Management and Appraisal System.* New York, Amacom.

PORTER L. W. *and* LAWLER E. E. *Managerial Attitudes and Performance.* Homewood, Ill., Irwin Dorsey.

PORTER M. E. (1985) *Competitive Advantage: Creating and sustaining superior performance.* New York, the Free Press.

PORTER M. E. (1997) 'Strategy'. Address at the Institute of

Personnel and Development's Annual Conference, Harrogate. October.

PRAHALAD C. K. *and* HAMEL, G. (1990) 'The core competence of the corporation'. *Harvard Business Review*. Vol. 68, No. 3. May–June. pp79–91.

PURCELL I. ET AL (1998) *see* Institute of Personnel and Development (1998).

RANDELL G. H. (1973) 'Performance appraisal: purpose, practices and conflicts'. *Occupational Psychology*. 47. pp221-224.

ROBERTSON I. T., SMITH M. *and* COOPER D. (1992) *Motivation*. 2nd edn. London, Institute of Personnel Management.

ROWE K. (1964) 'An appraisal of appraisals'. *Journal of Management Studies*. Vol. 1, No. 1. March. pp1–25.

RUCCI A. J., KIRN S. P. *and* QUINN R.T. (1998) 'The employee-customer-profit chain at Sears'. *Harvard Business Review*. January–February. pp82–97.

SCHAFFER R. H. (1991) 'Demand better results and get them'. *Harvard Business Review*. March–April. pp142–149.

SENGE P. M. (1990) *The Fifth Discipline: The art and practice of the learning organisation*. New York, Doubleday.

SILVERMAN D. (1970) *The Theory of Organisations: A sociological framework*. London, Heinemann.

SPARROW P. (1996) 'Too good to be true'. *People Management*. 5 December 1996. pp22–27.

SPENCER L. *and* SPENCER S. (1993) *Competence at Work*. New York, Wiley.

STEWART V. *and* STEWART A. (1982) *Managing the Poor Performer*. Aldershot, Gower.

STILES P., GRATTON L., TRUSS C., HOPE-HAILEY J. *and* McGOVERN P. (1997) 'Performance management and the psychological contract'. *Human Resource Management Journal*. Vol. 2, No. 1. pp57–66.

STOREY J. (1985) 'The means of management control'. *Sociology*. Vol. 19, No. 2. pp193–212.

TAMKIN P., BARBER L. *and* HIRSH W. (1995) *Personal Development Plans: Case studies of practice*. Brighton, the Institute for Employment Studies.

THOMAS C. (1995) 'Performance management'. *Croner Pay and Benefits Bulletin*. August. pp4–5.

THOR G. G. (1995) 'Using measurement to reinforce strategy', in H. Rishner and C. Fay (eds), *The Performance Imperative*. San Francisco, Calif., Jossey Bass.

TORRINGTON D. *and* HALL L.(1995) *Personnel Management:*

Human resource management in action. London, Prentice Hall.

TOWNLEY B. (1990) 'A discriminating approach to appraisal'. *Personnel Management*. December. pp34–37.

TOWNLEY B. (1990/1991) 'Appraisal into UK universities'. *Human Resource Management Journal*. Vol. 1, No. 2. pp27–44.

TOWNLEY B. (1993) 'Performance appraisal and the emergence of management'. *Journal of Management Studies*. Vol. 30, No. 2. March. pp221–238.

TURNOW W. W. (1993) 'Introduction to special issue on 360-degree feedback'. *Human Resource Management*. Summer/Fall. pp311–316.

VAN DE VLIET A. (1997) 'The new balancing card'. *Management Today*. July. pp78–79.

VROOM V. (1964) *Work and Motivation*. New York, Wiley.

WALTERS M. (1995) *The Performance Management Handbook*. London, Institute of Personnel and Development.

WALTERS M. (1995) 'Developing organisational measures', in M. Walters (ed.), *The Performance Management Handbook*. London, Institute of Personnel and Development.

WALTON R. E. (1985a) 'From control to commitment in the workplace'. *Harvard Business Review*. 63. pp76–84.

WALTON R. E. (1985b) 'Towards a strategy of eliciting employee commitment based on principles of mutuality', in R. E. Walton and P. R. Lawrence (eds), *Human Resource Management Trends and Challenges*. Boston, Mass., Harvard Business School Press.

WARD P. (1997) *360-Degree Feedback*. London, Institute of Personnel and Development.

WATERMAN R. (1994) *The Frontiers of Excellence*. London, Nicholas Brealey.

WEST M. A. *and* SLATER J. A. (1995) 'Teamwork; myths, realities and research'. *Occupational Psychology*. April. pp24–29.

WHEATLEY M. (1996) 'How to score performance management'. *Human Resources*. May–June. pp24–26.

WICK C. W. *and* LEON L. S. (1995) 'From ideas to action: creating a learning organisation'. *Human Resource Management*. Summer. pp299–311.

WILLIAMS S. (1991) 'Strategy and objectives', in F. Neale (ed.), *The Handbook of Performance Management*. London, Institute of Personnel and Development.

WINSTANLEY D. *and* STUART-SMITH K. (1996) 'Policing performance: the ethics of performance management'. *Personnel Review*. Vol. 25, No. 6. pp66–84.

WOOD S. (1996) 'High commitment management and organisation in the UK'. *The International Journal of Human Resource Management*. February. pp41–58.

ZIGON J. (1994) 'Measuring the performance of work teams'. *ACA Journal*. Autumn. pp18–32.

AUTHOR INDEX

SUBJECT INDEX